AF531260

Sociological Theory

Origin, Types of Sociology Theory

Sociological Theory

Origin, Types of Sociology Theory

C.R. Romesh

CENTRUM PRESS
NEW DELHI-110002 (INDIA)

CENTRUM PRESS
H.O.: 4360/4, Ansari Road, Daryaganj,
New Delhi-110002 (India)
Tel: 23278000, 23261597, 23255577, 23286875
B.O.: No. 1015, Ist Main Road, BSK IIIrd Stage,
IIIrd Phase, IIIrd Block, Bengaluru-560085 (INDIA)
Tel: 080-41723429
Email: centrumpress@gmail.com
Visit us at: www.centrumpress.com

Sociological Theory: Origin, Types of Sociology Theory

First Edition, 2011

ISBN 978-93-81293-71-3

PRINTED IN INDIA

Printed at Tarun Offset Printers, Delhi-110053

Contents

Preface

Sociology has a long prehistory going back to the Greeks. Ibn Khaldun, the eminent Berber scholar and statesman of the 14th century, was very likely the first thinker to formulate a clear conception of sociology. He did so under the name of the study of culture. Classical sociological theories are important not only historically, but also because they are living documents with contemporary relevance to both modern theorists and today's social world. The work of classical thinkers continues to inspire modern sociologists in a variety of ways. Many contemporary thinkers seek to reinterpret the classics to apply them to the contemporary scene. Sociologists develop theories to explain social phenomena. A *theory* is a proposed relationship between two or more *concepts*. In other words, a theory is explanation for why a phenomenon occurs. An example of a sociological theory is the work of Robert Putnam on the decline of civic engagement.

In the theory proposed above, the astute reader will notice that the theory includes two components: The data, in this case the findings that civic engagement has declined and TV watching has increased, and the proposed relationship, that the increase in television viewing has contributed to the decline in civic engagement. Data alone are not particularly informative. If Putnam had not proposed a relationship between the two elements of social life, we may not have realized that television viewing does, in fact, reduce people's desire to and time for participating in civic life. In order to understand the social world around us, it is necessary to employ theory to draw the connections between seemingly disparate concepts.

In defining Marxism a distinction has to be made between the writings and ideas of Karl Marx, the ideology of Marxism as a sociological perspective between his day and the present, and the politics of communism, socialism, and Labour's third way. Textbooks on sociology often contrast social systems or structuralism with social action perspectives. They frequently then differentiate between consensus theories and conflict theories. These distinctions may arise from the sociological cannon's axiomatic reliance on a few key historical thinkers providing a basis for almost all modern development of the subject.

The Enlightenment was a period of intellectual development and change in philosophical thought beginning in the eighteenth century. Enlightenment thinkers sought to combine reason with empirical research on the model of Newtonian science. They tried to produce highly systematic bodies of thought that made rational sense and that could be derived from real-world observation. Convinced that the world could be comprehended and controlled using reason and research, they believed traditional social values and institutions to be irrational and inhibitive of human development. Their ideas conflicted with traditional religious bodies like the Catholic Church, the political regimes of Europe's absolutist monarchies, and the social system of feudalism. They placed their faith instead in the power of the individual's capacity to reason. Early sociology also maintained a faith in empiricism and rational inquiry. A conservative reaction to the Enlightenment, characterized by a strong anti-modern sentiment, also influenced early theorists. The conservative reaction led thinkers to emphasize that society had an existence of its own, in contrast to the individualism of the Enlightenment. Additionally, they had a cautious approach to social change and a tendency to see modern developments like industrialization, urbanization, and bureaucratization as having disorganizing effects.

The present work on Sociological Theory provides an authentic, up-to-date and thought-provoking description of various trends and issues in Sociology Theory.

—*Editor*

1

Origins of Sociological Theory

SOCIOLOGICAL THEORY

Sociologists develop theories to explain social phenomena. A *theory* is a proposed relationship between two or more *concepts*. In other words, a theory is explanation for why a phenomenon occurs. An example of a sociological theory is the work of Robert Putnam on the decline of civic engagement. Putnam found that Americans involvement in civic life (e.g., community organizations, clubs, voting, religious participation, etc.) has declined over the last 40 to 60 years. While there are a number of factors that contribute to this decline (Putnam's theory is quite complex), one of the prominent factors is the increased consumption of television as a form entertainment. Putnam's theory proposes:

The more television people watch, the lower their involvement in civic life will be. This element of Putnam's theory clearly illustrates the basic purpose of sociological theory: it proposes a relationship between two or more concepts. In this case, the concepts are *civic engagement* and *television watching*. The relationship is an *inverse* one-as one goes up, the other goes down. What's more, it is an explanation of one phenomenon with another: part of the reason why civic engagement has declined over the last several decades is because people are watching more television. In short, Putnam's theory clearly encapsulates the key ideas of a sociological theory.

Sociological theory is developed at multiple levels, ranging from *grand theory* to highly contextualized and specific *micro-*

range theories. There are many *middle-range* and *micro-range* theories in sociology. Because such theories are dependent on context and specific to certain situations, it is beyond the scope of this text to explore each of those theories. The purpose of this chapter is to introduce some of the more well-known and most commonly used grand and middle-range theories in sociology.

Importance of Theory

In the theory proposed above, the astute reader will notice that the theory includes two components: The data, in this case the findings that civic engagement has declined and TV watching has increased, and the proposed relationship, that the increase in television viewing has contributed to the decline in civic engagement. Data alone are not particularly informative. If Putnam had not proposed a relationship between the two elements of social life, we may not have realized that television viewing does, in fact, reduce people's desire to and time for participating in civic life. In order to understand the social world around us, it is necessary to employ theory to draw the connections between seemingly disparate concepts.

Another example of sociological theorizing illustrates this point. In his now classic work, *Suicide*, Emile Durkheim was interested in explaining a social phenomenon, suicide, and employed both data and theory to offer an explanation. By aggregating data for large groups of people in Europe, Durkheim was able to discern patterns in suicide rates and connect those patterns with another concept (or variable): religious affiliation. Durkheim found that Protestants were more likely to commit suicide than were Catholics. At this point, Durkheim's analysis was still in the data stage; he had not proposed an explanation for the different suicide rates of the two groups. It was when Durkheim introduced the ideas of *anomie* and *social solidarity* that he began to explain the difference in suicide rates. Durkheim argued that the looser social ties found in Protestant religions lead to weaker social cohesion and reduced social solidarity. The higher suicide rates were the result of weakening social bonds among Protestants.

While Durkheim's findings have since been criticized, his study is a classic example of the use of theory to explain the relationship between two concepts. Durkheim's work also illustrates the importance of theory: without theories to explain the relationship between concepts, we would not be able to understand cause and effect relationships in social life.

Prominent Sociological Theories

As noted above, there are many theories in sociology. However, there are several broad theoretical perspectives that are prominent in the field (they are arguably paradigms). These theories are prominent because they are quite good at explaining social life. They are not without their problems, but these theories remain widely used and cited precisely because they have withstood a great deal of criticism.

As the dominant theories in sociology are discussed below, you might be inclined to ask, "Which of these theories is *the best*?" As is often the case in sociology, just because things are different doesn't mean one is better than another. In fact, it is probably more useful and informative to view these theories as *complementary*. One theory may explain one element of society better than another. Or, both may be useful for explaining social life. In short, all of the theories are correct in the sense that they offer compelling explanations for social phenomena.

Structural-Functionalism

Structural-Functionalism is a sociological theory that originally attempted to explain social institutions as collective means to meet individual biological needs. Later it came to focus on the ways social institutions meet social needs (structural-functionalism). Structural-functionalism draws its inspiration primarily from the ideas of Emile Durkheim. Durkheim was concerned with the question of how societies maintain internal stability and survive over time. He sought to explain social cohesion and stability through the concept of solidarity. In more "primitive" societies it was mechanical solidarity, everyone performing similar tasks, that held society together. Durkheim proposed that such societies tend to be segmentary, being composed of equivalent parts that are held together by shared values, common symbols, or systems of exchanges. In modern, complex societies members perform very different tasks, resulting in a strong interdependence between individuals. Based on the metaphor of an organism in which many parts function together to sustain the whole, Durkheim argued that modern complex societies are held together by organic solidarity (think interdependent *organs*).

The central concern of structural-functionalism is a continuation of the Durkheimian task of explaining the apparent stability and internal cohesion of societies that are necessary to ensure their continued existence over time. Many functionalists argue that social institutions are functionally integrated to form a stable system and that a change in one institution will precipitate a change in other institutions. Societies are seen as coherent, bounded and fundamentally relational constructs that function like organisms, with their various parts (social institutions) working together to maintain and reproduce them. The various parts of society are assumed to work in an unconscious, quasi-automatic fashion towards the maintenance of the overall social *equilibrium*. All social and cultural phenomena are therefore seen as being *functional* in the sense of working together to achieve this state and are effectively deemed to have a *life* of their own. These components are then primarily analysed in terms of the function they play. In other words, to understand a component of society, one can ask the question, "What is the function of this institution?" A *function*, in this sense, is the contribution made by a phenomenon to a larger system of which the phenomenon is a part.

Thus, one can ask of education, "What is the function of education for society?" The answer is actually quite complex and requires a detailed analysis of the history of education, but one obvious answer is that education prepares individuals to enter the workforce. By delineating the functions of elements of society, of the social structure, we can better understand social life.

Durkheim's strongly sociological perspective of society was continued by Radcliffe-Brown. Following Auguste Comte, Radcliffe-Brown believed that the social constituted a separate *level* of reality distinct from both the biological and the inorganic (here *non-living*). Explanations of social phenomena therefore had to be constructed within this social level, with individuals merely being transient occupants of comparatively stable social roles. Thus, in structural-functionalist thought, individuals are not significant in and of themselves but only in terms of their social status: their position in patterns of social relations. The social structure is therefore a network of statuses connected by associated roles.

Structural-functionalism was the dominant perspective of sociology between World War II and the Vietnam War.

Limitations

Structural-functionalism has been criticized for being unable to account for social change because it focuses so intently on social order and equilibrium in society. For instance, in the late 19th Century, higher education transitioned from a training center for clergy and the elite to a center for the conduct of science and the general education of the masses. In other words, education did not always serve the function of preparing individuals for the labour force. As structural-functionalism thinks about elements of social life in relation to their present function and not their past functions, structural-functionalism has a difficult time explaining why a function of some element of society might change or how such change occurs. However, structural-functionalism could, in fact, offer an explanation in this case. Also occurring in the 19th Century (though begun in the 18th) was the industrial revolution. The industrial revolution, facilitated by capitalism, was increasingly demanding technological advances to increase profit. Technological advances and advanced industry both required more educated workforces. Thus, as one aspect of society changed-the economy and production-it required a comparable change in the educational system, bringing social life back into equilibrium.

Another philosophical problem with the structural-functional approach is the ontological argument that society does not have *needs* as a human being does; and even if society does have needs they need not be met. The idea that society has *needs* like humans do is not a tenable position because society is only alive in the sense that it is made up of living individuals. Thus, society cannot have wants and/or needs like humans do. What's more, just because a society has some element in it at the present that does not mean that it must necessarily have that element. For instance, in the United Kingdom, religious service attendance has declined precipitously over the last 100 years. Today, less than 1 in 10 British attend religious service in a given week. Thus, while one might argue that religion has certain functions in British society, it is becoming apparent that it is not necessary for British society to function.

Another criticism often leveled at structural-functionalist theory is that it supports the status quo. According to some opponents, structural-functionalism paints conflict and challenge to the status quo as harmful to society, and therefore tends to be the prominent view among conservative thinkers.

Manifest and Latent Functions

Merton (1957) proposed a distinction between *manifest* and *latent* functions. *Manifest* functions are the intended functions of a phenomenon in a social system. *Latent* functions are the unintended functions of a phenomenon in a social system. An example of manifest and latent functions is education. The manifest purpose of public education is to increase the knowledge and abilities of the citizenry to prepare them to contribute in the workforce. A latent function of the public education system is the development of a hierarchy of *the learned*. The most learned are often also the most affluent. Thus, while education's manifest function is to empower all individuals to contribute to the workforce and society, it also limits some people by creating boundaries of entry into occupations.

Conflict Theory

A prominent sociological theory that is often contrasted with structural-functionalism is conflict theory. Conflict theory argues that society is not best understood as a complex system striving for equilibrium but rather as a competition. Society is made up of individuals competing for limited resources. Broader social structures and organizations (e.g., religions, government, etc.) reflect the competition for resources in their inherent inequalities; some people and organizations have more resources (i.e., power and influence) and use those resources to maintain their positions of power in society.

Conflict theory was developed in part to illustrate the limitations of structural-functionalism. The structural-functionalist approach argued that society tends toward equilibrium, focusing on stability at the expense of social change. This is contrasted with the conflict approach, which argues that society is constantly in conflict over resources. One of the primary contributions conflict theory presents over the structural-functional approach is that it is ideally suited for explaining social change, a significant problem in the structural-functional approach.

The following are three primary assumptions of modern conflict theory:

- Competition over scarce resources is at the heart of all social relationships. Competition rather than consensus is characteristic of human relationships.
- Inequalities in power and reward are built into all social structures. Individuals and groups that benefit from any particular structure strive to see it maintained.
- Change occurs as a result of conflict between competing interests rather than through adaptation. Change is often abrupt and revolutionary rather than evolutionary.

A heuristic device to help you think about society from a conflict perspective is to ask, "Who benefits from this element of society?" Using the same example as we did above, we can ask, "Who benefits from the current higher educational system in the U.S.?" The answer, of course, is the wealthy. Why? Because higher education in the U.S. is not free. Thus, the educational system often screens out poorer individuals not because they are unable to compete academically but because they cannot afford to pay for their education. Because the poor are unable to obtain higher education, this means they are also generally unable to get higher paying jobs which means they remain poor. This can easily translate into a vicious cycle of poverty. Thus, while the function of education is to educate the workforce, it also has built into it an element of conflict and inequality, favoring one group (the wealthy) over other groups (the poor). Thinking about education this way helps illustrate why both structural-functionalist and conflict theories are helpful in understanding how society works.

Conflict theory was elabourated in the United Kingdom by Max Gluckman and John Rex, in the United States by Lewis

A. Coser and Randall Collins, and in Germany by Ralf Dahrendorf, all of whom were influenced by Karl Marx, Ludwig Gumplovicz, Vilfredo Pareto, Georg Simmel, and other founding fathers of European sociology.

Limitations

Not surprisingly, the primary limitation of the social-conflict perspective is that it overlooks the stability of societies. While societies are in a constant state of change, much of the change is minor. Many of the broader elements of societies remain remarkably stable over time, indicating the structural-functional perspective has a great deal of merit.

As noted above, sociological theory is often complementary. This is particularly true of structural-functionalism and social-conflict theories. Structural-functionalism focuses on equilibrium and solidarity; conflict-theory focuses on change and conflict. Keep in mind that neither is better than the other; when combined, the two approaches offer a broader and more comprehensive view of society.

Symbolic Interactionism

In contrast to the rather broad approach toward society of structural-functionalism and conflict theory, Symbolic Interactionism is a theoretical approach to understanding the relationship between humans and society. The basic notion of symbolic interactionism is that human action and interaction are understandable only through the exchange of meaningful communication or symbols. In this approach, humans are portrayed as *acting* as opposed to being *acted upon*.

The main principles of symbolic interactionism are:

1. human beings act toward things on the basis of the meanings that things have for them
2. these meanings arise of out of social interaction
3. social action results from a fitting together of individual lines of action.

This approach stands in contrast to the strict behaviourism of psychological theories prevalent at the time it was first formulated (in the 1920s and 1930s). According to Symbolic Interactionism, humans are distinct from infrahumans (lower animals) because infrahumans simply respond to their environment (i.e., a stimulus evokes a response or stimulus-> response) whereas humans have the ability to interrupt that process (i.e., stimulus-> cognition-> response). Additionally, infrahumans are unable to conceive of alternative responses to gestures. Humans, however, can. This understanding should not be taken to indicate that humans never behave in a strict *stimulus-> response* fashion, but rather that humans have the capability of not responding in that fashion (and do so much of the time).

This perspective is also rooted in phenomenological thought. According to symbolic interactionism, the objective world has no reality for humans, only subjectively-defined objects have meaning. Meanings are not entities that are bestowed on humans and learned by habituation. Instead, meanings can be altered through the creative capabilities of humans, and individuals may influence the many meanings that form their society. Human society, therefore, is a social product.

Neurological evidence based on EEGs supports the idea that humans have a "social brain," that is, there are components of the human brain that govern social interaction. These parts of the brain begin developing in early childhood (the preschool years) and aid humans in understanding how other people think. In symbolic interactionism, this is known as "reflected appraisals" or "the looking glass self" and refers to our ability to think about how other people will think about us. A good example of this is when people try on clothes before going out with friends. Some people may not think much about how others will think about their clothing choices, but others can spend quite a bit of time considering what they are going to wear. And while they are deciding, the dialogue that is taking place inside their mind is usually a dialogue between their "self" (that portion of their identity that calls itself "I") and that person's internalized understanding of their friends and society (a "generalized other"). An indicator of mature socialization is when an individual quite accurately predicts how other people think about him/her. Such an individual has incorporated the "social" into the "self."

It should also be noted that symbolic interactionists advocate a particular methodology. Because they see *meaning* as the fundamental component of human and society interaction, studying human and society interaction requires *getting at* that meaning. Thus, symbolic interactionists tend to employ more qualitative rather than quantitative methods in their research.

Limitations

The most significant limitation of the symbolic-interactionist perspective relates to its primary contribution: it overlooks macro social structures (e.g., norms, culture) as a result of focusing on micro-level interactions. Some symbolic interactionists, however, would counter that if *role theory* is incorporated into symbolic interactionism-which is now commonplace-this criticism is addressed.

Impression Management

An extension of *role theory*, impression management is both a theory and process. The theory argues that people are constantly engaged in controlling how others perceive them. The process refers to the goal-directed conscious or unconscious effort to influence the perceptions of other people by regulating and controlling information in social interaction. If a person tries to influence the perception of her or his own image, this activity is called *self-presentation*.

Erving Goffman (1959), the person most often credited with formally developing impression management theory, cast the idea in a dramaturgical framework. The basic idea is that individuals in face-to-face situations are like actors on a stage performing roles. Aware of how they are being perceived by their audience, actors manage their behaviour so as to create specific impressions in the minds of the audience. Strategic interpersonal behaviour to shape or influence impressions formed by an audience is not a new idea. Plato spoke of the "great stage of human life" and Shakespeare noted that "All the world is a stage, and all the men and women merely players".

Social Constructionism

Social constructionism is a school of thought introduced into sociology by Peter L. Berger and Thomas Luckmann with their 1966 book *The Social Construction of Reality*. Social constructionism aims to discover the ways that individuals and groups create their perceived reality. Social constructionism focuses on the description of institutions and actions and not on analysing cause and effect. Socially constructed reality is seen as an on-going dynamic process; reality is reproduced by people acting on their interpretations of what they perceive to be the world external to them. Berger and Luckmann argue that social construction describes both subjective and objective reality-that is that no reality exists outside what is produced and reproduced in social interactions.

A clear example of social constructionist thought is, following Sigmund Freud and Emile Durkheim, religion. Religion is seen as a socially constructed concept, the basis for which is rooted in either our psyche (Freud) or man's need to see some purpose in life or worship a higher presence. One of the key theorists of social constructionism, Peter Berger, explored this concept extensively in his book, *The Sacred Canopy*.

Social constructionism is often seen as a source of the postmodern movement, and has been influential in the field of cultural studies.

Integration Theory

Recently, some sociologists have been taking a different approach to sociological theory by employing an integrationist approach-combining micro-and macro-level theories to provide a comprehensive understanding of human social behaviour. Numerous models could be presented in this vein. George Ritzer's Integration Model is a good example.

Ritzer proposes four highly interdependent elements in his sociological model: a macro-objective component (e.g., society, law, bureaucracy), a micro-objective component (e.g., patterns of behaviour and human interaction), a macro-subjective component (e.g., culture, norms, and values), and a micro-subjective component (e.g., perceptions, beliefs). This model is of particular use in understanding society because it uses two axes: one ranging from objective (society) to subjective (culture and cultural interpretation); the other ranging from the macro-level (norms) to the micro-level (individual level beliefs).

The integration approach is particularly useful for explaining social phenomenon because it shows how the different components of social life work together to influence society and behaviour.

If used for understanding a specific cultural phenomenon, like the displaying of abstract art in one's home, the integration model depicts the different influences on the decision. For instance, the model depicts that cultural norms can influence individual behaviour. The model also shows that individual level values, beliefs, and behaviors influence macro-level culture. This is, in fact, part of what David Halle finds: while there are art consumption differences based on class, they are not predicted solely by class. Displayers of abstract art tend not only to belong to the upper-class, but also are employed in art-production occupations. This would indicate that there are multiple levels of influence involved in art tastes – both broad cultural norms and smaller level occupational norms in addition to personal preferences.

HISTORICAL SOCIOLOGY

Historical sociology is a branch of sociology focusing on how societies develop through history. It looks at how social structure that many regard as natural are in fact shaped by complex social processes. The structure in turn shapes institutions and organizations, and they affect the society-resulting in phenomena ranging from gender bias, income inequality and war. Contemporary historical sociology is primarily concerned with how the state has developed since the Middle Ages, analysing relations between states, classes, economic and political systems.

The Use of History in Sociology

A common phrase regarding this subject is "Sociology is history with the hard work left out; history is sociology with the brains left out". As time has passed, History and Sociology have historically developed into two different specific academic disciplines. Historical data was used and is used today in mainly these three ways. There are many other ways and Sociologists can add different theories to it. The first one is: Examining a theory through a Parallel investigation. To correspond with the natural-science conceptions of laws, and to look at, or apply various historical material where you gather your resources in order to prove the theory that is applied. Or on the other hand sociologists for the parallel investigation theory could apply the theory to certain cases of investigation but in a different modalities of a more widely used process. The second theory that Sociologists mainly use: applying and contrasting certain events or policies. Analyzed by their specific, or what makes them in unique quality of a composition, certain events used by the Sociologist for comparative data can be contrasted and compared. For iterpretive Sociologists it is very common for them to use the 'Verstehen' tradition. And lastly, the third way sociologists typically relate is by taking a look at the causalities from a macro point of view. This is Mill's method: " a) principle of difference: a case with effect and cause present is contrasted with a case with effect and cause absent; and b) principle of agreement: cases with same effects are compared in terms of their (ideally identical) causes. There is an important debate on the usefulness of Mill's method for sociological research, which relates to the fact that historical research is often based on only few cases and that many sociological theories are probabilistic, not deterministic.. Today, historical sociology is measured by a conjunction of questions that are rich in detail

Path Dependence in Historical Sociology

Path dependence to some Sociologists is the theory that events that happened in past, have some or a lot of influence on events that happen in the future. However the Sociologist Mahoney has a different definition of path dependence. This theory suggests that "process, sequence, and temporality" have a valid reason for affecting path dependence and the meaning of past historical events. There are three path-dependent analyses with an explanation to how each theory works. "1) the study of causal processes that are especially sensitive, in a sequence, to early historical events, which are more important than later events; 2) these events are contingent occurrences that cannot be explained by prior events or initial conditions; and 3) that once contingent events take place, the path dependent sequence becomes a deterministic pattern."

The Debate Over General Theory in Sociology

A sociologist James Mahoney revisited the debate over general theory in Historical Sociology. By bridging the gaps of different assumptions, casual agents and causual mechanisms are connected to the empirical analysis, and this is seen as the general theory. "...the debate over general theory in historical sociology with the goal of clarifying the use of this kind of theory in empirical research. General theories are defined as postulates about causal agents and causal mechanisms that are linked to empirical analysis through bridging assumptions. These theories can contribute to substantive knowledge by helping analysts derive new hypotheses, integrate existing findings, and explain historical outcomes. To illustrate these applications, the article considers five different general theories that have guided or could guide historical sociology: functionalist, rational choice, power, neo-Darwinian, and cultural theories. A key conclusion that emerges is that scholars must evaluate both the overall merits of general theory and the individual merits of specific general theories".

Sociological Theory of Karl Marx

In defining Marxism a distinction has to be made between the writings and ideas of Karl Marx, the ideology of Marxism as a sociological perspective between his day and the present, and the politics of communism, socialism, and Labour's third way. Textbooks on sociology often contrast social systems or structuralism with social action perspectives. They frequently then differentiate between consensus theories (like functionalism) and conflict theories (like Marxism or feminism). These distinctions may arise from the sociological cannon's axiomatic reliance on a few key historical thinkers providing a basis for almost all modern development of the subject.

Who was Karl Marx?

Sociology can be thought of as a cannon of ideas and thought, stretching back into the nineteenth century. Its thinkers are "dependent on influences from elsewhere – they are not spontaneous individuals, geniuses who somehow spin their theories from thin air.". Karl Marx (1818 – 1883) was a university educated German and was influenced by the philosopher Hegel, French revolutionary and socialist politics and English economics. Hegel's writing provided a technical and theoretical basis for ideas concerning freedom, conflict and contradiction (dialectic logic) and man's place in the world. This combined with the French tenets of Equality, Fraternity and Liberty along with the pragmatic analyses of economics in England by Adam Smith and David Ricardo. His friend, financier and collabourator Frederick Engels, led Marx to see conflict rather than consensus in society. At the age of 30 he published the Communist Manifesto (1848). He opens saying "the history of all hitherto existing societies is the history of class struggle". By the time he wrote Das Kapital (1867) he had become more focused on the reality of capitalism and the nature of class struggle (and therefore of society) than the trans-historical and inevitable overthrow of capitalist, antagonistic modes of production. It is important to remember the historical perspective; he lived in a world without television, in which England led the world towards industrialization. Imperial Britain had acquired a quarter of the planet (and its resources) so it is not hard to see why he thought that "as capitalism consolidates its hold around the globe, non-capitalist classes are eliminated and the proletariat expands..."

What resources are available and who controls them influences (almost deterministically) the nature of the superstructure, which is made up of all the non-economic articles of society, such as legal, religious and educational systems. Marxism divides the capitalist economic structure into two broad class strata; the bourgeoisie and the proletariat. The bourgeoisie own the means of production, land and factories and buy labour for wages from the proletariat. The proletariat having no means of subsistence themselves, have no choice but to sell their labour for wages to the bourgeoisie. Everyone needs the results of production, food, shelter and commodities. The scarcity of resources leads to a society primarily defined by its economics or infrastructure. In this way Marx thought that the economic base of society provided the foundation for all other features or functions of society, the superstructure. How and to whom the responsibility falls to of first, the funding, production and distribution of agriculture, and second, the provision of all other goods, determines the ruling class and their interests. They, of course, act using their overwhelming economic interests to consolidate their power politically (and culturally according to Gramsci), as well as economically. The legal system, nuclear family and even personal tastes and entertainment are shaped by the ruling class ideology and Marx's description of capitalism in these terms vividly conveys the contradictions inherent in society. For example, he highlights the collective nature of production, whereby many hundred may work in a factory and yet only a very few own the factory and its equipment (capital) and thereby accrue profit. This is gained through the surplus effort of the workers over the wages paid to them, inspiring the term: 'wage slaves'. Many people work for the (overwhelming) benefit of very few. Neoliberals might argue that with modern stock markets, in fact many get to own the capital of business. Even if many workers do have pensions (the most frequent type of personal investment) and thereby a stake-holding, this is hidden behind the profit making and exploitative financial market that operates these investments. Only the already wealthy are in a position to genuinely benefit from the big financial institutions.

Marx could not have noticed the damaging of the environment by industrialisation himself, but Marxism certainly points to an ecological limit to the expansion of capitalism. Profits have to come from somewhere and as resources become more scarce, cheaper processing, environmentally friendly or not, will be employed to add value or profit when wages can be depressed no further. In the mean time capitalism has been buoyed up against rapid collapse ever more effectively by advertising. The power of persuasion using the modern media of TV and the Internet has allowed products as unhelpful and destructive as tobacco, guns and financial credit (debt) to be sold in great quantity. People are conduced by advertising to buy what they do not need and their position as wage slaves is consolidated by their growing addiction to consumerism. This false consciousness or reification (Lukàcs and Hegel) distracts the working classes from the true nature of their both economic and superstructural subjugation and their collective potential for overturning the domination by employing their combined class-consciousness to unite. The power of advertising to persuade people to buy that which they do not need is today nearly absolute. Marx may well have viewed television and the Internet as tools of the economic base as well as cultural artefacts. Antonio Gramsci popularised the term 'hegemony' to refer to the importance of popular culture in forming a collective class consciousness and referred to a need for a counter-hegemonic force in the form of intellectuals drawn from and representative of the working class. Both Hegel and George Lukacs might have criticised this view saying that as individuals undertake non-manual labour they lose direct contact with their human essence and as they loose touch become unable to understand the nature of society. This view would certainly have upset Stalin and Zedong but not 'El Che' Guevara, who insisted on digging and building at the weekends even when he was in charge of the national bank. In Russia Lenin's version of Marxism never truly followed the Communist template as his 'New Economic policy' allowed a limited capitalist investment to stimulate the economy and create a petty bourgeoisie. This was necessary because Russia was a largely rural country of peasants rather than an industrialised one with an alienated middle class. In fact Marx really envisioned Britain being ripe for his socialist revolution as in 1850 half of all manufactured goods globally were made there. The social suffering and damage of this massive development in rapidly overcrowding, and unplanned cities provided (so he thought) a large enough proletariat. Indeed, despite the lack of violent revolution, Britain now has a NHS and welfare state, as well as being nominally secular, democratic and largely socialist with the Labour party currently in government.

Many of the classic criticisms of Marxism arise either out of its macro-nature or the fact that it is about 150 years old. Since then new ideas have been incorporated into neo-marxist ideology most notably by Antonio Gransci and George Lukacs. Combining Marx's view of the economy as infrastructure with new manifestations of culture, Gramsci vividly saw the hegemony of the ruling class ideology flooding into peoples lives in ever more powerful and effective media (like new technology such as mobile 'phones and the internet). In fact the global dominance of capitalism today is so complete that the remaining (self-styled) communist regimes (all 5 of them) all receive the Internet, TV and radio signals and so are (probably fatally) exposed to the hegemony too. On the face of it postmodernism seems to blow Marxism apart simply by recognising the overwhelming complexity of society at any one moment in time. It is right that we will never be able to fully understand the reality of society and its functions, not least because such knowledge would introduce new unknown realities re-challenging our understanding. Conversely the numerically undeniable truth underwriting statistical mathematics proves some aspects of the modernist reality, in particular with regard to economics. Our absolute need to share scarce resources means that our lives are primarily concerned with acquiring the means to live.

Marxism largely ignores the subjugation of women (and other gender issues like homosexuality) and given their historical inability (equally to men) to contribute to the monetary economy it seems reasonable for a historically generated macro-view to ignore them. However, in his Communist Manifesto, Marx addresses patriarchy saying, "Bourgeois marriage is, in reality, a system of wives in common ... it is self-evident that the abolition of the present system of production must bring with it the abolition of free love springing from that system, i.e., of prostitution both public and private." He seems to envisage, with the abolition of class differences, no further innate repression of women as they represent a sub-class of the oppressed classes. Also ethnicity issues and racism are mostly ignored, although they are intrinsically involved when considering issues of class. Finally, the growth of the middle classes in the form of clerical and administrative jobs and the expanding service industry (at least in Britain and the "first world") has complicated the reality and definitions of class strata.

Having briefly outlined the origins of Karl Marx's thinking about Socialism the argument has progressed from the role of economics, the existence of contradictions, the nature of the ruling class ideology to some common criticisms. It becomes clear that the Marxist perspective in sociology is still an effective method for examining societies. The macro-nature of the Marxist perspective (and functionalist) neither claims to help explain micro-issues nor assist in thinking about them. That said, it still has limitations in both examining micro-issues and in addressing the twenty-first century world's post-modernist thinking. The neo-Marxism of Lukacs and Gramsci, in addressing hegemony and culture, help to move on with and beyond postmodernism. Society is complex and getting ever more so. As a template to understand the relations between people and the world in which they live Marxism dutifully conveys the genuine nature of suffering even today.

SOCIOLOGICAL THEORY OF ROLE THEORY

Role Theory posits that human behaviour is guided by expectations held both by the individual and by other people. The expectations correspond to different roles individuals *perform* or *enact* in their daily lives, such as secretary, father, or friend. For instance, most people hold pre-conceived notions of the role expectations of a secretary, which might include: answering phones, making and managing appointments, filing paperwork, and typing memos. These role expectations would not be expected of a professional soccer player. Individuals generally have and manage many roles. Roles consist of a set of rules or norms that function as plans or blueprints to guide behaviour. Roles specify what goals should be pursued, what tasks must be accomplished, and what performances are required in a given scenario or situation. Role theory holds that a substantial proportion of observable, day-to-day social behaviour is simply persons carrying out their roles, much as actors carry out their roles on the stage or ballplayers theirs on the field. Role theory is, in fact, predictive. It implies that if we have information about the role expectations for a specified position (e.g., sister, fireman, prostitute), a significant portion of the behaviour of the persons occupying that position can be predicted.

What's more, role theory also argues that in order to change behaviour it is necessary to change roles; roles correspond to behaviors and vice versa. In addition to heavily influencing behaviour, roles influence beliefs and attitudes; individuals will change their beliefs and attitudes to correspond with their roles. For instance, someone over-looked for a promotion to a managerial position in a company may change their beliefs about the benefits of management by convincing him/herself that they didn't want the additional responsibility that would have accompanied the position. Many role theorists as one of the most compelling theories bridging individual behaviour and social structure. Roles, which are in part dictated by social structure and in part by social interactions, guide the behaviour of the individual. The individual, in turn, influences the norms, expectations, and behaviors associated with roles. The understanding is reciprocal and didactic.

Structural-Functional Perspective

The functionalist approach sees a *role* as the set of expectations that society places on an individual. By unspoken consensus, certain behaviours are deemed *appropriate* and others *inappropriate*. For example, it is appropriate for a doctor to dress fairly conservatively, ask a series of personal questions about one's health, touch one in ways that would normally be forbidden, write prescriptions, and show more concern for the personal well-being of his clients. Electricians or shopkeepers may also show concern for the well-being of their clients, but if they start touching their clients, especially where doctors are allowed to touch, they'll get in trouble; they will have stepped outside of the norms associated with their roles.

In the functionalist conception, role is one of the important ways in which individual activity is socially regulated: roles create regular patterns of behaviour and thus a measure of predictability, which not only allows individuals to function effectively because they know what to expect of others, but also makes it possible for the sociologist to make generalisations about society. Collectively, a group of interlocking roles creates a social institution: the institution of law, for example, can be seen as the combination of many roles, including: *police officer*, *judge*, *criminal*, and *victim*.

Roles, in the functionalist perspective, are relatively inflexible and are more-or-less universally agreed upon. Although it is recognised that different roles interact (*teacher* and *student*), and that roles are usually defined in relation to other roles (*doctor* and *patient* or *mother* and *child*), the functionalist approach has great difficulty in accounting for variability and flexibility of roles and finds it difficult to account for the vast differences in the way that individuals conceive different roles. Taken to extremes, the functionalist approach results in *role* becoming a set of static, semi-global expectations laid down by a unified, amorphous society. The distinction between *role* and *norm* (or *culture*) thus becomes sterile. The functionalist approach has been criticized for its static understanding of roles. Even so, it remains a fundamental concept which is still taught in most introductory courses and is still regarded as important.

Intrestingly, this conception has crossed over from academic discourse into popular use. It has become commonplace to speak of particular *roles* as if they were indeed fixed, agreed upon by all, and uncontroversial (e.g., *the role of the teacher* or *a parent's role*). This everyday usage nearly always employs *role* in a normative way, to imply that *this is the proper behaviour* for a teacher or a parent, or even for an entire institution.

Interactionist Perspective

The interactionist definition of *role* is more fluid and subtle than the functionalist perspective. A *role*, in this conception, is not fixed or prescribed but something that is constantly negotiated between individuals.

One of the ways Mead explained the idea of roles was by using a development model for children. According to Mead, children adopt roles in the development of a self. In so doing, they pass through three stages:

1. preparatory stage-meaningless imitation by the infant; assumes roles but doesn't understand what they are
2. play stage-actual playing of roles occurs; but no unified conception of self
3. game stage-completion stage of self; child finds himself; must respond to simultaneous roles; the individual can act with a certain amount of consistency in a variety of situations because he/she acts in accordance with a generalized set of expectations and definitions he/she has internalized

Adults, of course, are beyond the game stage, but continue to adopt roles and adapt them through interpersonal interactions. This can be most easily seen in encounters where there is considerable ambiguity. For instance, let's assume person X has a friend who is also a lawyer; we'll call him Y. If X approaches Y as a friend but then asks for legal advice, this forces Y to either switch roles completely or merge the roles temporarily. Until Y decides on his course of action, role ambiguity will exist.

Additional Approaches

- structural-little attention given to norms; attention is focused on social structures conceived as stable organizations of sets of persons (called social positions or statuses) who share the same, patterned behaviors (roles)
- organization-focuses on social systems that are preplanned, task-oriented, and hierarchical; roles in such organizations are assumed to be associated with identified social positions and to be generated by normative expectations
- cognitive role theory-focuses on relationships between role expectations and behaviour (from Biddle 1986)

Propositions

Role Theory includes the following propositions:

1. people spend much of their lives participating as members of groups and organizations
2. within these groups, people occupy distinct positions
3. each of these positions entails a role, which is a set of functions performed by the person for the group
4. groups often formalize role expectations as norms or even codified rules, which include what rewards will result when roles are successfully performed and what punishments will result when roles are not successfully performed
5. individuals usually carry out their roles and perform in accordance with prevailing norms; in other words, role theory assumes that people are primarily conformists who try to live up to the norms that accompany their roles
6. group members check each individual's performance to determine whether it conforms with the norms; the anticipation that others will apply sanctions ensures role performance.

Extensions of the Theory

Role Theory has been a fruitful approach to understanding

humans and society. As a result, various derivatives and additional concepts have developed.

Role Confusion

Role confusion is a situation where an individual has trouble determining which role he/she should assume. For example, if a graduate student were to attend a department party at a professor's home, the student may find it difficult to determine if he/she should act as a student toward the professor, exhibiting deference or respect, or as a friend or associate, showing collegiality and familiarity.

Role Conflict

Role Conflict results when an individual encounters tensions as the result of incompatible roles. For instance, a mother who is employed full-time may experience role conflict because of the norms that are associated with the two roles she has. She may be expected to spend a great deal of time taking care of her children while simultaneously trying to advance her career.

Role Strain

Role Strain refers to the felt difficulty in fulfilling role obligations. In contrast to *role conflict*, where tension is felt between two competing roles, the tension in role strain comes from just one role. Returning to the example of a mother, if she were to find that she is unable to fulfil her obligations as defined by, say, an overly demanding spouse (or religion, or child), she would experience role strain. The *role expectations* may be beyond what she is able to achieve or may push her to the limits of her abilities.

Role Distance

Role Distance is the effectively expressed pointed separateness between the individual and his putative role. The individual is not denying the role but the virtual self that is implied in the role for all accepting performers. The concept of *role distance* provides a sociological means of dealing with one type of divergence between obligation and actual performance. For example, the *maturing* adolescent who is forced to ride a merry-go-round may display role distance by acting as though the ride does not challenge her physical abilities or frighten her. This may be displayed by riding backwards or leaning dangerously from her horse.

Immediate audiences figure very directly in the display of role distance; actors need an audience or a co-conspirator for role distancing to work. There are two ways of establishing role distance:

1. isolating one's self from the contamination of the situation, which can be displayed through indifference (e.g., a waiter saying, "I'm just doing this to put myself through college.")
2. joking about the situation (e.g., the young merry-go-round rider saying, "I can do this with my eyes closed.").

It is often possible to determine incidents in which *role distance* might be displayed solely on the grounds of the performers' gross age-sex characteristics. A seventeen year-old boy riding a merry-go-round (especially with peers) will likely display significant role distance.

Role Embracement

Role Embracement refers to the complete adoption of a role. When a role is truly embraced, the self disappears completely into the role. Three things seem to be involved in the earnestness with which people assume roles or the degree to which they embrace a role:

1. an admitted or expressed attachment to the role
2. a demonstration of qualifications and capacities for performing it
3. an active engagement or spontaneous involvement in the role activity at hand, that is, a visible investment of attention and muscular effort.

Limitations

Role theory has a hard time explaining social deviance when it does not correspond to a pre-specified role. For instance, the behaviour of someone who adopts the role of bank robber can be predicted-she will rob banks. But if a bank teller simply begins handing out cash to random people, role theory would be unable to explain why. Another limitation of role theory is that it does not and cannot explain how role expectations came to be what they are. Role theory has no explanation for why it is expected of male soldiers to cut their hair short, but it could predict with a high degree of accuracy that if someone is a male soldier they will have short hair. Additionally, role theory does not explain when and how role expectations change.

CONFLICT THEORY

In sociology and biology, conflict theory states that the society or organization functions so that each individual participant and its groups struggle to maximize their benefits, which inevitably contributes to social change such as changes in politics and revolutions. The theory is mostly applied to explain conflict between social classes in ideologies such as socialism and communism. The theory refutes functionalism, which considers that societies and organization function so that each individual and group plays a specific role, like organs in the body. There are radical basic assumptions (it is only conflict, which might explain social change), or moderate ones (custom and conflict are always mixed).

In understanding conflict theory, competition plays a key part.

The following are four primary assumptions of modern conflict theory:

1. Competition. Competition over scarce resources (money, leisure, sexual partners, and so on) is at the heart of all social relationships. Competition rather than consensus is characteristic of human relationships.
2. Structural inequality. Inequalities in power and reward are built into all social structures. Individuals and groups that benefit from any particular structure strive to see it maintained.
3. Revolution. Change occurs as a result of conflict between competing interests rather than through adaptation. It is often abrupt and revolutionary rather than evolutionary.
4. War. Even war is a unifier of the societies involved, as well as war may set an end to whole societies.

Conflict theory was elabourated e. g. in the United Kingdom by Max Gluckman and John Rex, in the United States by Lewis

A. Coser and Randall Collins, and in Germany (later the United Kingdom) by Ralf Dahrendorf, all of them being less or more influenced by Karl Marx, Ludwig Gumplovicz, Vilfredo Pareto, Georg Simmel, and other founder fathers of European sociology.

SOCIOLOGICAL THEORY OF EMILE DURKHEIM

Emile Durkheim (1858-1917) is claimed as the father of sociology by renowned american sociologist "Talcott Parsons". His contributions make it clear why he deserves the title.

Biographical Sketch

Emile Durkheim was born into the traditional Jewish family in the village of Epinal in the Vosges near Strasbourg, France. He lost faith in God at an early age and turned towards the secular view of religion. The disastrous Franco-Prussian war of 1870 made a major impression on Durkheim, which can be seen in his fascination with the study of group solidarity. He went to attend Ecole Normale Superior at Paris whose impact can be seen in his scientific and mathematical bent in research. His works revolve around two themes, "Domination of collectivism over individualism" and "Application of scientific methods to study social phenomenon".

Intellectual Influence

Durkheim was influenced by many scholars from french, english and german traditions. Montesquieu's spirit of laws influenced him to study the changes in society in terms of other factors like Law. Which led him to create a distinction of societies based on repressive law and restitutive law. Other Major influences being Rousseau, Condorcet, Emile Boutrox, Wilhelm Wundt, Ferdinand Tonnies, Fustel de coulenges, Charles Renouvier, Georg Simmel and August Comte. He had a running intellectual fued with his colleague Gabriel Tarde. This fued also contributed to his intellectual thinking defending his positivistic approach from socio-psychological approach of Tarde.

Contributions

Durkheim began by publishing articles, first on the German academic life. In 1893 came his first monumental work on the *The Social Division of Labour*. He published his second major study *The Rules of Sociological Method* in 1895 and completed his trilogy in 1897 with *Suicide*. His final book was entitled, *Totemism: The Elementary Forms of Religious Life* in 1912. He created a distinct identity to sociology as a discipline with his concept of distinct social reality which can be understood and explained in terms of social facts. He made sociology a study of social facts thus effectively creating a clear scope for the subject culling it out of What was earlier studied by psychology and philosophy.

His second book "The Rules of sociological Method", he clearly states the methods that are to be followed by a sociologist while studying the society. In this book he discusses three methods of carrying out research in a positive science like sociology. These methods are observation, experimentation and generalization. This book formed the framework which was later demonstrated by durkheim in letter and spirit through in studies. His Study of suicide reaffirms his belief that causal relationship can be established between social phenomenon. Next study of Religion demonstrates the utility of functional explanation in sociology. In his third book, *Le Suicide* He had used considerable statistical ingenuity to reject the early theories for giving extra social factors such as climate, heredity, mental alienation as causes of suicide, and established a causal relationship between suicide and lack of cohesion. To support his own findings he used the empirical data collected from many societies and cultures. Durkheim identified three basic types of suicide: *Egoistic suicide, Altruistic suicide, and Anomic suicide* based on the empirical evidences and added *Fatalistic Suicide* based on historical evidence. This work stands as a landmark in the sociological tradition as the first work which successfully combines theory with empirical evidence.

In his last major book,*Totemism: The Elementary Forms of Religious Life (*1912), he gave the description and detailed analysis of simplistic form religion, Totemism as practiced by Aboriginal Australian tribes. He derived general theory of religion from the study of the simplest and most primitive of religious institutions like totemism. He began by refuting the existing theories of Animism by *Tylor* and naturism by *Max Mueller* on the grounds of them promoting religion as an illusion with reliance on spirit and supernatural forces. Religion according to Durkheim is very much real, permanent and transcendent. The essence of religion according to him is divided into *Sacred* and *Profane*. Durkheim defines religion as a unified system of beliefs and practices relative to sacred things,that is to say things set apart and forbidden-beliefs and practices that unite in one simple moral community called a Church, all those who adhere to it.

ETHNOMETHODOLOGY

Ethnomethodology is a perspective within sociology that focuses on the way people make sense of their everyday world. People are seen as rational actors, but employ practical reasoning rather than formal logic to make sense of and function in society. The theory argues that human society is entirely dependent on these methods of achieving and displaying understanding. The approach was developed by Harold Garfinkel, based on Alfred Schütz's phenomenological reconstruction of Max Weber's verstehen sociology.

Like Durkheim, the fundamental sociological phenomenon for ethnomethodologists is the social fact. But, unlike Durkheim, the social fact is not external of the individual. The social fact is the product of the social member's methodological activities; it is their understanding of their everyday world. Members, here, are understood not simply as individuals but any social entity (i.e., individuals and organizations) that can produce a social fact. In short, members of society (individuals and organizations) make sense of and function in society by creating social facts or understandings of how society works. In this sense, ethnomethodology is at the same time both macro and micro oriented in that members can produce social facts at either level, for either the personal structure (the individual's level of everyday meaning) or the organizational/institutional structure (the organization's level of everyday meaning).

One of the key points of the theory is that ethnomethods or social facts are *reflexively accountable*. *Accounts* are the ways members describe or explain specific situations. *Accounting* is the process of describing or explaining social situations or how members make sense of their everyday world. Ethnomethodologists are interested in both the account and the method by which the account is made meaningful to the recipient of the account, and tend to emphasize the latter. The interest is not in determining if the account is accurate or otherwise judging the account but rather in exploring how the account is conveyed. For example, the explanation given by a husband for arriving home late at night is an account. The ethnomethodologist is interested in both the account and the methods used to convey that account to the recipient, in this case, the wife. Whether the account is factual or not does not interest the ethnomethodologist.

Sociology, generally, seeks to provide accounts of society. Ethnomethodologists view such accounts-sociological ones-the same way they view the account given by the husband above. In other words, ethnomethodologists break down the accounts given by other sociologists (and other scientists, for that matter) the same way they break down the accounts of interpersonal interaction in romantic relationships.

Ethnomethodologists are not interested in whether or not the accounts given by sociologists are accurate but rather are interested in the accounts that are given and the methods used to develop and convey those accounts.

The accounts people use to explain their behaviour or help them understand social interactions are generally taken for granted (e.g., you don't have to ask permission to use the restroom in your own home). To illustrate how these accounts are usually taken for granted, ethnomethodologists have used research methods in the past that 'breach' or 'break' the everyday routine of interaction in order to reveal the work that goes into maintaining the normal flow of life. Some examples include:

- pretending to be a stranger in one's own home
- blatantly cheating at board games
- attempting to bargain for goods on sale in stores

In most of these situations, the individuals who are unaware that the researcher is intentionally breaching social norms attempt to explain the *breacher's* behaviour by providing accounts for them. These interventions demonstrate the creativity with which ordinary members of society are able to interpret and maintain the unspoken social order that ethnomethodologists study.

Impact of Ethnomethodology

While ethnomethodology is often seen as being removed from more mainstream sociology, it has proven to be influential. For instance, ethnomethodology notes that words are reliant for their meaning based on the context in which they are used; they are *indexical*. This has led to insights into the objectivity of social science and the difficulty in establishing a description of human behaviour which has an objective status outside the context of its creation. Ethnomethodology has also influenced the Sociology of Scientific Knowledge by providing a research strategy that precisely describes the methods of its research subjects without the necessity of evaluating their validity. This proved to be useful to researchers studying social order in labouratories who wished to understand how scientists conducted their experiments without either endorsing or criticising their activities.

Ethnomethodology has had an impact on linguistics and particularly on pragmatics. Ethnomethodological studies of work have played a significant role in the field of human-computer interaction, informing design by providing engineers with descriptions of the practices of users. Additionally, ethnomethodologically informed management and leadership studies are newly emerging fields.

EXCHANGE THEORY

Social Exchange Theory (sub of Reinforcement):-assumes freedom of choice and situations that require decision making; cost/benefit analysis-people are hedonistic-they try to maximize rewards and minimize costs-views social relationships primarily as exchanges of goods and services among persons-include equity theory here as: predicting the conditions under which people try to change or restructure their relationships; a state of equity exists in a relationship when participants feel that the rewards they receive are proportional to the costs they bear

Social exchange theory is a social psychological perspective that explains social change and stability as a process of negotiated exchanges between parties. Social exchange theory posits that all human relationships are formed by the use of a subjective cost-benefit analysis and the *comparison of alternatives*. For example, when a person perceives the costs of relationship as outweighing the perceived benefits, then the theory predicts that the person will choose to leave the relationship.

The early permuatations of Social Exchange Theory stem from Gouldner's (1960) norm of reciprocity, which simply argues that people aught to return benefits given to them in a relationship. Later modifications to this theory focus attention on relational development and maintenance rules. For social exchange theorists, when the costs and benefits are equal in a relationship, then that relationship is not equitable. The notion of equity is a core part of social exchange theory.

Social exchange theory is intimately tied to rational choice theory, and features all of its main assumptions. Rational choice theory is a way of looking at deliberations between a number of potential courses of action, in which "rationality" of one form or another is used either to decide which course of action would be the best to take, or to predict which course of action actually will be taken. Such a perspective finds itself in models for both human behaviour and behaviour of non-human but nonetheless potentially rational entities, such as corporations.

Obviously, what is taken as "rational" is of chief importance here. This varies with context:

- The technical meaning in economics is about preferences: preferences are defined to be rational if they are complete and transitive. That is, that the decision maker is able to compare all of the alternatives, and that these comparisons are consistent.
- If uncertainty is involved, then the independence axiom is often assumed in addition to rational preferences.
- Rationality can also mean that the decision maker always chooses the most preferred option, as in the Utility Maximization Problem.

Often, to simplify calculation and ease prediction, some rather unrealistic assumptions are made about the world. These can include:

- An individual has precise information about exactly what will occur under any choice made. (Alternatively, an individual has a reliable probability distribution describing what will happen under any choice made.)

- An individual has time and ability to weigh every choice against every other choice.
- An individual is fully aware of all possible choices.

Assumptions such as these have sparked criticism from a number of camps. Some people have tried to create models of bounded rationality, which try to be more psychologically plausible without giving up completely on the idea that some kind of reason underlies decision-making processes.

SOCIOLOGICAL THEORY OF MAX WEBER

Max Weber (1864-1902) was born in Erfurt, the son of a prosperous and influential lawyer who was active in politics. Like his friend Simmel, Weber was brought up in Berlin. He studied law, history, economics, and philosophy and achieved early recognition, becoming a professor at the age of 30. Then he suffered a nervous breakdown which forced him to give up teaching. After he recovered, he spent most of his life in private study. His writings were extensive; although many volumes have been translated into English, a considerable amount remains untranslated. Weber believed that the same forms of social organization develop independently in different cultured, and his enormous historical knowledge enabled him to demonstrate the one point again and again. He was discussing religious congregations and the balance between preaching and pastoral care in such congregations. "Among those religious functionaries whose pastoral care has influenced the everyday life of the laity and the behaviour of political officials in an enduring and often decisive manner have been the counselling rabbis of Judaism, the father confessors of Catholicism, the pietistic pastors of souls in Protestantism, the directors of souls in Counter Reformation Catholicism, the Brahminic purohitas at the court, the gurus and gosains in Hinduism, and the muftis and dervish sheikhs in Islam. One of Weber's lifelong concerns was to show how the major segments of a society influenced each other in their historical development. His first important work, The Protestant Ethic and. The Spirit of Capitalism, demonstrated how the religious values held by the luritan sects of the Reformation, especially their asceticism and their belief that God arbitrarily elects certain souls for salvation, contributed to the development of industrial capitalism in England and northern Europe by providing motives for hard work, austere living, and the accumulation of wealth. Although it was not his sole purpose, Weber refuted Marx's contention that all beliefs and values were mere superstructure, explainable by reference to the organization of production, by showing that beliefs and values could be equally well used to explain the development of a system of production. Because he provided an alternative explanation of the rise of capitalism and a different set of predictions about its future, Weber has been called "the Marx of the bourgeoisie." But his historical analyses go far beyond this one point; he was able to show the mutual dependence of economic systems, forms of government, social stratification, and religious beliefs in Greece and Rome, in the Middle Ages, in the ancient Near East, in India, China, Japan, and medieval Russia, indeed wherever civilization had left written records.

The Perception of Charisma

In Weber's word the word "charisma" is denoted to a quality of an individual personality, which makes him distinguish from other persons in a society. This quality may be a supernatural, superhuman, or at least specifically exceptional power. We may say in simple that it is God gifted. These traits, as such, are not accessible to the ordinary person, but are regarded as of divine origin or as exemplary, and on the basis of them the individual concerned is treated as a leader. In primitive circumstances this peculiar kind of deference is paid to prophets, to people with a reputation for therapeutic or legal wisdom, to leaders in the hunt, and heroes in war. It is very often thought of as resting on magical powers. Max Weber treated every type of this quality in his theory for explanation whether it is unenthusiastic or Enthusiastic. He also included intellectual, and Heroes (such as Alexander the Great etc.). Charismatic authority is different from bureaucratic and traditional authority in performing the everyday routine and the profane sphere. Bureaucrat authority is specifically rational in the sense of being bound to intellectual analyzable rules, while charismatic authority is specifically irrational in this sense of being foreign to all rules. Traditional authority is bound to the precedents handed down from the past and to this extent is also oriented to rule while the charismatic authority repudiates to past and is in this sense a specifically revolutionary force. It recognizes the appropriation of positions of power by virtue of the possession of property either on the part of a chief or of socially privileged groups. The on basis of legitimacy for it is personal charisma, so long as it is proved, this, is, as long as it receives recognition and is able to satisfy the followers disciples. But this lasts only so long as the belief in its charismatic inspiration remains. The charismatic revolutionary force alters the situations of action by changing men's attitudes and intellectualizes the individual. Charisma, on the other hand, may involve a subjective or internal re orientation born out of suffering, conflicts or enthusiasm. It may then resin in a radical alteration of the central system of attitudes and directions d action, with a completely new orientation of all attitudes toward the different problems and structures of the "world."

Motives for Transformation of Charismatic Authority

Under charismatic realm the social relationships directly involved are strictly personal, based on the validity and practice of charismatic personal qualities. If this is not to remain a purely transitory phenomenon, but to take on the character of a permanent relationship forming a stable community of disciples, or a band of followers, or a party organization, or any sort of political or hierocratic organization, it is necessary for the character of charismatic authority to become radically changed. Charismatic authority exists only in the process of originating. It cannot remain stable, but becomes either traditionalized or rationalized, or a combination of both. What are the motives necessary for this transformation? (1) The material interests of the followers in the continuation and the continual reactivation of the community or in simple words we can say the economic and social life is necessary for follower and they can not remain uncommitted from their social life. (2) Both traditional and administrative authority have an interest in continuing it in such a way that both from an ideal and a material point of view, their own status is put on a stable everyday basis. This means, above all, making it possible to participate in normal family relationships and at least to enjoy a secure social position, in place of the kind of discipleship which is cut off from ordinary worldly connections, notably in the family and in economic relationships.

Solution for the Problem of Succession

These interests generally become conspicuously evident with the disappearance of the personal charismatic leader, and with the problem of succession which inevitably arises. The way in which this problem is met if it is met at all and the charismatic group continues to exist is of crucial importance for the character of the subsequent social relationships. The principal possible types of solution to problem appeared during the process of succession:

Selection of New Charismatic Leader

The search for a new charismatic leader on the basis of criteria of the qualities which will fit him for the position of authority. A example of this is the choice of new Dalai Lama or new Bull of Apis.

Revelation Process

By revelation manifested in oracles, lots, divine judgments, or other techniques of selection. In this case, the legitimacy of the new leader is dependent on the legitimacy of the technique of his selection. This involves a form of legalization. It is said that at times the Schofetim of Israel had this character. Saul is said to have been chosen by the old war oracle.

Designation by Charismatic Leader

By the designation on the part of the original charismatic leader of his own successor and his recognition on the part of the followers. This is' a very common form. Originally, the Roman magistracies were filled entirely in this way. The system survived most clearly into later times in the appointment of "dictators" and in the institution of the "interrex." In this case, legitimacy is acquired through the act of designation.

Pre Designation of Successor by Selection

Designation of a successor by the charismatically qualified administrative staff and his recognition by the community. In its typical form, this process should quite definitely not be interpreted as "election," or "nomination," or anything of the sort. It is not a matter of free selection, but of one which is strictly bound to objective duty. It is not to be determined merely by majority vote, but is a question of arriving at the correct designation, the designation of the right person who is truly endowed with charisma. It is quite possible that the minority and not the majority should be right in such a case. It is obligatory to acknowledge a mistake, and persistence in error is a serious offense.

Making a wrong choice is a genuine wrong requiring expiation. Originally it was a magical offense. Nevertheless, in such a case it is easy for legitimacy to take on the character of an acquired right which is justified by standards of the correctness of the process by which the position was acquired, for the most part, by its having been acquired in accordance with certain formalities, such as coronation. This was the original meaning of the coronation of bishops and kings in the Western world by the clergy or the nobility with the "consent" of the community. There are numerous analogous phenomena all over the world. The fact that this is the origin of the modem conception of "election" raises problems which will have to be gone into later.

Inherit Quality or Kinship

By the conception that charisma is a quality transmitted by heredity; thus that it is participated in by the kinsmen of its bearer, particularly by his closest relatives. This is the case of hereditary charisma. The order of hereditary succession in such a case need not be the same as that which is in force for appropriated rights, but may differ from it. It is also sometimes necessary to select the proper heir within the kinship group by some of the methods just spoken of; thus in certain Negro states brothers have had to fight for the succession. In China, succession bad to take place in such a way that the relation of the living group to the ances spirits was not disturbed. The rule either of seniority or of designation by the follower has been very common in the Orient. Hence, in the house of Osman, it has been obligatory to eliminate all other possible candidates. Only in medieval Europe and in Japan universally, elsewhere only sporadically, has the principle of primogeniture, as governing the inheritance of authority, become clearly established. This has greatly facilitated the consolidation of political groups in that it has eliminated struggle between a plurality of candidates from the same charismatic family. In Asia there have been very numerous hereditary priesthoods; also, frequently, the hereditary charisma of kinship groups has been treated as a criterion of social rank and of eligibility for fifes and benefices.

Transmitted Dogma

The concept that charisma may be transmitted by formal procedure means from one bearer to another or may be created in a new person. The concept was originally supernatural. It involves a dissociation of charisma from a particular character, making it an objective, transferable entity.

In particular, it may become the charisma of office. In this case the belief in legitimacy is no longer directed to the individual, but to the acquired qualities and to the effectiveness of the ritual acts. The most important example is the transmission of priestly charisma by anointing, consecration, or the laying on of hands and of royal authority, by anointing and by coronation. The caratter indelibly thus acquired means that the charismatic qualities and powers of the office are emancipated from the personal qualities of the priest.

SOCIAL LEARNING THEORY

Observational learning or social learning refers to learning that occurs as a function of observing, retaining and replicating behaviour observed in others. It is most associated with the work of psychologist Albert Bandura, who implemented some of the seminal studies in the area and initiated social learning theory. Although observational learning can take place at any stage in life, it is thought to be particularly important during childhood, particularly as authority becomes important.

Because of this, social learning theory has influenced debates on the effect of television violence and parental role models. Bandura's Bobo doll experiment is widely cited in psychology as a demonstration of observational learning and demonstrated that children are more likely to engage in violent play with a life size rebounding doll after watching an adult do the same.

Observational learning allows for learning without any change in behaviour and has therefore been used as an argument against strict behaviourism which argued that behaviour change must occur for new behaviours to be acquired.

Required Conditions

Bandura called the process of social learning *modelling* and gave four conditions required for a person to successfully model the behaviour of someone else:

- Attention to the model:A person must first pay attention to a person engaging in a certain behaviour (the model).
- Retention of details: Once attending to the observed behaviour, the observer must be able to effectively remember what the model has done. He talked a lot about sponge cake.
- Motor reproduction: The observer must be able to replicate the behaviour being observed. For example, juggling cannot be effectively learned by observing a model juggler if the observer does not already have the ability to perform the component actions (throwing and catching a ball).
- Motivation and Opportunity: The observer must be motivated to carry out the action they have observed and remembered, and must have the opportunity to do so. For example, a suitably skilled person must want to replicate the behaviour of a model juggler, and needs to have an appropriate number of items to juggle to hand.

Effect on Behaviour

Social learning may effect behaviour in the follow ways:

- Teaches new behaviours
- Increases or decreases the frequency of which previously learnt behaviours are carried out
- Can encourage previously forbidden behaviours
- Can increase or decrease similar behaviours. For example, observing a model excelling in piano playing may encourage an observer to excel in playing the saxophone.

SYMBOLIC INTERACTIONISM

This approach stands in contrast to the strict behaviourism of psychological theories prevalent at the time it was first formulated (in the 1920s and 1930s), behaviourism and ethology, and also contrasts with structural-functionalism. According to Symbolic Interactionism, humans are distinct from infrahumans (lower animals) simply respond to their environment (i.e., a stimulus evokes a response or stimulus-> response) whereas humans have the ability to interrupt that process (i.e., stimulus-> cognition-> response). Additionally, infrahumans are unable to conceive of alternative responses to gestures. Humans, however, can. This understanding should not be taken to indicate that humans never behave in a strict *stimulus-> response* fashion, but rather that humans have the capability of not responding in that fashion (and do so much of the time).

This perspective is also rooted in phenomenological thought. According to symbolic interactionism, the objective world has no reality for humans, only subjectively-defined objects have meaning. Meanings are not entities that are bestowed on humans and learned by habituation. Instead, meanings can be altered through the creative capabilities of humans, and individuals may influence the many meanings that form their society (Herman and Reynolds 1994). Human society, therefore, is a social product. It should also be noted that symbolic interactionists advocate a particular methodology. Because they see *meaning* as the fundamental component of human/society interaction, studying human/society interaction requires *getting at* that meaning. Thus, symbolic interactionists tend to employ more qualitative rather than quantitative methods in their research.

Additional Concepts

In symbolic interactionist thought, there is a difference between infrahuman and human society. In infrahuman life, cooperation is physiologically determined. In other words, it is not a cognitive process; it results from instinct and biological programming rather than conscious thinking. In human society, cooperation is cognitive and conscious. Human cooperation can only be brought about by:

- each acting individual ascertaining the intention of the acts of others

- each acting individual deciding on his/her own response on the basis of that intention

Another distinction drawn between infrahumans and humans is in the types of communication employed. Infrahuman communication is gestural; it takes place immediately, without any interruption of the act for interpretation or assigning meaning. In contrast to infrahuman communication, human communication is meaningful in that gestures are symbolic and do not invoke immediate responses-humans must interpret gestures and assign them meaning. Because human communication involves interpretation and the assignment of meaning, it is only possible when there is consensus in meaning. Meanings for symbols must be shared.

Shared meaning necessarily takes place through role-taking; in order to complete an act, the actor must put himself in the position of the other person. Behaviour is viewed as *social* not simply when it is a response to others, but rather when it has incorporated in it the behaviour of others. Human beings respond to themselves as other persons respond to them, and in so doing they imaginatively share the conduct of others.

Self

The self refers to the conscious, reflective personality of an individual. It is the entity the person envisions when he/she thinks about who they are. In order to understand the concept of self, it is important to understand that the development of self is only possible through role-taking. In order to look upon your *self*, you have to be able to take the role of another, which, in turn, allows you to reflect upon your *self*. Because role-taking is a necessary part of self-development, it is concurrent with the development of self.

According to Mead (1967), the self develops in a series of three stages:

1. preparatory stage-meaningless imitation by the infant
2. play stage-actual playing of roles occurs; but no unified conception of self develops
3. game stage-this is the completion stage of self-development; the child finds who he or she is; the child also must respond to simultaneous roles; the individual

can act with a certain amount of consistency in a variety of situations because he/she acts in accordance with a generalized set of expectations and definitions he/she has internalized

The *self* consists of two parts, the *I* and the *Me*. The *I* is the impulsive tendency of the individual. The *I* is the spontaneous, unorganized aspect of human existence. The *Me* is the incorporated other within the individual. The incorporated or generalized other supplies an organized set of attitudes and definitions, understandings and expectations (or meanings) that are common to the group to which the individual belongs.

According to Mead's presentation of the *I* and the *Me*, action begins in the form of the *I* and ends in the form of the *Me*; the *I* gives propulsion while the *Me* gives direction. Additionally, the *I*, being creative and spontaneous, provides for change in society. The *Me*, being regulatory, works to maintain society. Thus, in the concept of *self* is a powerful and comprehensive understanding of how humans function in society and, in turn, how society functions. The concept also depicts the relationship between the individual and society (Meltzer 1978).

According to Meltzer (1978), there are three implications of selfhood:

1. the possession of self makes of the individual a society in miniature; humans can engage themselves in interaction; they can view themselves in a new way
2. the ability to act toward oneself makes possible an inner experience which need not reach overt expression; humans can have a mental life
3. an individual with a self can direct and control his behaviour

It is also important to recognize that the self and the mind are twin emergents in the social process...

Mind

The *Mind* or mental component of man emerges out of human communication. The mind is only present when significant symbols (as opposed to gestures that do not have meaning but simply evoke responses) are being used in communication. In this sense, *mind* is a process manifested whenever the individual is interacting with himself using significant symbols. The mind is also the component of the individual that interrupts responses to stimuli. It is the mind that attempts to pre-vision the future by exploring possible outcomes of actions before proceeding with actions. In minded behaviour, the individual carries on an internal conversation.

SYSTEMS THEORY

Systems theory or general systems theory or systemics is an interdisciplinary field which studies systems as a whole. Systems theory was founded by Ludwig von Bertalanffy, William Ross Ashby and others between the 1940s and the 1970s on principles from physics, biology and engineering and later grew into numerous fields including philosophy, sociology, organizational theory, management, psychotherapy (within family systems therapy) and economics among others. Cybernetics is a closely related field. In recent times complex systems has increasingly been used as a synonym.

Systems theory focuses on complexity and interdependence. A system is composed of regularly interacting or interdependent groups of activities/parts that form a whole. Part of systems theory, *system dynamics* is a method for understanding the dynamic behaviour of complex systems. The basis of the method is the recognition that the structure of any system — the many circular, interlocking, sometimes time-delayed relationships among its components — is often just as important in determining its behaviour as the individual components themselves. Examples are chaos theory and social dynamics.

Systems theory has also been developed within sociology. The most notable scientist in this area is Niklas Luhmann. The systems framework is also fundamental to organizational theory as organizations are dynamic living entities that are goal-oriented. The systems approach to organizations relies heavily upon achieving negative entropy through openness and feedback. In recent years, the field of *systems thinking* has been developed to provide techniques for studying systems in holistic ways to supplement more traditional reductionistic methods. In this more recent tradition, systems theory is considered by some as a humanistic counterpart to the natural sciences.

History

Subjects like complexity, self-organization, connectionism and adaptive systems had already been studied in the 1940s and 1950s, in fields like cybernetics through researchers like Norbert Wiener, William Ross Ashby, John von Neumann and Heinz Von Foerster. They only lacked the right tools, and tackled complex systems with mathematics, pencil and paper. John von Neumann discovered cellular automata and self-reproducing systems without computers, with only pencil and paper. Aleksandr Lyapunov and Jules Henri Poincare worked on the foundations of chaos theory without any computer at all. All of the "C"-Theories below-cybernetics, catastrophe theory, chaos theory,...-have the common goal to explain complex systems which consist of a large number of mutually interacting and interwoven parts. Cellular automata (CA), neural networks (NN), artificial intelligence (AI), and artificial life (ALife) are related fields, but they do not try to describe general complex systems. The best context to compare the different "C"-Theories about complex systems is historical, which emphasizes different tools and methodologies, from pure mathematics in the beginning to pure computer science now. Since the beginning of chaos theory when Edward Lorenz accidentally discovered a strange attractor with his computer, computers have become an indispensable source of information. One could not imagine the study of complex systems without computers today.

Timeline

- 1960 cybernetics (W. Ross Ashby, Norbert Wiener) Mathematical theory of the communication and control of systems through regulatory feedback. Closely related: "control theory" and "general systems theory" founded by Ludwig von Bertalanffy and W. Ross Ashby
- 1970 catastrophe theory (Rene Thom, E.C. Zeeman) Branch of mathematics that deals with bifurcations in dynamical systems, classifies phenomena characterized by sudden shifts in behaviour arising from small changes in circumstances.
- 1980 chaos theory (David Ruelle, Edward Lorenz, Mitchell Feigenbaum, Steve Smale, James A. Yorke....) Mathematical theory of nonlinear dynamical systems

that describes bifurcations, strange attractors, and chaotic motions.

- 1990 complex adaptive systems (CAS) (John H. Holland, Murray Gell-Mann, Harold Morowitz, W. Brian Arthur,..) The "new" science of complexity which describes emergence, adaptation and self-organization was established mainly by researchers of the SFI and is based on agents and computer simulations and includes multi-agent systems (MAS) which have become an important tool to study social and complex systems. CAS are still an active field of research.

2

Development of Sociological Theory

The social conditions of the nineteenth and early twentieth centuries were of the utmost significance to the development of sociology. The chaos and social disorder that resulted from the series of political revolutions ushered in by the French Revolution in 1789 disturbed many early social theorists. While they recognized that a return to the old order was impossible, they sought to find new sources of order in societies that had been traumatized by dramatic political changes. The Industrial Revolution was a set of developments that transformed Western societies from largely agricultural to overwhelmingly industrial systems. Peasants left agricultural work for industrial occupations in factories. Within this new system, a few profited greatly while the majority worked long hours for low wages. A reaction against the industrial system and capitalism led to the labour movement and other radical movements dedicated to overthrowing the capitalist system. As a result of the Industrial Revolution, large numbers of people moved to urban settings. The expansion of cities produced a long list of urban problems that attracted the attention of early sociologists.

Socialism emerged as an alternative vision of a worker's paradise in which wealth was equitably distributed. Karl Marx was highly critical of capitalist society in his writings and engaged in political activities to help engineer its fall. Other early theorists recognized the problems of capitalist society but sought change through reform because they feared socialism more than they feared capitalism. Feminists were especially active during the French and American Revolutions, during the abolitionist movements and political rights mobilizations of the mid-nineteenth century, and especially during the Progressive Era in the United States. But feminist concerns filtered into early sociology only on the margins. In spite of their marginal status, early women sociologists like Harriet Martineau and Marianne Weber wrote a significant body of theory that is being rediscovered today. All of these changes had a profound effect on religiosity. Many sociologists came from religious backgrounds and sought to understand the place of religion and morality in modern society.

Throughout this period, the technological products of science were permeating every sector of life, and science was acquiring enormous prestige. An ongoing debate developed between sociologists who sought to model their discipline after the hard sciences and those who thought the distinctive characteristics of social life made a scientific sociology problematic and unwise.

Rise of Sociological Theory

The Enlightenment was a period of intellectual development and change in philosophical thought beginning in the eighteenth century. Enlightenment thinkers sought to combine reason with empirical research on the model of Newtonian science. They tried to produce highly systematic bodies of thought that made rational sense and that could be derived from real-world observation. Convinced that the world could be comprehended and controlled using reason and research, they believed traditional social values and institutions to be irrational and inhibitive of human development. Their ideas conflicted with traditional religious bodies like the Catholic Church, the political regimes of Europe's absolutist monarchies, and the social system of feudalism. They placed their faith instead in the power of the individual's capacity to reason. Early sociology also maintained a faith in empiricism and rational inquiry.

A conservative reaction to the Enlightenment, characterized by a strong anti-modern sentiment, also influenced early theorists. The conservative reaction led thinkers to emphasize that society had an existence of its own, in contrast to the individualism of the Enlightenment. Additionally, they had a cautious approach to social change and a tendency to see modern developments like industrialization, urbanization, and bureaucratization as having disorganizing effects.

Development of French Sociology

Claude Henri Saint-Simon (1760-1825) was a positivist who believed that the study of social phenomena should employ the same scientific techniques as the natural sciences. But he also saw the need for socialist reforms, especially centralized planning of the economic system. Auguste Comte (1798-1857) coined the term "sociology." Like Saint-Simon, he believed the study of social phenomena should employ scientific techniques. But Comte was disturbed by the chaos of French society and was critical of the Enlightenment and the French Revolution. Comte developed an evolutionary theory of social change in his law of the three stages. He argued that social disorder was caused by ideas left over from the idea systems of earlier stages. Only when a scientific footing for the governing of society was established would the social upheavals of his time cease. Comte also stressed the systematic character of society and accorded great importance to the role of consensus. These beliefs made Comte a forerunner of positivism and reformism in classical sociological theory.

Emile Durkheim (1858-1917) legitimized sociology in France and became a dominant force in the development of the discipline worldwide. Although he was politically liberal, he took a more conservative position intellectually, arguing that the social disorders produced by striking social changes could be reduced through social reform. Durkheim argued that sociology was the study of structures that are external to, and coercive over, the individual; for example, legal codes and shared moral beliefs, which he called social facts.

In *Suicide* he made his case for the importance of sociology by demonstrating that social facts could cause individual behaviour. He argued that societies were held together by a strongly held collective morality called the collective conscience. Because of the complexity of modern societies, the collective conscience had become weaker, resulting in a variety of social pathologies. In his later work, Dukheim turned to the religion of primitive societies to demonstrate the importance of the collective consciousness.

Development of German Sociology

German sociology is rooted in the philosopher G.F.W. Hegel's (1770-1831) idea of the dialectic. Like Comte in France, Hegel offered an evolutionary theory of society. The dialectic is a view that the world is made up not of static structures but of processes, relationships, conflicts, and contradictions. He emphasized the importance of changes in consciousness for producing dialectical change. Dialectical thinking is a dynamic way of thinking about the world.

Karl Marx (1818-1883) followed Ludwig Feuerbach (1804-1872) in criticizing Hegel for favouring abstract ideas over real people. Marx adopted a materialist orientation that focused on real material entities like wealth and the state. He argued that the problems of modern society could be traced to real material sources like the structures of capitalism. Yet he maintained Hegel's emphasis on the dialectic, forging a position called dialectical materialism that held that material processes, relationships, conflicts, and contradictions are responsible for social problems and social change. Marx's materialism led him to posit a labour theory of value, in which he argued that the capitalist's profits were based on the exploitation of the labourer. Under the influence of British political economists, Marx grew to deplore the exploitation of workers and the horrors of the capitalist system. Unlike the political economists, his view was that such problems were the products of an endemic conflict that could be addressed only through radical change. While Marx did not consider himself to be a sociologist, his influence has been strong in Europe. Until recently, American sociologists dismissed Marx as an ideologist.

The theories of Max Weber (1864-1920) can be seen as the fruit of a long debate with the ghost of Marx. While Weber was not familiar with Marx's writings, he viewed the Marxists of his day as economic determinists who offered single-cause theories of social life. Rather than seeing ideas as simple reflections of economic factors, Weber saw them as autonomous forces capable of profoundly affecting the economic world. Weber can also be understood as trying to round out Marx's theoretical perspective; rather than denying the effect of material structures, he was simply pointing out the importance of ideas as well. Whereas Marx offered a theory of capitalism, Weber's work was fundamentally a theory of the process of rationalization. Rationalization is the process whereby universally applied rules, regulations, and laws come to dominate more and more sectors of society on the model of a bureaucracy.

Weber argued that in the Western world rational-legal systems of authority squeezed out traditional authority systems, rooted in beliefs, and charismatic authority, systems based on the extraordinary qualities of a leader. His historical studies of religion are dedicated to showing why rational-legal forms took hold in the West but not elsewhere. Weber's reformist views and academic style were better received than Marx's radicalism in sociology. Sociologists also appreciated Weber's well-rounded approach to the social world.

Georg Simmel (1858-1918) was Weber's contemporary and co-founder of the German Sociological Society. While Marx and Weber were pre-occupied with large-scale issues, Simmel was best known for his work on smaller-scale issues, especially individual action and interaction. He became famous for his thinking on forms of interaction (i.e., conflict) and types of interacts (i.e., the stranger). Simmel saw that understanding interaction among people was one of the major tasks of sociology. His short essays on interesting topics made his work accessible to American sociologists. His most famous long work, *The Philosophy of Money*, was concerned with the emergence of a money economy in the modern world. This work observed that large-scale social structures like the money economy can become separate from individuals and come to dominate them.

Origins of British Sociology

British sociology was shaped in the nineteenth century by three conflicting sources: political economy, ameliorism, and social evolution. British sociologists saw the market economy as a positive force, a source of order, harmony, and integration in society. The task of the sociologist was not to criticize society but to gather data on the laws by which it operated. The goal was to provide the government with the facts it needed to understand the way the system worked and direct its workings wisely. By the mid-nineteenth century this belief manifested itself in the tendency to aggregate individually reported statistical data to form a collective portrait of British society. Statistical data soon pointed British sociologists toward some of the failings of a market economy, notably poverty, but left them without adequate theories of society to explain them. Ameliorism is the desire to solve social problems by reforming individuals. Because the British sociologists could not trace the source of problems such as poverty to the society as a whole, then the source had to lie within individuals themselves.

A number of British thinkers were attracted to the evolutionary theories of Auguste Comte. Most prominent among these was Herbert Spencer (1820-1903), who believed that society was growing progressively better and therefore should be left alone. He adopted the view that social institutions adapted progressively and positively to their social environments. He also accepted the Darwinian view that natural selection occurred in the social world. Among Spencer's more outrageous ideas was the argument that unfit societies should be permitted to die off, allowing for the adaptive upgrading of the world as a whole. Clearly, such ideas did not sit well with the reformism of the ameliorists.

OTHER DEVELOPMENTS

Vilfredo Pareto (1848-1923) thought that human instincts were such a strong force that Marx's hope to achieve dramatic social changes with an economic revolution was impossible. Pareto offered an elite theory of social change that held that a small elite inevitably dominates society on the basis of enlightened self-interest. Change occurs when one group of elites begins to degenerate and is replaced by another. Pareto's lasting contribution to sociology has been a vision of society as a system in equilibrium, a whole consisting of balanced independent parts.

After his death, Marx's disciples became more rigid in their belief that he had uncovered the economic laws that ruled the capitalist world. Seeing the demise of capitalism as inevitable, political action seemed unnecessary. By the 1920's, however, Hegelian Marxists refused to reduce Marxism to a scientific theory that ignored individual thought and action. Seeking to integrate Hegel's interest in consciousness with the materialist interest in economic structures, the Hegelian Marxists emphasized the importance of individual action in bringing about a social revolution and reemphasized the relationship between thought and action.

Classical Sociological Theory

Classical sociological theories are important not only historically, but also because they are living documents with contemporary relevance to both modern theorists and today's social world. The work of classical thinkers continues to inspire modern sociologists in a variety of ways. Many contemporary thinkers seek to reinterpret the classics to apply them to the contemporary scene.

THREE-COMPONENT THEORY OF STRATIFICATION

The three-component theory of stratification, more widely known as Weberian Stratification or Three Class System, was developed by German sociologist Max Weber with class, status and party as distinct ideal types. Weber developed a multidimensional approach to Social stratification that reflects the interplay among wealth, prestige, and power.. "Weber argued that power can take a variety of forms. A person's power can be shown in the social order through their status, in the economic order through their class, and in the political order through their party. Thus, class, status and party are each aspects of the distribution of power within a community." (Hurst, 202) Class, Status and party have a great deal of effect not only within their individual areas but also have a great deal of influence over the other areas as well.

- Wealth: includes property such as buildings, lands, farms, houses, factories and as well as other assets-Economic situation
- Prestige: the respect with which a person or status position is regarded by others-Status Situation
- Power: the ability of people or groups to achieve their goals despite opposition from others.-Parties.

There are two basic dimensions of power: The possession of power and the exercising of power.

Possession of Power

According to Weber, the ability to possess power derives

from the individual's ability to control various "social resources." "The mode of distribution gives to the propertied a monopoly on the possibility of transferring property from the sphere of use as "wealth" to the sphere of "capital," that is, it gives them the entrepreneurial function and all chances to share directly or indirectly in returns on capital." These resources can be anything and everything and might include things like land, capital, social respect, physical strength, intellectual knowledge, etc.

Exercising of Power

The ability to exercise power takes a number of different forms, but all involve the idea that it means the ability to get your own way with others, regardless of their ability to resist you."For example, if we think about an individual's chances of realizing their own will against someone else, it is reasonable to believe that the person's social prestige, class position, and membership in a political group will have an effect on these chances." In terms of understanding the relationship between power and social stratification, Weber theorized the various ways in which societies are organized in hierarchical systems of domination and subordination using the several major concepts.

Class Power

"Class, at its core, is an economic concept; it is the position of individuals in the market that determines their class position. And it is how one is situated in the marketplace that directly affects one's life chances." This was theorized by Weber on the basis of "unequal access to material resources." For example, if someone possesses something that you want or need then this makes him potentially more powerful than you. He is in a dominant position and you are in a subordinate position because he controls access to a desired social resource. A classic illustration here is the relationship between an employer and employee.

Social Power (Status)

"The existence of status groups most often shows itself in the form of (1) endogamy or the restricted pattern of social intercourse, (2) sharing of food and other benefits within groups,

(3) status conventions or traditions, and (4) monopolistic acquisition of certain economic opportunities or the avoidance of certain kinds of acquisitions. If you respect someone or view him as your social superior, then he will potentially be able to exercise power over you (since you will respond positively to his instructions/commands). In this respect, social status is a social resource simply because he may have it while you may not.. "Not all power, however entails social honour: The Typical American Boss, as well as the typical big speculator, deliberately relinquishes social honour. Quite generally, "mere economic" power, and especially "naked" money power, is by no means a recognized basis or social honour."

Political Power (Party)

"Parties are associations that aim at securing "power within an organization [or the state] for its leaders in order to attain ideal or material advantages for its active members." This form of power can be related to the way in which the State is organized in modern social systems (involving the ability to make laws, for example). If you can influence this process of law creation then you will be in a potentially powerful position. Thus, by your ability to influence a decision-making process you possess power, even though you may not directly exercise that power personally. Political parties are the organizational means to possess power through the mechanism of the State and they include not just formally organized parties, but any group that is organized to influence the way in which power is exercised legitimately through the machinery of the State. "Since parties aim at such goals as getting their programs developed or accepted and getting positions of influence within organizations, it is clear that they operate only within a rational order within which these goals are possible to attain and only when there is a struggle for power"

Social Action

Social action is in direct relation to "Political or Party Power" in combination with the class situation. The influence of laws is based on the social action of members of the classes. "The direction of interests may vary according to whether or not social action of a larger or smaller portion of those commonly affected by the class situation, or even an association among them, e.g., a trade union, has grown out of the class situation, from which the individual may expect promising results for himself." "The degree in which "social action" and possibly associations emerge from the mass behaviour of the members of a class is linked to general cultural conditions, especially to those of an intellectual sort. It is also liked to the extent of the contrasts that have already evolved." We can also see this in another quote "Class-conscious action is most likely if, first, "the connection between the causes and consequences of the 'class situation'" are transparent, or clear. If individuals can plainly see that there is a connection between the structure of the economic system and what happens to them in terms of life chances, class action is more likely" The greater the numbers within these class positions will increase the chance that they will rise up in action.

Mobility

The greater the numbers within these class positions will increase the chance that they will rise up in action. "it is noncontroversial that the class situation in which each individual finds himself represents a limitation on his scope, tends to keep him within the class. It acts as an obstacle to any rise into a higher class, and as a pair of water wings with respect to the classes below...Class type, relations with class fellows, power over outward resources adapted to the class situation, and so on." In the capitalist society movement between classes is a possibility. Hence the use of the term "The American Dream" to show the ability of people to ascend to a higher class through hard work and ingenuity. "Class composition is forever changing, to the point where there may be a completely new set of families." He saw four classes-the propertied class, non-propertied class, petit bourgeoisie and the manual labourer class.

SOCIOLOGY AND HISTORICAL MATERIALISM

The process of becoming and being in our world is a never-ending, materially unified whole. This evolutionary process can be divided into two sections according to their order of emergence and their level of development. The first period comprises the development of the physical universe from its observable beginnings up to the advent of the first humans.

According to the latest hypothetical calculations, this cosmic evolution took at least twenty billion years. The second period covers the origins and growth of our species from the point where our primate progenitors graduated from the animal state to the present. This process of humanisation has lasted almost two million years.

The natural sciences from astrophysics and geology to biology and zoology deal with one or another sector of the evolution of the material world apart from the social existence of mankind. The social sciences from archaeology and anthropology to political economy and history have as their objects of investigation one or another of the aspects of social life arising from the activities of human beings. Sociology is one of the social sciences. What are its special features and its relations to other branches of social investigation?

Other social sciences, such as archaeology, economics, demography, law, linguistics, psychology, logic, study special aspects and restricted areas of human activity and achievement. Linguistics, for example, deals solely with the phenomena of human speech and its structural elements. These sciences that seek to discover the laws of a delimited domain of social life necessarily have a narrow, one-sided character. But society is not actually partitioned into domains completely cut off from one another nor is its development split into absolutely disjointed stages. Human life has developed continuously from its origins to the present. Each stage of human history and its social organisation has had an integrated constitution depending upon its mode of production and its appropriate place in the sequence of the historical process.

Sociology is that branch of scientific knowledge which investigates the evolution of society in its entirety and the content of social life in its fullness. It endeavours to discover the laws governing the progress of social life from the most primitive and simple form of social organisation to its most complex and mature structures. Both the laws of nature and the laws of society are historical in character since they are drawn from phenomena engaged in constant change. But social phenomena are qualitatively different from the purely natural events out of which they have grown and in which they remain rooted. Social facts are produced by our species, which obtains its means of existence in a unique manner through cooperative labour. Man's activities of production and their results invest the laws of social development with characteristics distinctively different from those governing other living creatures.

The laws of social evolution have retained certain traits in common with the laws of organic evolution, since up to now these have operated without conscious collective direction or control. That is why Marx regarded "the evolution of the economic formation of society Öas a process of natural history", as he wrote in the preface to the first edition of Volume 1 of *Capital*. But the dominant features of the social-historical process are fundamentally different from those prevailing in the rest of reality. The broad scope and aims of sociology make it the most general of the social sciences. It seeks to synthesise the findings of the rest of the social sciences into a comprehensive conception of the dynamics of the historical process.

Sociology plays a role in regard to the social sciences comparable to scientific cosmology, which comprehensively explains the evolution of the physical universe, or synthetic biology, which aims to provide a coherent picture of the whole realm of living matter. To the degree that sociology succeeds in comprehending the laws of human development, it provides the other social sciences with a general method of investigation which can serve as a guide to their more specialised studies. There is an unbreakable interdependence and constant interaction between sociology and the more specialised departments of social science, each of which has its relative autonomy. The data provided by these in turn enrich and extend the ideas and method of sociology as it grows.

Sociology seeks to answer such questions as: What is society and in what respects does it differ from nature? How did social life originate? How and why does it change? What are the most powerful driving forces in its development? Through what stages has social evolution passed? What forms of organisation has society acquired? What are the standards of social progress? What relations do the various aspects of the social structure have to one another? What laws regulate the replacement of one grade of social development by the next and the transformation of one type of social organisation into another?

Sociology and the Philosophy of History

The generality that distinguishes sociology as a science stands out most clearly in contrast with history. These two branches of knowledge are so intimately interlinked that at certain points on their boundaries they are barely separable. History relates what men did at a certain time and place and under certain specific circumstances, however extensive the period and theatre of operations. Sociology takes up where history leaves off. Proceeding from the results of historical research, it seeks to find in them and through them the inner connections and causal laws of the actual historical process. Considerable historical data had to be amassed before sociology became possible.

Sociology and history have the broadest scope of all the social sciences. These two used to merge at that border line which has been designated as "the philosophy of history". This term, invented by Voltaire, refers to the systematic theoretical interpretation of the historical process as a whole, what Hegel called Universal History. This side of the study of history was energetically pursued by those West European thinkers of the 17th and 18th centuries who sought to extend to social phenomena the methods which were revolutionising research into the physical world. They proceeded on the premise that the world of man, no less than the world of nature, was a rational system whose principles of development could be found out and should be known. So they set out to ascertain the causal laws which determined human history.

Although some of their speculations went wide of the mark, these explorers of the logic of the historical process gathered materials and cleared the way for those eminent theorists in the 19th century from Saint-Simon to Marx who placed the study of society on solid scientific foundations. These theoretical inquiries into the motive forces of history were prompted and promoted by practical aims. The philosophers of the Enlightenment who heralded the French revolution, and their successors of the Napoleonic and Restoration periods who came after the revolution, looked for the efficient agents of history in order to change society according to their lights. Just as the physical scientists had acquired control over nature through deeper insight into its modes of operation, so these thinkers aspired to control the reconstruction of society by understanding and managing the main factors that shaped the course of history.

The authors of the conjectures associated with the philosophy of history were ideological precursors and progenitors of sociology. Whatever was valid in their contributions and conclusions on the whole of human history became incorporated into the science of society. The philosophy of history as such, however, belongs to the prescientific stage of sociological knowledge. It bears the same relation to scientific sociology as alchemy to chemistry and astrology to astronomy. Its hypotheses were stimulating and indispensable so long as the prime motive forces of social development were unknown and being sought for. But once historical materialism uncovered the true laws of social evolution and progressive research guided by scientific principles could replace guesswork, the old purely speculative philosophical approach to sociology was rendered obsolete and retrogressive.

TYPES OF SOCIOLOGICAL THEORY

Sociology has a long prehistory going back to the Greeks. Ibn Khaldun, the eminent Berber scholar and statesman of the 14th century, was very likely the first thinker to formulate a clear conception of sociology. He did so under the name of the study of culture.

He wrote: "History is the record of human society, or world civilisation; of the changes that take place in the nature of that society, such as savagery, sociability, and group solidarity; of revolutions and uprisings by one set of people against another with the resulting kingdoms and states, with their various ranks; of the different activities and occupations of men, whether for gaining their livelihood or in the various sciences and crafts; and, in general, of all the transformations that society undergoes by its very nature."

But sociology is a comparatively recent department of social science. Such sciences as economics and history developed on an independent basis much earlier and faster. Sociology was constituted as a distinct branch of learning only after the French revolution. It was given its own name over 150 years ago by August Comte. Since then sociology has developed in different directions and given rise to a motley host of theoretical approaches. The diverse schools can be roughly classified into three major categories: the materialist, the idealist, and the eclectic or dualistic tendencies.

Idealists rely upon mental, superstructural or purely subjective factors for the prime explanation of social-historical phenomena. Thus the Swiss writer, Bachofen, who first called attention to the system of kinship through the mothers, said in the introduction to his book *Das Mutterrecht* : " Religion is the only efficient lever of all civilisation. Each elevation and depression of human life has its origin in a movement which begins in this supreme department." The American anthropologist, Alexander Goldenweiser, stated in his work on *Early Civilisation* : "Thus the whole of civilisation, if followed backward step by step, would ultimately be found resolvable, without residue, into bits of ideas in the minds of individuals."

The British biologist Julian Huxley encompasses the whole span of social development with a similar explanation: "Human evolution occurs primarily in the realm of ideas and their results—in what anthropologists call *culture* Ö" Historical idealism is prevalent not only in the sciences but in all areas of culture. Thus the literary critic, Alfred Kazin, reviewing *The Life of the Mind in America: From the Revolution to the Civil War* by Perry Miller, asserts: "In the end, the national mind is the national force." This is diluted Hegelianism.

The materialists, on the other hand, teach that everything in social life comes from objective and observable material causes of a physical or man-made character. Thus, in *The Nature of Things*, the Roman poet-philosopher Lucretius attributed the discovery of the uses of metals to men's thoughtful notice of their melting by forest fires and moulding in the bed from which the lump of silver and gold, copper or lead, was lifted. He was reaching toward a materialist explanation for the metallic revolution which had given immense impetus to human progress several thousands of years before him. In the 14th century Ibn Khaldun sought to explain the emergence of the civilised state from the primitive tribal community along the following essentially materialist lines: To satisfy the physical needs for food, procreation and protection which they shared with plants and animals, men were impelled to cooperate, learn to make tools and weapons and establish small and simple communities. The development of cooperation and the division of labour led to producing more than was required for sheer survival. The subsequent fierce conflicts over possession of this surplus of wealth threatened the existence of men. To curb their animal appetites and create civil order, they set up a powerful and able ruler who forced the aggregate to obey his directives. Thus kingship and the state came into existence as the necessary outcome of economic opulence.

The interplay of natural and man-made factors in shaping the course of history was emphasised by the 18th century French thinker Montesquieu, who picked out geography and government as the main determinants of social phenomena. The influence of the first factor prevailed in the earlier stages of human development; the second came forward as civilisation progressed. But both continue to work together upon the mental life of man and generate his predominant characteristics. Thus heat and despotism made certain Asiatic peoples placid and docile while cold and democracy made some Europeans active in mind and body. Besides such efforts to apply either idealist or materialist procedures in a more or less consistent and clear-cut manner, we find an array of thinkers who shuttle between these opposing modes of reasoning and arrive at the most incongruous conclusions in their works. The literature of the social sciences is saturated with such eclecticism in theory and method; it is the habitual, normative viewpoint of contemporary Western scholarship.

A characteristic expression of this dualism was provided by Charles Beard, the American liberal historian. His last word on historical philosophy was that ideas and interests were the twin motive forces of civilisation. If it be asked which is predominant as a rule and in the long run, he answered that this cannot be ascertained in advance. All depends upon the concrete circumstances of the given case. The door was thus flung open for ideological considerations to prevail over material conditions both in particular and in general.

Although the idealist approach to history is false in principle, it is not all wrong. It takes into account certain features of the development of society. Ideas, opinions, religions, individual action, are all parts of history and contribute to its making. The point is that they are not the decisive factors in social life and therefore cannot serve to explain the rest They are secondary and derivative elements which themselves stand in need of explanation. The idealistic conception is misleading because it is shallow; it does not get to the inner core, the essential causes, of social phenomena. Every materialist school of historical explanation has had erroneous and inadequate notions. But their procedure was valid in essence because it oriented social investigation in the right direction. The materialists looked for the motive forces and root causes of social evolution in the influence and changes of the material conditions of human existence and kept digging deeper and deeper into these. With Marx and Engels they succeeded in reaching bedrock: They located the basis of society in the mode of production which arises out of the given state of man's struggle with nature for the means of life and further development.

Historical Materialism

Historical materialism is a particular type of sociological theory. It is the sociological method of Marxism. It investigates the same phenomena as rival schools of sociology but in a more probing, many-sided, rigorously scientific way that gives more insight into the total life of society and more foresight about its trends of development. Historical materialism is not the whole of Marxist theory. It forms a special branch arising from the application of its dialectical and materialist principles to the evolution of society. This is disputed by certain revisionist interpreters of Marxism, like Sidney Hook and Jean-Paul Sartre, who contend that the Marxist domain is restricted to social phenomena, to the life of man, and cannot be extended to nature. The Russian Marxist Plekhanov, more correctly stated that it had an all-embracing universal jurisdiction.

Plekhanov divided the unified and systematic structure of Marxist thought into three parts: 1. *Dialectical materialism*, the most general approach to reality, which covers nature, society and the mind and which aims to discover the general laws governing the modes of motion in all three interacting sectors of existence; 2. *Historical Materialism*, the application of these laws to the development of mankind and the discovery of the specific laws involved in social existence; 3. *Scientific socialism*, the application of the laws of historical materialism to that particular stage of social evolution in which capitalism takes shape, fulfils and exhausts its potential, and passes over to the higher formation of socialism. Thus dialectical materialism is a school of philosophy, logic and theory of knowledge; historical materialism, of sociology; and scientific socialism, of political economy and revolutionary practice.

Historical materialism is accurately named. It did not acquire either element of its designation by chance. Its title formulates the essential features which demarcate this method from other ways of interpreting social phenomena: On the one hand, its derivation of all the higher manifestations of culture from their economic foundations opposes it to the historical idealisms which have been the chief adversary of materialist thought in history and sociology. On the other hand, there have been tendencies which analysed social processes and structures materialistically but disregarded or minimised their evolutionary aspects. These unhistorical materialisms attributed the basic elements of social formations either to an unchangeable nature or to some fixed traits of human nature.

The distinctiveness of Marxist sociology comes from its fusion of the materialist approach to society with a thoroughgoing evolutionary outlook. It teaches that everything in social life is subject to modification and transformation in accord with causes of a physical or historical character.

An idealistic philosophy of history may also be evolutionary, as in Hegel, but it vests the ultimate causal agencies in nonmaterial factors such as spirit, mind or God. Marxism in fact originated by detaching the evolutionary outlook projected by Hegel in his dialectical logic from its idealistic context and by removing the nonhistorical elements from preceding materialist theories. Many critics insist that this marriage of dialectical method with materialist principles is impossible. Nonetheless, their indivisible combination constitutes the pith of the Marxist mode of thought in sociology as in all other fields.

THE CLASS CHARACTER OF SOCIOLOGY

Sociology could not have arisen or prospered in a homogenous, harmonious, equilibrated, unchanging, social medium. The accelerated economic changes, social instability and class antagonisms characteristic of commercial civilisation were needed to impel men to look for the forces which moved and transformed society. The earliest systematic observations and critical reflections on the course and causes of social change were made by Greek thinkers in those city-states torn by class conflict where revolutions and counterrevolutions periodically upset and replaced the form of rule. Plato set forth the specifications for his ideal republic in the quest for stability as the obverse of the restless regimes of the commercial slave society around him. Aristotle carefully analysed the causes of revolution with an eye to preventing, not promoting, them.

Ibn Khaldun brought forth his new science of culture, the first extended essay in sociology, in response to the decline and disintegration of the Islamic states of North Africa and Spain during the 14th century. Living in a time of distress and desolation when nomadic incursions and the Black Death had ruined the Maghreb he keenly felt the need for a deeper understanding of history. "When the universe is being turned upside down, we must ask ourselves whether it is changing its nature, whether there is to be a new creation and a new order in the world. Therefore today we need a historian who can declare the state of the world, of its countries and people, and show the changes that have taken place in customs and beliefs", he wrote. Since his time inquiry into the causes of social progress and regress has been quickened whenever and wherever the social order has been unsettled, turned topsy-turvy, and the historical destiny of peoples has been radically redirected. The upheavals in social relations and political institutions issuing from the development of the bourgeois-democratic revolutions in England, France and North America provided both the incentives and data for the research and reflections which crystallised in the creation of sociology as a separate science in the 19th century.

Conceived, nurtured and functioning in a setting of clashing social interests, the social sciences could not avoid having a class character. In order to serve as tools and weapons in the contest of social forces, they have been bent to class purposes. This bias can be observed from ancient times. It is obvious in Aristotle's *Politics*. Like other Greek aristocrats, he viewed the state as founded on households where the male is master over wives, children, slaves and all property; the concept of sexual, civic or universal equality is conspicuously absent in Aristotle's social thought.

Coming to our own time, those Anglo-American sociologists who ignore evolution in society, disregard revolutionary changes in social organisation, and focus exclusively on functional correlations in small-scale static structures are equally class-conditioned in their outlook. They present the viewpoint of the liberal middle-class intellectual or progressive. How is the patently class character of social science and its practitioners to be reconciled with the tests of scientific objectivity? This is one of the most vexing problems in the sociology of knowledge. If the vision of the investigator is inescapably blurred and distorted by class motivations, how can any valid truths be attained in the social sciences?

Karl Mannheim offered an ingenious solution. He held that the ideologists of the bourgeoisie and the proletariat are prohibited from being clear-sighted and impartial because they must defend overwhelming material interests. Their views are clouded by a deceptive "false consciousness" and a utopianism, which, despite its unrealism, is in practice the generator of political action and social progress.

Fortunately for science, the relativism and subjectivism of the representatives of the major classes can be offset by the capacity of socially detached and politically uncommitted intellectuals to comprehend and appraise social phenomena without prejudice. Thus Mannheim tried to resolve the contradiction between prejudiced spokesmen for contending social forces and the demands of science by vesting the virtues of objectivity in an uprooted but fair-minded intellectual elite with which he identified himself. Marxism handles this problem in a more correct and consistent way. It acknowledges that the thinkers of every social regime and layer without exception are animated by class considerations, however little or much they may be aware of the influence on them. This class outlook can hamper their work and warp their conclusions. But it is not an insuperable barrier to the acquisition of genuine knowledge and indeed under certain circumstances may prompt and speed its development.

Every successive ruling class—and the rising class which challenges its supremacy—has created a general conception of the world and society conforming to its needs. These ideologies intermingle accurate descriptions and correct explanations of phenomena with prejudices derived from the special situation and outlook of the class formation they speak for. This twofold character permeates Aristotle's *Politics*, which, through his aristocratic angle of vision, conveys valuable information and valid generalisations on the economic, sociological and political features of the Greek city-states. The demands which a given social order or class imposes upon its ideologists have differential effects upon their capacities to extend knowledge at different points of their historical evolution. When the basic interests of a class accelerate economic development and promote political and cultural progress, the beneficial influence of its predispositions and preoccupations radiates through the sciences and spurs the advance of knowledge.

The science of mineralogy received its strongest impetus from the direct economic interest of the Western European mine owners in the study of rocks. The father of mineralogy, the German physician Georg Bauer (1490-1555), better known under his Latinised name, Agricola, who lived and worked in one of the mining centres of the continent, wrote on the geographical distribution of various economically useful metals, the growth of metallurgy and its machinery in Germany and Austria, and the classification of the minerals known in his time. After him more and more attention was directed to the study of rocks for their potential economic value and many institutions of learning established teaching positions in mineralogy. The growth of this science led to increased knowledge of the history of the earth and eventually to the need for ascertaining a time scale for prehistory. Thus the progress made in positive knowledge and the accrued benefits to mankind transcended and outlasted the drive for private profit which gave birth to mineralogy. The same considerations are true of the social sciences. The businessmen, financiers and statesmen of the early bourgeois era needed more extensive and exact statistics for trade, insurance, banking, government tax and administrative purposes. Their interests brought the science of statistics into being during and after the 17th century.

Yet this branch of knowledge has an objective basis and scientific validity which goes beyond the special class motives inseparable from its origins and development.

In order to conduct a successful struggle against precapitalist institutions and ideas, the rising bourgeoisie had to probe more deeply into the structure of society and the motive forces of history. Its economists studied foreign trade, the role of money and the forms of capital and labour, amassing materials and devising theories for placing economics on solid scientific foundations. Its political thinkers developed theories of popular sovereignty and representative government in opposition to monarchical and theocratic views. Their critical and creative thought introduced lasting enlightenment into these fields of social science.

As one type of social regime has supplanted another in the onward march of civilisation, there has been a cumulative growth of knowledge about society. The comprehension of social relations and their modes of transformation arrived at by the most penetrating theorists of one stage of social and scientific development and its dominant class has been reevaluated, sifted and corrected by the leading ideologists of the next higher social formation. Thus the political economy of the working class took off from a critical reworking of the doctrines of the classical bourgeois economists, just as its philosophy combined the principles of previous materialists with the logical method of the German philosophers from Kant to Hegel. In this way the deficiencies and inherent limitations of the outmoded stage were reduced and removed while the store of genuine knowledge was amplified and improved by the fresh findings of the representatives of the more progressive class forces.

The incentives for objective research and judgment in sociology are lessened and the advance of the science slowed down when the major efforts of a class become dedicated to preserving an obsolete system of production and a reactionary political structure. The statesmen and economists of Southern slavery added very little to the sum of knowledge even about the laws regulating their own peculiar social regime. This blindness to the real forces stirring within society and their trends of development has afflicted all decadent and outdated ruling classes. Because they had acted as the dominant power in national politics for decades, the representatives of the slavocracy believed they could continue to hold sway after the economic, social and political balance of forces in the country had decisively shifted against them. The test of the Civil War burst this illusion. Today the statesmen and ideologists of the major capitalist power expect the United States to exercise the same prolonged supremacy over world affairs that England did 100 years ago, regardless of the growing weight of the anticapitalist states and forces in this century. Their vision and prevision of world history is impaired, not sharpened, by their class position and prejudices.

The best understanding of society at the disposal of the world working class is contained and codified in the tenets of historical materialism. This is the most comprehensive and integrated system of sociological laws and the most profound interpretation of historical development. It incorporates the verified knowledge of history and society bequeathed from the past with the contributions made by the masters of Marxism. The needs of the working class in its struggle for emancipation impose exacting demands and a severe objectivity upon its ideologists. As two world wars and fascism have demonstrated, the working class has to pay heavily for every failure of cognition about the dynamics of contemporary society. It suffers from every instance of ignorance, subjectivity and shortsightedness in the socioeconomic analyses of its leaders and scholars.

This puts a premium on finding out the reality of social and political conditions and ascertaining the precise movements of the diverse social forces. False ideas have to be constantly corrected by the results of actual experience in the arena of struggle on a world scale; a more objective and rounded picture of the concrete situation in all its interacting aspects has to be worked out if the historical aims of the socialist movement are to be fulfilled. These vital stimuli emanating from the movement for liberation from bondage to class society are the lifeblood of the progress of historical materialism. This method teaches that theory and practice, science and experience go hand in hand throughout history. But the two do not evolve symmetrically; their progress is extremely uneven. The understanding of peoples and classes about their situation and tasks has usually lagged far behind their actual relations and the possibilities of changing them. This gap has never been greater than in the atomic age. Although the world is ready to receive socialism, a considerable section of the working class in the West is not ready to achieve it. Yet the very salvation of humanity depends upon its capacity to intervene as the dominant and decisive force in redirecting the history of our time. The enlightenment and guidance provided by historical materialism can do much to alter the gross imbalance between the immense untapped revolutionary potential of the working people and their present inadequate level of consciousness. From the 1840s to the 1960s the victories and defeats, advances and setbacks of the masses in their strivings to change the course of history and reconstruct society on new foundations has amplified the method and enriched the content of historical materialism. The greatest value of all science comes from its usefulness in practice. The science of the social process formulated in historical materialism must also meet and pass this supreme test.

The history of the past century has given many proofs of its superior capacities to decipher the past, analyse current events, and forecast the variants of social and political development Its truth and potency will be irrefutably vindicated as the application of its ideas enables the revolutionary forces to forge a policy which can bring about with the greatest speed and efficiency the abolition of the old order and the building of a better world.

3

A Historical Sketch of Sociological Theory

EARLY AMERICAN SOCIOLOGY

Much of early American sociology was defined by the influence of Herbert Spencer (1820-1903); various strands of Social Darwinism; and political liberalism-with the latter paradoxically contributing to the discipline's conservativism. William Graham Sumner (1840-1910) and Lester F. Ward (1841-1913) exemplify these tendencies in late nineteenth-and early twentieth-century American sociological theory, but their work has certainly not passed the test of time. Other early American sociologists, especially from the Chicago School, did have an enduring impact on sociological theory. W.I. Thomas (1863-1947), Robert Park (1864-1944), Charles Horton Cooley (1864-1929), and George Herbert Mead (1863-1931) profoundly shaped the theoretical landscape of symbolic interactionism, and their ideas predominated until the institutionalization of sociology at Harvard University in the 1930s. While for many years sociologists have emphasized these three theoretical orientations, scholars of sociology have recently pointed to the significance of early women sociologists such as Jane Addams (1860-1935), Charlotte Perkins Gilman (1860-1935), and Beatrice Potter Webb (1858-1943), as well as the race theory of W.E.B. Du Bois (1868-1963).

Rise and Decline of Structural Functionalism

Pitirim Sorokin (1889-1968) was a central figure in the founding of sociology at Harvard University during the 1930s.

Sorokin was soon overshadowed, however, by Talcott Parsons (1902-1979). Parsons is a key figure in the history of sociological theory in the United States because he introduced European thought to large numbers of American sociologists and developed a theory of action and, eventually, structural functionalism. Parsons helped to legitimize grand theory in the United States, and produced many graduate students who carried his ideas to other departments of sociology in the U.S. The rise of structural functionalism to a dominant position in the 1940s and 1950s led to the decline of the Chicago School. While structural functionalism was gaining ground in the United States, the Frankfurt school of critical theory was emerging in Europe. With the rise to power of Adolf Hitler and the National Socialists in Germany, many of the critical theorists fled to the United States, where they came into contact with American sociology. Thinkers such as Max Horkheimer (1895-1973), Theodor Adorno (1903-1969), and Herbert Marcuse (1898-1979) propounded a kind of Marxian theory that was heavily influenced by the work of G.W.F. Hegel (1770-1831), Max Weber (1864-1920), and Sigmund Freud (1856-1939). Much of the critical theorists' work, however, was neglected until the 1960s.

During the 1940s, '50s, and '60s, many criticisms and challenges to structural functionalism emerged. Radical sociologists such as C. Wright Mills (1916-1962) and conflict theorists attacked structural functionalism for its grand theory, purported political conservatism, inability to study social change, and lack of emphasis on social conflict. Other theorists, such as Erving Goffman (1922-1982) and George Homans (1910-), developed dramaturgical analysis and exchange theory, respectively. The sociological phenomenology of Alfred Schutz (1899-1959) prompted a great deal of interest in the sociology of everyday life, which is exemplified by Harold Garfinkel's (1917-) ethnomethodology.

The Rise and Fall of Marxian Theory

During the 1970s and 1980s, a number of scholars revived Marxist perspectives in studies of historical sociology and economic sociology, while others began to question the viability of Marxian theory given the atrocities committed in the name of Marxism and the collapse of the Soviet Union and other

Marxist regimes. Ritzer and Goodman suggest that neo-Marxian theory will see something of a renaissance as a consequence of the inequalities of globalization and the excesses of capitalism.

Late Twentieth-Century Social Theory

In the last thirty years or so, a number of theoretical perspectives have emerged. First, and perhaps most significant, is the rise of feminist theory. Second, structuralism, post-structuralism, and post-modernism gained considerable ground-most notably in the work of Michel Foucault (1926-1984). Third, in the United States, many sociological theorists have developed an interest in the micro-macro link. Fourth, the debate over the relationship between agency and structure-which developed mainly in Europe-has made its way into sociological theory in the U.S. Finally, in the 1990s a number of sociological thinkers have taken an interest in theoretical syntheses.

Early Twenty-First-Century Theory

While the future of sociological theory is unpredictable, a number of perspectives have come to the forefront in recent years. Multicultural social theory, for example, has exploded in the past 20 years. Post-modernism continues to be influential, though some post-post-modernists are making headway. Finally, theories of consumption are shifting the focus of sociology away from its productivist bias and toward consumers, consumer goods, and processes of consumption.

STRUCTURAL FUNCTIONALISM

Although popular, even dominant, after World War II, structural functionalism is today generally of only historical interest. Emerging as an offshoot of organicism, structural functionalists were mainly societal functionalists who were interested in large-scale social structures and institutions within society, how they interrelate, and their constraining effects on actors. One of the earliest and better known applications of structural functionalism was the *functional theory of stratification*. This theory argued that stratification was universal and necessary for society, and that it was therefore functional. Stratification here refers to positions rather than individuals and to the way that individuals are placed in the appropriate position. Since some positions are more important, more pleasant, and require different skills, a system of stratification is necessary to make sure all roles are fulfilled. Much like other versions of structural functionalism, this theory is criticized as conservative and lacking in empirical support.

Talcott Parsons

The single greatest contributor, and practitioner, of structural functionalism was Talcott Parsons (1902-1979). The heart of Parsons's theory is built on the four functional imperatives, also known as the AGIL system:

1. The adaptive function, whereby a system adapts to its environment.
2. The goal-attainment function, i.e., how a system defines and achieves its goals.
3. The integrative function, or the regulation of the components of the system.
4. Latency, or pattern maintenance function, i.e., how motivation and the dimensions of culture that create and sustain motivation are stimulated.

Complementing this are *four action systems*, each of which serve a functional imperative: the *behavioural organism* performs the adaptive function; the *personality system* performs goal attainment; the *social system* performs the integrative function; and the *cultural system* performs pattern maintenance. Parsons saw these action systems acting at different levels of analysis, starting with the behavioural organism and building to the cultural system.

He saw these levels hierarchically, with each of the lower levels providing the impetus for the higher levels, with the higher levels controlling the lower levels. Parsons was concerned primarily with the creation of social order, and he investigated it using his theory based on a number of assumptions, primarily that systems are interdependent; they tend towards equilibrium; they may be either static or involved in change; that allocation and integration are particularly important to systems in any particular point of equilibrium; and that systems are self-maintaining. These assumptions led him to focus primarily on order but to overlook, for the most part, the issue of change. The basic unit of Parsons's social system is the *status-role complex*. Actors are seen as a collection of statuses and roles relatively devoid of thought. Parsons's interest was in the large-scale components of social systems, such as collectivities, norms, and values. Parsons also thought that social systems had a number of functional prerequisites, such as compatibility with other systems, fulfilment of the needs of actors, support from other systems, inducing adequate levels of participation from its members, controlling deviance, controlling conflict, and language. Parsons was particularly interested in the role of norms and values. He focused on the socialization process, whereby society instills within individuals an outlook in which it is possible for them to pursue their own self-interest while still serving the interests of the system as a whole. It was through socialization that Parsons believed that actors internalized the norms of society. Physical or coercive systems of control were seen as only a secondary line of defense.

The cultural system is at the very pinnacle of action systems. For instance, Parsons believed that culture had the capability of becoming a part of other systems, such as norms and values in the social system. Culture is defined as a patterned, ordered system of symbols that are objects of orientation to actors, internalized aspects of the personality system, and institutionalized patterns. The symbolic nature of culture allows it to control other action systems. The personality system generates personality, defined as the organized orientation and motivation of action in the individual actor, built by need-dispositions and shaped by the social setting. Again Parsons presents a passive view of actors.

In order to deal with change, Parsons turned to a form of evolutionary theory, focusing on differentiation and adaptive upgrading. He suggested *three evolutionary stages*: primitive, intermediate, and modern. This perspective suffers from a number of flaws, primarily because it sees change as generally positive and does not deal with the process of change, but rather points of equilibrium across periods of change.

One way that Parsons does inject a real sense of dynamism into his theory is with the concept of the generalized media of interchange. Although this concept is somewhat ambiguous, it can be thought of as resources, particularly symbolic resources, for which there is a universal desire (e.g., money, influence, or political power). The suggestion that individuals might act to influence the social distribution of such resources (as media entrepreneurs) adds dynamism to what is often seen as a static theory.

ROBERT MERTON

Robert Merton(1910-2003) attempted to rectify some of the weaknesses within structural functionalism. Specifically, he criticized the underlying assumptions of functionalism and added complexity to how structural functionalism dealt with the relationship between structures and functions. Dispensing with the notion that all parts of the system are functional, highly integrated, and indispensable, he created a system of concepts to deal with the ways in which structures may be related to the whole. For instance, he suggested that some social facts might be dysfunctional, meaning they may have negative consequences for other social facts. Overall, he thought that it was possible to have an idea of the balance of a structure by taking into account dysfunctions, functions, and nonfunctions. He also added additional complexity by asserting that this sort of analysis may be performed at various levels of functional analysis, as "functions" might be a matter of perspective. For instance, slavery was functional for some and dysfunctional for others. Merton was also concerned with the intended and unintended functions of structures, or *manifest and latent functions*, and their unanticipated consequences. He added nuance to structural functionalism by noting that dysfunctional structures can exist within systems, depending on their relationship to other systems. Thus not all structures are positive, nor are all of them indispensable. Merton also took up Emile Durkheim's (1857-1917) notion of anomie. He suggested that when individuals cannot act in accordance with normalized values or realize normalized goals because of the obstacles created by social structures, it produces deviant behaviour.

Criticisms

There are a number of criticisms of structural functionalism: it is ahistorical; it is unable to deal effectively with the process of change or conflict; and it is conservative. It is viewed as ambiguous and lacking in adequate methods. Structural functionalism inhibits certain forms of analyses, such as comparative analysis. Structural functionalism has also been described as both illegitimately teleological and tautological. The former implies that structural functionalists rely too heavily on the notion that social structures have purposes or goals. This notion is posited to justify the existence of particular structures without adequate theoretical reasons or empirical backing. Tautology suggests that the conclusion of a theory makes explicit what is implicit in the premise of the theory. Thus, structural functionalism defines the whole in terms of the parts and the parts in terms of the whole.

Neofunctionalism

Neofunctionalism was an attempt by theorists such as Jeffrey Alexander, among others, to revive the stronger tenets of structural functionalism. Neofunctionalism attempted to synthesize portions of structural functionalism with other theories. It highlighted the interactional patterning of the elements that constitute society, attended to both action and order, understood integration as a possibility rather than as fact, adopted various portions of Parsons's action systems, and traced the process of social change that resulted from differentiation within action systems.

Conflict Theory

Associated primarily with the work of Ralf Dahrendorf (1929-), conflict theory arose primarily as a reaction against structural functionalism and in many ways represents its antithesis. Where structural functionalism sees a near harmony of purpose from norms and values, conflict theory sees coercion, domination, and power. Dahrendorf saw both theories as addressing different situations, depending upon the focus of the study. According to Dahrendorf, functionalism is useful for understanding consensus while conflict theory is appropriate for understanding conflict and coercion. For Dahrendorf the distribution of authority was a key to understanding social conflict. Authority is located not within people but within various positions. Authority is created by the expectation of certain types of action associated with particular positions, including subordination of others and subordination to others. Various positions of authority exist within associations. The fault lines that spring up around competing loci of authority generate conflicting groups. The conflict between these groups pervades their interaction, with the result that authority is often challenged and tenuous. Much as Merton looked at latent and manifest functions, Dahrendorf identified latent and manifest interests, or unconscious and conscious interests. The connection between these two concepts was a major problematic for conflict theory. Dahrendorf posited the existence of three types of groups: *quasi-groups*, *interest groups*, and *conflict groups*. Dahrendorf felt that, under ideal circumstances, conflict could be explained without reference to any other variables. Conflict theory has been criticized for being ideologically radical, underdeveloped, and unable to deal with order and stability. Both functionalism and conflict theory share the weakness of being able to explain only portions of social life.

Conflict Sociology

Randall Collins developed a form of conflict theory that focuses far more on micro-level interactions than does Dahrendorf. It criticized previous conflict theories and theories of stratification as "failures," and attempted to focus on the role of individual action in the process of stratification. His theory of stratification is rooted in Marxist, phenomenological, and ethnomethodological concerns, focusing on material arrangements and exploitation in real-life situations. Collins extended his theory to deal with various dimensions of stratification, such as gender and age inequality, as well as looking at stratification within formal organizations.

INTERPRETATIONS OF KARL MARX

There are a variety of interpretations of Karl Marx's (1818-1883) theory of capitalism. This arises from both its unfinished nature and Marx's shifting points of emphasis across his lifetime. The focus of Marx's work, however, was undoubtedly on the historical basis of inequality, and specifically inequality under capitalism. Marx's critiques of the capitalist system-its tendency towards crises, the necessity of inequality-are still relevant today.

The Dialectic

Marx's powerful critique has as it basis a unique approach

to reality-the dialectic. Taking from G.W.F. Hegel (1770-1831), Marx believed that any study of reality must be attuned to the contradictions within society and, indeed, he sees contradiction as the motor of historical change. Unlike Hegel, Marx believed that these contradictions existed not simply in our minds (i.e., in the way we understand the world), but that they had a concrete material existence. At the heart of capitalism was the contradiction between the demands of the capitalist to earn a profit and the demands of the worker, who wants to retain some profit to subsist. Over time, the workings of the capitalist system would exacerbate this contradiction, and its resolution can be had only through social change.

The Dialectical Method

The dialectical approach does not recognize the division between social values and social facts. To do so leads away from any real understanding of the problems people face. Additionally, the dialectical method does not envision the social world as being dominated by a cause-and-effect relationship; instead, it looks at the reciprocal relations among social factors within the totality of social life. These relations include not only contemporary phenomena but also the effects of history, as dialecticians are concerned with how the past shapes the present and how the present lays the seeds for the future. Because of this complex set of relations, which often fold back in on themselves, the future is both indeterminate and contingent on individual action. Indeed, this relationship between actors and structures is at the heart of Marx's theory. Structures both constrain and enable individuals, having the potential of both helping them to fulfil themselves and contributing to their exploitation.

Human Nature

Marx's insights into actors and structures must be understood in the context of his views on human nature, which is the basis for his critical analysis of the contradictions of capitalism. Marx viewed human nature as historically contingent, shaped by many of the same relations that affect society. In his view, a contradiction exists between our human nature and work in the capitalist system. Though we have powers that identify us as unique animals, our species being, the possibilities for realizing human potential within the capitalist system are frustrated by the structures of capitalism itself. Unlike most social theories that have implicit assumptions about human nature, Marx elabourates a concept of human nature that also informed his view of how society should look. An important factor in this is Marx's ideas about labour. By objectifying our ideas and satisfying our needs, labour both expresses our human nature and changes it. Through this process, individuals develop their human powers and potentials.

THE STRUCTURES OF CAPITALIST SOCIETY

Marx wrote in response to the rapid changes taking place in Europe in response to industrialization, particularly in Germany. This period of dislocation and poverty is the context for Marx's notion of alienation, and his critiques were designed to show that capitalism was the basis for alienation and to develop a plan for action for overcoming the structures of capitalism. Marx understood that inherent within capitalism was also a system of power: it is both economic and political; it both coerces and exploits workers. Actions undertaken in the name of economic necessity disguise political decisions For example, although it is an accepted economic method for dealing with inflation, raising interest rates protects the wealthy, while causing unemployment among the poor. The political decision to privilege the wealthy at the expense of workers is hidden behind economics.

Commodities

Marx's understanding of commodities (products of labour intended for exchange) is central to understanding his ideas about the nature of capitalism. Commodities produced to subsist and to satisfy their needs have use value. Under capitalism, where workers produce for others and exchange commodities for money, products have exchange value. Because it is often unclear where a commodity's value comes from, it takes on an independent, external reality. Marx called this the fetishism of commodities, when the value of an object or commodity is believed to be tied to something "natural" or independent of human action, such as markets. Thus, the reality that value originates from labour and the satisfaction of needs is obscured. Marx used the term reification to describe the process whereby social structures become naturalized, absolute, independent of human action, and unchangeable. Just as the fetishism of commodities obscures the relationship between commodities, value, and human labour, reification obscures the underlying relationships within the capitalist system and allows supposedly natural and objective social structures to dominate people.

Capital, Capitalists, and Proletariat

Under capitalism, there are two main groups: the *proletariat*, who are wage-labourers, and the *capitalists*, who own the means of production. Whereas workers are wholly dependent upon wages, capitalists are dependent upon money invested to create more money. Capital is unique to the circulation of commodities under capitalism. Under non-capitalist forms of exchange, commodities are traded for money, which is then traded for another commodity (C_1-M-C_2). The primary reason for exchange is to obtain a commodity for use. Under capitalism, money is used to purchase a commodity, which is then sold to create a greater amount of money (M_1-C-M_2). The purpose of this form of exchange is to create greater and greater sums of money.

Exploitation

Exploitation is a set of social relations on which capitalism is built. Capitalists exploit workers by paying them less in wages than the value they produce. While a worker may earn eight dollars a day in wages, s/he may produce ten dollars a day worth of value, creating what Marx called surplus value. Capital grows by exploiting workers to generate ever greater amounts of surplus value, usually by lowering workers' wages. In addition, capitalists constantly compete with one another over capital by finding new ways to generate profit and surplus value in order to maintain an edge. Marx calls this drive the general law of capitalist accumulation. Capitalism is not the only historical epoch in which individuals are exploited, but it is the only one in which the mechanisms of exploitation are hidden behind independent, objectified, and reified structures, such as the market.

Class Conflict

The conflict created by the contradictory positions of two groups, the proletariat and the capitalists, is at the heart of capitalism. Because these represent groups in conflict, Marx called them classes. For Marx, every period of history contained fault lines upon which potential conflict could result, and, thus, every historical period had its own class formations. Because capitalists are continually accumulating capital while also competing with other capitalists, Marx believed that more and more members of society would eventually become proletarians in a process he called proletarianization. Society would then be characterized by a very small number of capitalists exploiting a large number of poor proletarians subsisting on low wages. Marx called this group of proletarians the industrial reserve army. Thus, the normal operation of the capitalist system, through competition and exploitation, produces an ever greater number of workers who will eventually rise up to overthrow the system.

Capitalism as a Good Thing

Despite his criticisms, Marx was aware of the benefits of capitalism, and generally understood it to be a good thing. The productive capacity of capitalism could free people from need, and it delivered people from the traditions that have dominated them throughout history. Marx criticized capitalism from a future-oriented perspective, based upon his understanding of what capitalism, as a revolutionary force in modern society, was capable of, and what its limits were.

Marx thought that capitalism had fully developed itself and that it was ready to enter a new mode of production, communism.

THE MATERIALIST CONCEPTION OF HISTORY

Marx's future-oriented perspective has its basis in his materialist conception of history. He suggests that the ways societies provide for their material well-being affects the type of relations that people will have with one another, their social institutions, and the prevailing ideas of the day. Marx uses the term "the forces of production" to refer to the ways in which people provide for their needs. He uses the term "relations of production" to describe social relationships that dominate the productive capacities of a society. Under capitalism, the forces of production lead to a set of relations of production which pit the capitalist and the proletariat against one another. To change the relations of production, Marx felt revolution was necessary. Revolution arises from exploited classes agitating for change in the relations of production that favor transformations in the forces of production.

Ideology

The relations of production act to dissuade revolutionary behaviour, as do the prevalent ideas within society. Many of these ideas cloud the true relationships that underlie capitalist society. Marx called these kinds of ideas ideologies. The first type of ideology is emergent from the structure of society, and can be seen in things like the fetishism of commodities, or money. The second type is used by the ruling class to hide the contradiction of this system when it becomes apparent. These explain away the contradiction by making them seem coherent (as in religion or philosophy), making them seem the product of personal pathologies, or making them seem a reflection of the contradiction within human nature itself and, therefore, immutable. Marx used equality and freedom, our ideas of which stem from the nature of commodity exchange in capitalist society. These mask the fact that we are neither equal with one another nor able to freely control our labour or the products of our labour. Capitalism inverts our notion of equality and freedom: it is capital that is freely and equally exchanged, not individuals who are free and equal.

Marx also viewed religion as an ideology. Just as freedom and equality are ideas to be cherished, religion also contains positive dimensions, but it has been used to disguise the true set of relations that undergird capitalism.

Criticisms

Marx has faced a number of criticisms. Most importantly, actual existing communism failed to fulfil its promise. Though these experiments may have distorted Marx's thought, Marxist theory certainly did not reflect its practice. Second, history has shown that workers have rarely been in the vanguard of revolutionary movements, and indeed have resisted communism in some places. Third, Marx failed to adequately consider gender as factor in the reproduction of labour and commodity production. Fourth, some have accused Marx of focusing far too much on production, without giving enough attention to the act of consumption. Last, Marx's historical materialist approach uncritically accepts Western notions of progress.

VARIETIES OF NEO-MARXIAN THEORY

Since the time of Karl Marx's writing, a variety of theories have emerged that bear the Marxian legacy, although in many different ways.

Economic Determinism

Although it is often said that Marx was an economic determinist, or, rather, that he focused narrowly on how the economic dimension of society determined the shape of the rest of society, this view overlooks Marx's dialectical inclinations. A number of the so-called revisionist Marxists, including Friedrich Engels (1820-1895), Karl Kautsky (1850-1938), and Eduard Bernstein (1850-1932), espoused an economically deterministic brand of Marxism, influenced primarily by the boom and busts that characterized this period of capitalism.

Hegelian Marxism

One reaction to the growth of economic determinism was a renewed focus on Marx's philosophical writings, particularly their Hegelian roots. Although a number of Marx's early writings, which were primarily philosophical in their orientation, were unpublished and therefore unavailable to scholars at the time, Georg Lukács (1885-1971) managed to anticipate much of what was to be revealed of Marx's philosophical perspective. In particular, Lukács focused on two major concepts-*reification* and *class consciousness*. With reification he extended Marx's notion of the fetishism of commodities to include the process by which any portion of social life could be made a "thing," rather than just commodities. Lukács also developed the notion of class consciousness, or the belief systems shared by those who occupy the same class position within society. Conversely, those who occupy the same class position may be unaware of their common lot, and may possess a *false consciousness*. Although classes are a part of every historical epoch, to Lukács it was only under capitalism that a class could achieve true class consciousness and be a truly revolutionary force. Lukács discussed the ways in which the nature of the capitalist system is obscured. He thought that once these were revealed, society would become a battleground in the conflict between those who wished to conceal the class character of society and those who wished to expose it.

Another important Hegelian Marxist is Antonio Gramsci (1891-1937). Gramsci rejected deterministic Marxist formulations, focusing instead on how revolution was contingent on action on the part of the masses, assuming they became conscious of the nature of capitalism and their role in it. This they could do only by using the analysis provided to them by intellectuals. Perhaps the most important contribution Gramsci made to Neo-Marxian theory has been the concept of *hegemony*, which he referred to as the cultural leadership exercised by the ruling class. Thus, revolutionary forces must not only change the material bases of society, but they must also wrest from its oppressors the cultural leadership of society.

Critical Theory

Critical theory grew up around a group of German neo-Marxists who were unhappy with the economic determinism of turn-of-the-century Marxism. Rather than focusing on the material dimensions of society, the critical school focused primarily on culture. As its name suggests, critical theory is predominantly known for offering critiques of various dimensions of society. Central to this were its critiques of positivism (it leads to passivity), sociology (for its scientism), modern society (rationalization and the absence of reasonableness, as in the rationality), and culture (the pacifying and repressive effects of mass culture disseminated by the culture industry). The critical school has been credited with refocusing attention on subjective phenomena, despite Marx's materialist tendencies. For example, the critical school also had an interest in ideology and its role in domination. They were also dialecticians who attempted to relate the parts of society to its whole, or its totality. Critical theory has been criticized for its lack of historical focus, its weak treatment of economic factors, and its lack of faith in the working class as a revolutionary force.

A slightly different variant found within the critical school tradition is the work of Jurgen Habermas(1929-). Habermas believes that Marx oversimplified the social component of species-being. Habermas takes as his starting point the necessity of communicative action in the realization of species-being, which emerges from the distinction between purposive-rational action (work) and communicative action (interaction). While Marx's central problematic was the alienation of workers, Habermas's is the alienation of communication, or the "distortion" of communication. Habermas is concerned with the technological dominance of life through the rationalization of purposive-action. However, unlike other theorists, Habermas argues that rationalization can have a positive effect if it rationalizes communication, which would lead to a communication free from domination, creating a form of emancipatory communication. Habermas's idea of a rational society is a society constructed of free communication, where ideas are weighed on their merits and unaltered by ideology.

Neo-Marxian Economic Sociology

Noting that the period in which Marx formulated his critique of capitalism was a specific period in the development of capitalism, a number of theorists have attempted to develop work that more accurately portrays the workings of the capitalist system as it exists today. This can be seen as a shift away from focusing on the era of competitive capitalism and towards looking at what has been called *monopoly capitalism*. Paul Baran and Paul Sweezy are the major contributors to this line of work, particularly in their book *Monopoly Capitalism*. Monopoly capitalism involves a transformation in the ways in which companies operate. Under monopoly capitalism, firms compete on the basis of advertising and marketing rather than price. Further, markets are dominated by a small number of very large firms. Lastly, there are many owners, in the form of stockholders, and managers play a much larger role in the operation of the capitalist firms. Similar work has been done by Harry Braverman. Braverman took a microscopic view and looked at changes in the labour process. He emphasized that the control of workers required task specialization, the separation of knowledge and execution, and scientific management techniques. The overall effect of these strategies is to increase productivity while decreasing the cost of labour. Machinery also plays a role in this process. Braverman was one of the first neo-Marxists to deal with white-collar clerical workers, as he tried to show that they faced a set of strategies of control very similar to that faced by manual labourers.

One important line of research surrounds the transition from Fordism to post-Fordism. Fordism is characterized by the assembly line and mass-production techniques, whereas post-Fordism involves small, flexible production runs and high technology. The importance of the Fordism/post-Fordism debate is related to the argument of whether our current society is modern or postmodern. While some have argued that post-Fordism is an improvement over Fordism, this overlooks the fact that both exist simultaneously across the world and that empirical studies have shown increased stress levels for those working in post-Fordist environments.

Historically Oriented Marxism

Perhaps the single most important contributor to historical Marxism has been Immanuel Wallerstein (1930-). Unlike other Marx-influenced thinkers, Wallerstein focused on world-systems as his unit of analysis. The current capitalist world economy is but one of three possible world-systems, along with the world empire and a socialist world government, the latter of which has never existed. Wallerstein breaks down the world system into *core*, *periphery*, and *semi-periphery*. The core dominates the world economy and exploits the others. The periphery provides raw materials, and the semi-periphery is a mix of the two. The world-system eventually incorporated every nation, and was structured by three processes: geographical expansion, the worldwide division of labour, and the development of the core states. The world-systems perspective has been criticized for under-developing a central Marxist problematic, since it focuses on relations within the world system rather than relations between classes.

Neo-Marxian Spatial Analysis

A number of Marxists, influenced by the work of Michel Foucault (1926-1984), have turned to an analysis of the production of space. Henri Lefebvre (1901-1991) focuses on the ways in which space is used to reproduce the capitalist system and the class structure that underpins it. For Lefebvre, notions of space propagated by elites are used to achieve and maintain dominance, distorting the use of space that would flow from people's natural experience of it. Edward Soja attempts to integrated space, geography, and time. He developed the notion of *trialectics* to understand cities as historical-social-spatial phenomena, with an emphasis on the spatial dimension. David Harvey highlights the attention Marx paid to the spatial dimension, and the strength and weaknesses of his positions. For Harvey, the necessity of capitalist expansion puts space near the center of Marx's theory. Marx is faulted for paying little attention to the problematics inherent in the territorial organization of states and for ignoring the way space differentiates strata of the working class.

Post-Marxist Theory

Post-Marxists may be characterized by their nihilistic approach to the history of Marxist thought, to the extent that they dispose of much of Marx's philosophical underpinnings, as well as repudiating the existence of any truly Marxist "method." John Roemer's analytical Marxism attempts to employ modern positivistic methods of analysis to create a better "scientific" Marxism. This includes incorporating rational-choice and game-theoretic orientations. Erik Olin Wright has tried to bring robust, complex, empirical methods to the investigation of Marxist themes. This has led him to break from Marx in at least one way, illustrated in his notion of contradictory locations within class relations. This suggests that individuals may hold multiple, sometimes contradictory, class positions. Marxian theory as a field has not escaped the wide-ranging influence of postmodern thought. It has led to a focus on the relationship between discourse and ideology, time-space compression, and the continuity between Fordism/post-Fordism and modernity/postmodernity. More generally, Ronald Aronson has gone so far as to suggest that Marxism as a coherent theory is dead. The fall of the Soviet Union, and communism more generally, is seen as the ultimate historical test of Marxian thought, and it has failed. The birth of so many variants of Marxism has destroyed its powerful coherence in totality. Aronson views these new modifications as pure theory, and not as an expression of the unification of theory and practice that was central to Marx's work. Because of this, he does not believe that these new formulations should be called Marxist.

THE THEORETICAL BASIS OF MARXIAN SOCIALISM

Marx's socialism is frequently called scientific socialism, because its followers believe that it rests upon a scientific theory of social evolution. This theory is best stated in Marx's own words, as he gives it in his Critique of Political Economy, namely, that "the method of the production of material life determines the social, political, and spiritual life process in general." We find it stated in other words, though in substance the same, by Engels, Marx's friend and coworker.

Engels says, "In every historical epoch, the prevailing mode of economic production and exchange, and the social organization necessarily following from it, form the basis upon which is built up, and from which alone can be explained, the political and intellectual history of that epoch." In other words, according to Marx and his followers, the economic element in human society determines all other elements; if the other elements cannot be fully derived from the economic, their form and expression is at least determined by the economic. This is the so-called "materialistic conception of history" upon which Marxian socialists believe their program to have a firm scientific foundation.

The followers of Marx, indeed, declare that with this principle Marx explains social evolution quite as fully as Darwin explained organic evolution through natural selection; and they do not hesitate to compare Marx's work in the social sciences with Darwin's work in the biological sciences. It may certainly be agreed that this social philosophy which we have already said is best characterized as "economic determinism," is the logically necessary foundation of economic socialism.

If the change of the economic or industrial order of human society is going to work such wonders as the socialists claim, then it must follow that the economic element is the fundamental and determining element in the social life. If what is wrong with human society is chiefly wrong economic conditions, then the changing of those conditions should, of course, change the whole social superstructure. It would seem, therefore, that the dominantly economic program of Marxian socialists must stand or fall with the economic interpretation of social organization and evolution which Marx proposed. If it can be shown that

Marx's philosophy of human society is essentially unsound, then the proposition to regenerate human society simply by economic reorganization is also unsound.

Criticism of Marxian Socialism

The student has already been told that human society is a complex of living organisms, responding now this way, now that, to external stimuli in the environment. These stimuli in the environment we have roughly, but inaccurately, spoken of as causes, though they are not causes in a mechanical sense. The responses which are given to these stimuli by individuals and groups vary greatly according to heredity, instincts, and habits,—the inner nature, in other words, of the organisms composing society. Now, the stimuli in the environment which give rise to the activities of individuals and societies, though not in any mechanical way, may be classified into several great groups, such as the economic, the reproductive, the political, the religious, and so on.

The economic stimuli would be those that have to do with the processes of production, distribution, and consumption of wealth; that is, the economic stimuli are those which are concerned with economic values.

Now, while the student has not been even introduced to the psychological theory of human society, he perhaps knows enough of individual human nature to see that there is no reason in the nature of things why one's responses to economic stimuli, those connected with economic values, should determine his response to all other stimuli; and this is what scientific sociology and scientific psychology exactly find; namely, that there is no reason for believing that economic stimuli determine in any exact way or to any such extent, as Marx thought, responses to other stimuli. It is true that our habits of response to a certain class of stimuli affect to a certain extent our habits of response to all other classes. Thus it follows that the economic phase of human society affects to a very great degree all other phases of human society. But this is simply the doctrine of the unity of personality and the interdependence of all phases of the social life, and it is very different from Marx's theory that the economic determines all the other phases; for under the doctrine of social interdependence we can see it is quite as reasonable to state that the religious and political phases of the social life determine the economic as it is to state that the economic determines the political and religious. Let us bring the discussion down to more concrete terms.

The student has seen that in every social problem there are a multitude of factors or stimuli (causes) at work, and that in no problem is the economic factor so all important that it may be said that the other factors are simply subsidiary. On the contrary, in such a problem as crime the methods of production and distribution of material goods, while important factors in the problem of crime, in no way determine that problem; and ideal conditions of the production and distribution of wealth would in no way solve the problem of crime. So, too, the negro problem is hardly touched by the question of the forms of industry or the economic organization of society. We might go on with a whole list of social problems and show that in every case the economic factor is no more important than many other factors, and that the economic reorganization of society would in some cases scarcely affect these problems at all.

The social problem, therefore,—the problem of the relations of men to one another,—is not simply nor fundamentally an economic problem; rather it is fundamentally a biological and psychological problem, —if you please, a moral problem. This brings us to a second criticism of socialism, namely, that it proposes to reorganize human society upon an economic basis, not upon a biological basis. The program of the socialist looks forward to the satisfaction of economic needs, but it has failed to take into account the biological requirements for existence. It would be far more scientific to reorganize society upon the basis of the needs of the family than to reorganize it simply upon the basis of industry. The reproductive process which the economic socialists ignore, or leave unregulated almost entirely, is far more important for the continued existence of human society than all its economic processes,—if by the reproductive process we mean the rearing as well as the birth of offspring; and if by the economic process we mean merely the forms and methods of the production and distribution of material goods.

In other words, the socialistic program leaves the future out of account, and aims simply to satisfy the present generation with a just distribution of material goods. If it could be shown that a just distribution of material goods would insure the future of the race and of civilization, then, of course, the socialist plea would be made good. But this is just what is doubtful. On the whole, it must be said that the socialist program is based upon the wishes and desires of the adult, not upon the needs of the child or of the race. The extreme emphasis which Marxian socialism throws upon economic and industrial conditions in human society is, therefore, not justified by the scientific facts which we know about collective human life. Rather it must be said that this is the vital weakness of Marxian socialism,—that it over-emphasizes the economic element. Of course, we are not saying that control over economic conditions is not necessary to collective control over the general conditions of existence, which society is undoubtedly aiming at, but it is saying that conceivably collective control over the social life process might be upon some other basis than the economic. It might emphasize, for example, the health and continuity of the race, or individual moral character, far more than the distribution of economic values. Modern economic socialism proposes simply to carry a step further our already predominatingly economic social organization by frankly recognizing the economic as the basis of all things in the social life.

Modern economic socialism is, therefore, rightfully judged as materialistic. It is really an expression of the industrial and commercial spirit of the present age. When the perspective of life becomes shifted again to the more important biological and spiritual elements in life, socialism will lose its prevailingly economic character, or it will cease to exist. It must be emphasized here that all the material and economic progress of the modern world has not added greatly to the happiness or betterment of man. It is true that material progress is important, yes, necessary for spiritual progress. But material progress alone does not lead to spiritual progress, and therefore mere material progress can never add anything to the real happiness and social betterment of the race. On the contrary, it is possible to conceive of a society in which every one has an economic surplus,—a society rolling in wealth, approximately equally divided, and yet one in which human misery in its worst forms of vice and crime, pessimism and self-destruction, prevail. It is an old truth that making men "better-off" does not necessarily make them "better," and one which cannot be too often emphasized, but one which the modern socialist gets angry at when it is mentioned to him. It is therefore a matter of comparative indifference, from the standpoint of the happiness and ultimate survival of the race, whether economic goods are distributed relatively evenly in human society or not.

We say comparative indifference, because, of course, no one can be indifferent to the material needs of life, inasmuch as thev are the basis of its higher development. But after a certain minimum is assured it is extremely doubtful whether a surplus will be of benefit or not, and this minimum necessary for the higher spiritual development of the social life can be secured through the reform of present society without trying the doubtful social revolution which the socialists advocate. This brings us to a third criticism of Marxian socialism. Traditionally Marxian socialism has been revolutionary socialism. The vast mass of the socialist party to-day look forward to some revolution which will, as they say, "socialize the instruments of production," that is, transfer capital from private ownership and management to public ownership and management. Probably rightly, many socialists hold that such a wholesale transfer from private to public ownership would be the only way in which a socialistic regime could be successfully inaugurated.

But if this revolution were accomplished it is evident that it is highly uncertain whether its results would be permanent. For all that we have learned concerning human society leads us to say that social organization at any particular time is very largely a matter of habit. Now collective habits are less easily changed than individual habits, because any change in collective habits practically necessitates the consent of all the individuals who make up the social group. We know also that even in individual life old habits are not easily supplanted by new ones and that there is always a tendency to revert to the old. All historical evidence shows that revolutions are always followed by periods of reaction, and that this reaction is usually proportionate to the extent and suddenness of change in social organization. Some modern socialists have argued from de Vries's mutation theory in biology that in social evolution we must expect mutations also, and that, therefore, the great changes in human society are normally accomplished by means of revolution. But this argument rests wholly on analogy, and arguments from analogy in science are practically worthless. It may be asserted, on the other hand, that all the great changes in human society which have been desirable have come about only after prolonged preparation and after a series of gradual steps which led up to the final change.

The Greco-Roman world, for example, was becoming ripe for Christianity before Christianity finally appeared and became triumphant. The centuries from the fourteenth to the sixteenth had prepared for the protestant reformation in the countries of modern Europe before the reformation became an established fact. Thus, radical reconstruction of the social life by means of revolution is scarcely possible.

The instincts and habits of individual human nature upon which the social order rests cannot be easily changed by revolutionary programs in legislation or in institutions. The only probable result of such an attempt would be the collapse of the new social order, because it would have insufficient foundations in individual character upon which to rest. The idea of ushering in the social millennium through some vast social revolution is therefore chimerical. It is not the place in this book to take up the practical objections to economic socialism. These practical objections are for the most part of a political and economic nature, and they accordingly can be better dealt with in treatises on politics and economics than in one on sociology. It is perhaps sufficient to say that the political and economic objections to socialism are not less weighty than the sociological objections.

Government, for example, exists in human society to regulate, and not to carry on directly, all social activities. If the state were in its various forms called upon to own and manage all productive wealth in society, it is extremely probable that such an experiment would break down of its own weight, since the state would be attempting that which, in the nature of things, as the chief regulative institution of society, it is not fitted to do. But it is not our purpose, as has just been said, to go into the political and economic objections to economic or Marxian socialism. To understand these the student must consult the leading works on economic and political science.

Substitutes for Economic Socialism

Certain steps sociology and all social sciences already indicate as necessary for larger collective control over the conditions of social existence. These steps, however, aim not at instituting a new social order, but at removing certain demonstrated causes of social maladjustment which exist in present society; and as in the solution of special social problems we have seen reason to reject "short-cuts" and "cure-alls," so in a scientific reconstruction of human society we have good reason to reject the social revolution which the followers of Marx advocate, and to offer as a substitute in its stead some social reforms which will make more nearly possible a normal social life.

Perhaps the necessary steps for bringing about such a normal social life have never been better summed up than by Professor Devine in his book on Misery and its Causes. Rather than offer a program of our own we shall, therefore, give a brief resume of the conditions which Professor Devine names as essential to normal social life, believing that these offer a program upon which all sane social workers and reformers can unite. Professor Devine names ten conditions essential to a normal social life:

(1) The securing of a sound physical heredity, that is, a good birth for every child, by a rational system of eugenics;

(2) The securing of a protected childhood, which will assure the normal development of the child, and of a protected motherhood, which will assure the proper care of the child;

(3) A system of education which shall be adapted to social needs, inspired by the ideals of rational living and social service;

(4) The securing of freedom from preventable disease;

(5) The elimination of professional vice and crime;

(6) The securing of a prolonged working period for both men and women;

(7) A general system of insurance against the ordinary contingencies of life which now cause poverty or dependence;

(8) A liberal relief system which will meet the material needs of those who become accidentally dependent;

(9) A standard of living sufficiently high to insure full nourishment, reasonable recreation, proper housing, and the other elementary necessities of life;

(10) A social religion which shall make the service of humanity the highest aim of all individuals.

It is sufficient to say, in closing this chapter, that if these ten essentials of a normal social life could be realized—and there is no reason why they cannot be—there would be no need to try the social revolution which Marxian socialism advocates. There can be no question that the ultimate aim of the social sciences is to provide society with the knowledge necessary for collective control over its own life processes. Sociology and the special social sciences are aiming, therefore, in an indirect way to accomplish the same thing which political socialism aims at accomplishing through economic revolution. There would seem to be no danger in trusting science to work out this problem of collective control over the conditions of existence. There are no risks to run by the scientific method, for it proceeds step by step, adequately testing theories by facts as it goes along.

The thing to do, therefore, for those who wish to see "a humanity adjusted to the requirements of its existence" is to encourage scientific social research along all lines. With a fuller knowledge of human nature and human society it will be possible to indicate sane and safe reconstructions in the social order, so that ultimately humanity will control its social environment and its own human nature even more completely than it now controls the forces of physical nature.

EMILE DURKHEIM: SOCIOLOGY AS A DISCIPLINE AND SOCIAL FACTS

Emile Durkheim(1858-1917) is considered one of the "fathers" of sociology because of his effort to establish sociology as a discipline distinct from philosophy and psychology. This effort is evident in the two main themes that permeate Durkheim's work: the priority of the social over the individual and the idea that society can be studied scientifically. Durkheim's concept of social facts, in particular, differentiates sociology from philosophy and psychology. *Social facts* are the social structures and cultural norms and values that are external to, and coercive over, individuals. Social facts are not attached to any particular individual; nor are they reducible to individual consciousness. Thus, social facts can be studied empirically. According to Durkheim, two different types of social facts exist: material and immaterial. Durkheim was most interested in studying the latter, particularly morality, collective conscience, collective representation, and social currents.

The Division of Labour

In this work Durkheim discusses how modern society is held together by a division of labour that makes individuals dependent upon one another because they specialize in different types of work. Durkheim is particularly concerned about how the division of labour changes the way that individuals feel they are part of society as a whole. Societies with little division of labour (i.e., where people are self-sufficient) are unified by *mechanical solidarity*; all people engage in similar tasks and thus have similar responsibilities, which builds a strong collective conscience. Modern society, however, is held together by *organic solidarity* (the differences between people), which weakens *collective conscience*. Durkheim studied these different types of solidarity through laws. A society with mechanical solidarity is characterized by repressive law, while a society with organic solidarity is characterized by restitutive law.

Suicide

Durkheim's goal to differentiate sociology from psychology is perhaps best seen in this work on how social facts can be used to explain suicide rates. This work is also important because of the historical comparative method that Durkheim uses to show that suicide rates vary across societies and over time. According to Durkheim, suicide cannot simply be explained by individual psychological problems-otherwise suicide rates would be static. Durkheim argues that two social facts, in particular, influence suicide rates: integration, or the strength of attachment people feel to society, and regulation, or the degree of external constraint on people. Durkheim distinguishes between four types of suicide that correlate to these two social facts. Egoistic suicide is a result of a lack of integration; altruistic suicide is a result of too much integration; anomic suicide is a result of too little regulation; and fatalistic suicide is a result of too much regulation.

Elementary Forms of Religious Life

This is perhaps Durkheim's most complex work, as he attempts to provide both a sociology of religion and a theory of knowledge. In this work, Durkheim studies primitive society to demonstrate that an enduring quality of all religions, even the most modern, is the differentiation between the sacred and the profane. The sacred is created through rituals, and what is deemed sacred is what morally binds individuals to society. This moral bond then becomes, according to Durkheim, a cognitive bond that shapes the categories we use to understand the social world.

The development of religion is not simply based on the differentiation between the sacred and the profane, but also on religious beliefs, rituals, and the church. The latter two conditions are particularly important to Durkheim because they connect the individual to the social; individuals learn about the sacred and religious beliefs through participating in rituals and the church. The most primitive form of religion is totemism, which is connected to the least complex form of social organization, the clan. The totem is the actual representation of the clan-it is the material representation of the nonmaterial, collective morality of the clan.

Totemism is important to Durkheim's theory of knowledge in that it is one of his categories of understanding: classification. Other categories of understanding include time, space, force, causality, and totality. These six categories may be abstract concepts, but they are all derived from social experiences, particularly rituals. Durkheim acknowledges that it is possible for moral and cognitive categories to change or be created anew through what he calls collective effervescence, or periods of great collective exaltation.

Cult of the Individual

Although Durkheim focused much of his attention on the social, he did not dismiss the idea of individualism. Indeed, he believed that in modern society the individual has become sacred, and he called the modern form of collective conscience the cult of the individual. According to Durkheim, humans are constituted by two beings or selves: one is based on the isolated individuality of the body, and the other is based on the social. These two beings may be in a continual state of tension, and they are connected in that individuality develops as society develops. For example, it is only in modern society, characterized by the division of labour, that people even come to understand themselves as distinct individuals. Durkheim argued that individuality has both positive and negative consequences. Egoism, or the selfish pursuit of individual interests, is at odds with moral individualism, the ability to sacrifice self-interest for the rights of all other individual human beings.

Moral Education and Social Reform

Durkheim believed that society is the source of morality; therefore, he also believed that society could be reformed, especially through moral education. According to Durkheim, morality is composed of three elements: discipline, attachment, and autonomy. Discipline constrains egoistic impulses; attachment is the voluntary willingness to be committed to groups; and autonomy is individual responsibility. Education provides children with these three moral tools needed to function in society. Adults can also acquire these moral tools by joining occupational associations. According to Durkheim, these associations would include members of a particular occupation regardless of class position and could provide a level of integration and regulation, both of which tend to be weakened by the division of labour.

Criticisms

Durkheim is often criticized for being a functionalist and a positivist. However, his historical comparative methodology puts him at odds with functionalists and positivists who believe that invariant social laws exist that can explain social phenomenon across all societies. Durkheim does tend to emphasize the objective nature of social facts; thus, he neglects the subjective interpretations that social actors may have of a particular social phenomenon and the agency of individuals in general to control social forces. Furthermore, Durkheim's basic assumption about human nature-that people are driven by their passion for gratification that can never be satisfied-is not empirically substantiated in any of his work. Finally, Durkheim's understanding of the relationship between morality and sociology has been critiqued as being conservative.

MAX WEBER'S METHODOLOGY

Max Weber (1864-1920) argued against abstract theory, and he favoured an approach to sociological inquiry that generated its theory from rich, systematic, empirical, historical research. This approach required, first of all, an examination of the relationships between, and the respective roles of, history and sociology in inquiry. Weber argued that sociology was to develop concepts for the analysis of concrete phenomena, which would allow sociologists to then make generalizations about historical phenomena. History, on the other hand, would use a lexicon of sociological concepts in order to perform causal analysis of particular historical events, structures, and processes. In scholarly practice, according to Weber, sociology and history are interdependent. Weber contended that understanding, or *verstehen*, was the proper way of studying social phenomena. Derived from the interpretive practice known as hermeneutics, the method of *verstehen* strives to understand the meanings that human beings attribute to their experiences, interactions, and actions. Weber construed *verstehen* as a methodical, systematic, and rigorous form of inquiry that could be employed in both macro-and micro-sociological analysis.

Weber's formulation of causality stresses the great variety of factors that may precipitate the emergence of complex phenomena such as modern capitalism. Moreover, Weber argued that social scientists, unlike natural scientists, must take into account the meanings that actors attribute to their interactions when considering causality. Weber, furthermore, sought a middle ground between nomothetic (general laws) and idiographic (idiosyncratic actions and events) views in his notion of a probabilistic adequate causality. Weber's greatest contribution to the conceptual arsenal of sociology is known as the ideal type. The *ideal type* is basically a theoretical model constructed by means of a detailed empirical study of a phenomenon. An ideal type is an intellectual construct that a sociologist may use to study historical realities by means of their similarities to, and divergences from, the model. Note that ideal types are not utopias or images of what the world ought to look like.

Weber urged sociologists to reflect on the role of values in both research and the classroom. When teaching, he argued, sociologists ought to teach students the facts, rather than indoctrinating them to a particular political or personal point of view. Weber did argue, however, that the values of one's society often help to decide what a scholar will study. He contended that, while values play this very important role in the research process, they must be kept out of the collection and interpretation of data.

Max Weber's Substantive Sociology

Max Weber's sociology is fundamentally a science that employs both interpretive understanding and causal explanations of social action and interaction. His typology of the four types of social action is central to comprehending his sociology. According to Weber, social action may be classified as means-ends rational action, value-rational action, affectual action, or traditional action. Any student of Weber must keep in mind that these are ideal types. Weber developed a multidimensional theory of stratification that incorporated class, status, and party. Class is determined by one's economic or market situation (i.e., life chances), and it is not a community but rather a possible basis for communal action. Status is a matter of honour, prestige, and one's style of life. Parties, according to Weber, are organized structures that exist for the purposes of gaining domination in some sphere of social life. Class, status, and party may be related in many ways in a given empirical case, which provides the sociologist with a very sophisticated set of conceptual tools for the analysis of stratification and power.

Weber also made a profound contribution to the study of obedience with his ideal types of legitimate domination or authority. Rational-legal authority rests on rules and law. Traditional authority rests on belief in established practices and traditions-i.e., authority is legitimate because it is exercised the way it has always been exercised. Charismatic authority rests on belief in the extraordinary powers or qualities of a leader. All of these forms of authority must take into account the point of view of those obeying commands. Moreover, each form of authority is associated with a variety of structural forms of organization and administration. Legal authority, for example, is often associated with bureaucracy, while traditional authority is associated with gerontocracy, patriarchalism, patrimonialism, and feudalism. Charismatic authority may be associated with a charismatic form of organization. The dilemma of charismatic authority, however, consists of the difficulty of maintaining charisma when the charismatic leader dies. In other words, charismatic organizations tend to routinize charisma, which invariably gives rise to either traditional or rational-legal authority. Weber also argued that rationalization is a long-term historical process that has transformed the modern world. His typology of forms of rationality is central to this argument. He argued that there are four types of rationality: practical, theoretical, formal, and substantive. He was most concerned with processes of formal and substantive rationalization, especially as propelled by capitalism and bureaucracy. Weber argued that rationalization has occurred in many spheres, including the economy, law, religion, politics, the city, and art.

Weber's arguments regarding rationalization are exemplified in his studies of religion and capitalism. These sophisticated and voluminous studies inquire into the ways in which religious ideas, the spirit of capitalism, and capitalism as an economic system, are interrelated. In short, according to Weber, Calvinism as a rational, methodical system of religious beliefs and practices was an important factor in the emergence of modern capitalism in the Western world. The economic ethics of other religions, such as Hinduism and Confucianism, inhibited the emergence of modern capitalism in India and China. Once modern capitalism emerged in the Western world, however, it spread the effects of rationalization worldwide.

While Weber's work has had a profound impact on sociology-as well as other disciplines-it is not without its critics. Some critics question the consistency and applicability of Weber's method of *verstehen*. Others are puzzled by Weber's methodological individualism as it is applied to macro-sociology. Some critics have rebuked Weber for failing to offer any alternatives to rationalization, capitalism, and bureaucracy.

Finally, many critics decry Weber's unflagging pessimism about the future of rationalization and bureaucracy.

GEORG SIMMEL

Georg Simmel (1858-1918) is best known as a microsociologist who played a significant role in the development of small-group research. Simmel's basic approach can be described as "methodological relationism," because he operates on the principle that everything interacts in some way with everything else. His essay on fashion, for example, notes that fashion is a form of social relationship that allows those who wish to conform to do so while also providing the norm from which individualistic people can deviate. Within the fashion process, people take on a variety of social roles that play off the decisions and actions of others. On a more general level, people are influenced by both objective culture (the things that people produce) and individual culture (the capacity of individuals to produce, absorb, and control elements of objective culture). Simmel believed that people possess creative capacities (more-life) that enable them to produce objective culture that transcends them. But objective culture (more-than-life) comes to stand in irreconcilable opposition to the creative forces that have produced it in the first place.

Primary Concerns

Simmel's interest in creativity is manifest in his discussions of the diverse forms of social interaction, the ability of actors to create social structures, and the disastrous effects those structures have on the creativity of individuals. All of Simmel's discussions of the forms of interaction imply that actors must be consciously oriented to one another. Simmel also has a sense of individual conscience and of the fact that the norms and values of society become internalized in individual consciousness. In addition, Simmel has a conception of people's ability to confront themselves mentally, to set themselves apart from their own actions, which is very similar to the views of George Herbert Mead. Simmel is best known in contemporary sociology for his contributions to our understanding of patterns or forms of social interaction. Simmel made clear that one of his primary interests was association among conscious actors and that his intent was to look at a wide range of interactions that may seem trivial at some times but crucially important at others. One of Simmel's dominant concerns was the form rather than the content of social interaction. From Simmel's point of view, the sociologist's task is to impose a limited number of forms on social reality, extracting commonalities that are found in a wide array of specific interactions.

Along these lines, Simmel attempts to develop a geometry of social relations. The crucial difference between the dyad (two-person group) and triad (three-person group) is that a triad presents a greater threat to the individuality of group members. In a larger society, however, an individual is likely to be involved in a number of groups, each of which controls only a small portion of his or her personality. Distance also determines the form of social interaction. For example, the value of an object is a function of its distance from an actor. Simmel considered a wide range of social forms, including exchange, conflict, prostitution, and sociability. One of the main focuses of Simmel's historical and philosophical sociology is the cultural level of social reality, which he called objective culture. In Simmel's view, people produce culture, but because of their ability to reify social reality, the cultural world and the social world come to have lives of their own and increasingly dominate the actors who created them. Simmel identified a number of components of objective culture, including tools, transportation, technology, the arts, language, the intellectual sphere, conventional wisdom, religious dogma, philosophical systems, legal systems, moral codes, and ideals. The absolute size of objective culture increases with modernization. The number of different components of the cultural realm also grows. What worried Simmel most was the threat to individual culture posed by the growth of objective culture.

The Philosophy of Money

In *The Philosophy of Money*, Simmel assesses the impact of the money economy on the inner world of actors and the objective culture as a whole. Simmel saw money as linked with social phenomena such as exchange, ownership, greed, extravagance, cynicism, individual freedom, style of life, culture, and the value of personality. In general, he argued that people create value by making objects, separating themselves from those objects, and then seeking to overcome distance, obstacles, and difficulties. Money serves both to create distance from objects and to provide the means to overcome it. Money provides the means by which the market, the economy, and ultimately society, acquire a life of their own that is external to and coercive of the actor. Simmel saw the significance of the individual declining as money transactions became an increasingly important part of society. A society in which money becomes an end in itself can cause individuals to become increasingly cynical and to have a blase attitude.

Objective Culture

The increasing division of labour in modern societies leads to an improved ability to create the various components of the cultural world. But at the same time, the highly specialized individual loses a sense of the total culture and loses the ability to control it. As objective culture grows, individual culture atrophies. The massive expansion of objective culture has had a dramatic effect on the rhythm of life. For example, our means of communication are more efficient, meaning that slow and unpredictable communication has been replaced with readily available mail, telephone, and e-mail service. On the positive side, people have much more freedom because they are less restricted by the natural rhythm of life. On the negative side, problems arise because the growth of objective culture generates cultural malaise, cultural ambivalence and, ultimately, a tragedy of culture.

Secrecy

Simmel's work on secrecy is characteristic of his work on social types. Simmel defines secrecy as a condition in which one person is intentionally hiding something while another person is seeking to reveal what is being hidden. Simmel examines various forms of social relationships from the point of view of reciprocal knowledge and secrecy. According to Simmel, confidence is an intermediate state between knowledge and ignorance about a person. Acquaintanceship is a relationship in which there is far more discretion and secretiveness than there is among intimates. Friendship is not based on total intimacy, but rather involves limited intimacy based on common intellectual pursuits, religion, and shared experiences. Marriage is the least secretive form of relationship. Simmel sees the secret as one of man's greatest achievements because it makes for a strong "we-feeling" among those who know the secret. But the secret is always accompanied dialectically by the possibility that it can be discovered. Simmel thought that the social structure of modern society permits and requires a high degree of secrecy. The money economy, for example, allows people to hide transactions, acquisitions, and changes in ownership.

Criticisms

Simmel is most frequently criticized for the fragmentary character of his work. He did not devise a systematic sociology on a par with Marx, Durkheim, or Weber. Marxists criticize Simmel for not seeing a way out of the tragedy of culture-an analytic equivalent to Marx's concept of alienation.

4

Sociological Theories and Perspectives

THEORY OF SOCIAL DEVELOPMENT

For the scholar, development is a particular activity of society seen in certain periods. For the social being it is an ever-present, non-stop activity whose intensity varies with periods and circumstances. This is true of survival, growth, development and evolution. These are all the same activity at root with varying degrees of energy, intensity, organisation, result and aims. That is why we say that these four phenomena exist in each of them. Evolution can be termed as fast moving survival and survival is evolution at its slowest pace. Development begins as a physical activity. The energy released by the physical is always the lowest and the conscious awareness of the being is also at the lowest in the physical and highest in the mind. The true centre of energy is vital. It is the vital that energizes the body as well as the mind. Still, the physical work releases the energy in low volumes. Mind, by lending its comprehension to the vital, is capable of energising it several-fold. As the development experience started with the physical and essentially remains in that plane, development is necessarily slow and unconscious.

Man, having started his life in the body and not in the mind, experiences work and life. Body is not conscious and is subconscious. It learns by doing. Learning succeeds doing. This is also so because existence and survival compel man to act and to do. He has to eat, drink and sleep. His act of eating over the centuries makes him learn how to gather food more efficiently. The compelling need of thirst sets him in quest of water. He cannot wait to learn about food and drink. Long practical experience leads to knowledge of the process. That is true till now. The cities man has built, the religion he soared to, the science he has discovered and all he has achieved today are achievements in experience, not experiences that issued out of knowledge. A few thousand years of man's existence which is studded with rich experiences have not led him to know the knowledge-basis of those experiences. Medical theory is of recent origin. No theory of history is yet born. Science is striving its best to found itself on a theory. As for social development, we do not have any indications of thinkers trying to evolve a theory. Hundreds of theories have been discovered and have gained social acceptance, but they are of partial phenomena, rather a particular phenomenon. There seems to be no theory or even an attempt at it.

As man starts his experiences in the physical plane and moves to the vital and mental planes later, a theory can emerge only when his activities reach the mental plane. They have not yet reached that elevated, exalted plane. What has happened is the physical plane is getting saturated with physical experiences. Saturation leads to maturity and maturity will lead to moving to the higher planes. A theory can only emerge when the experiences reach the mental plane. The world's developmental experience has not only saturated the physical plane in several countries but also has saturated the vital plane. As both planes are nearing saturation, the mind can act. Perhaps only when the whole of humanity is essentially covered by physical experience will the mind sail into action.

As the experiences of the physical and vital planes are exhausted, saturated and the planes are mature with experience, it is time to evolve a theory. Also, in the past man has never attempted development as a conscious effort. The hundreds of developmental failures are an indication that no conscious attempt has been resorted to. This again is an indication that the time has come for conceptualisation. What the body is forced to do, it experiences as movement. The vital chooses to do what the body feels compelled to do. The vital experiences in energy what the body experiences in matter. At the next stage the same is experienced by the mind as comprehension. Theory is the mind in its comprehension codifying what the body experiences in physical substance-matter. The twentieth century seems to be the watershed between developmental experience and a theory of development. Two or three events of importance stand out. One is the backlash of expanding development in the form of pollution which indicates that in some fashion the development effort cannot go further. For humanity to accept development as a full time vocation, it must have assured peace. War, as known by this century, has been abolished for all intents and purposes. The nervous energy of mankind engaged in the tension of the cold war has now been released. Assured peace and the stalling of the further spread of development augur well for the emergence of a theory.

At least from two highly placed persons the idea was mooted. One was chief of the UNDP advisory board and the other the UN chief. The latter described the evolution of a theory of development as an intellectual challenge of this century. People placed at the helm of world affairs looking for a theoretical framework for the guidance of their main activities is certainly a symptom that the mind of humanity may be ready for that conceptualisation. Great national events have shaken the world decade after decade. Several of them were successfully tackled and a catastrophe averted, but several others had their sway. The Great Depression, the two World Wars, the Green Revolution, emergence of Japan, the demise of empires, and the spread of education were there. Wherever tragedies were averted, they were not done so consciously. Without exception all human victories of the Green Revolution type have been unconscious.

Theoretical knowledge validates past practical experience. If that validation is logically perfect, theoretically it enables one to project the theory into the future for purposes of prediction. Logically perfect theories, like that of Marx, may lead to practical disaster. But when a logical theory has the advantage of being tested against past experience, it is validated in theory and practice, thus enabling it to be a future instrument of development. In this way theory can accelerate future development. It is the process of an unconscious equipment becoming a conscious instrument. The unconscious element in our equipment leaves several chinks in our armour, making us vulnerable to the environment and future forces, physical and non-physical. Becoming conscious means the body is guided by the mind or mind uses the power of the body. Naturally it becomes more powerful by the mind sharing the power of the body, and speedier by the body using the speed of the vital and mind. Nations, corporations, and organisations can plan with a knowledge they do not have now. That planning cannot go astray because it is comprehensive. Without being conscious one cannot be comprehensive. Economists the world over talk of development as the development of wealth, infrastructure, comforts, conveniences, technology, and resources possessed. They see land, oil, natural resources, buildings, roads, airport, education etc. as development. But these are the results of development, not development. Again, community development, national extension service, hybrid seeds, fertilizers, and liberalisation are spoken of as development. These are strategies, programmes and projects. They are the means to development but not development itself. A social energy helps develop. A certain will of the society releases that energy. Sometimes that energy is directed to become a social force. That direction is given by the social attitude and social goals. An organisation in the society converts that force into social power. The available social skills convert that social power into the social results mentioned above. The process by which the social energy is converted into social results is a social process. It is this process that is called development.

Development is a process and not a programme or a policy. Will, energy, direction, force, organisation, power, and skill all go to accomplish development. All together they make up the development organisation which incidentally includes a part known as organisation too. It is this that serves as the lynch pin for development. In a sense this developmental organisation is the backbone or social structure that enables the process of development to complete itself. Over long centuries society developed the million fingers of this central organisation by an unconscious process of slow trial and error. Without any knowledge of the goal or process, it seeks to be consciously organised at a centre. The organisation itself does not seem to be aware of its whole existence or its centre or the relationship of the centre to its terminal fingers. Only the ends are visible to man, and perhaps also to the self-awareness of the organisation only the ends are revealed, not the whole.

Physical work generates vital energy and gives rise to subconscious knowledge i.e., knowledge in the physical. Being subconscious and physical it does not confine itself to one individual but is spread all over the collective. The collective physical existence by exertion collects a little subconscious knowledge. At the point of saturation it shows in one pioneering individual who is conscious. Thus the collective subconscious knowledge becomes individual conscious knowledge. Its next stage is the conversion of the knowledge into effective work through external means. That external means is the social organisation we described above. Organisation is the collective subconscious knowledge becoming a social instrument of work through the pioneering conscious individual.

Organisation is the mind's comprehension systematising the physical experience into an instrument of social action.

That organisation is composed of systems and subsystems which are truly the skills of the organisation. For its functioning it needs what are called infrastructures that enable the organisation to achieve its goals. Infrastructures exist as physical components, vital attitudes crystalising into institutions, and mental beliefs that guide the mass of men as rules, laws, customs and usages. As the society grows it sheds lower skills and acquires higher skills. By skills of the society we mean the organisation and its systems. As in the path of every progress, achievements of the past, however glorious, have a way of becoming obstacles for future progress. Neither the shining monarchies of the past, nor the wisdom of Socrates, nor even the findings of Newton can hold forever with the same aura. Developmental effort proceeding unconsciously has the painful necessity of breaking down the obstacles to make the transition complete. Conscious development, guided by a theory has the option of transforming the past obstacles into future opportunities.

LEVELS OF INFRASTRUCTURE

Infrastructure is the support for the main structure of development in physical, social, mental, and psychological forms.

It is a part, sometimes subordinate, sometimes that which makes the structure meaningful. It is known as infrastructure as it underlies the main structure. This being a widely known term, we would like to accept it as it is and define it as it is meant among the scholars of development. To go into the origin of the word and make it theoretically precise is not possible, because occasionally the sum total of infrastructures act as the cumulative structure without any structure being there, as in education. The field of education is filled with the physical buildings of schools and colleges, the vital component of students and teachers, the mental part of the school organisation, the syllabus, the lessons, etc. and the psychological values of discipline, pursuit of knowledge, and dedication to learning. All these are physical, vital, mental, and psychological infrastructures of education which when removed leave no structure by itself. We may consider the UGC, the department of education, and the university as the structure at the core and the rest as infrastructure. It may be a matter of convenience, not a principle that can be defined precisely.

Our subject is development of society or social development. It may be proper to define society as the structure and everything which supports society as the infrastructure. By extension we can say the departments of society like economics, education, defence, administration etc. are the structures that hold society together while dozens of infrastructures support the main structures. The imprecision arises from the insufficiency of the language as well as a lack of clear demarcations in the process of development. For the present let us settle for what is available and define it well enough to serve our purpose of presenting our principles in a coherent fashion. The field of education provides enough examples of what we mean by infrastructure. If it is to be made comprehensive, an example from each of the fields of commerce, defence, administration, social existence, finance, and corporate life should be given.

Infrastructure is needed to make the activity possible. Without a building for the school, or students or teachers there will be no education. Education of children being the activity and children being the vital infrastructure of education, an overlapping of thought occurs adding to the obstacle of creating precise definitions. Education is the process of knowledge transmitted to the children by the teachers. Teachers and children are part of the vital infrastructure. Infrastructure makes the activity possible, is essential for the activity to be completed and is often part of the activity. To think of transport without roads, warfare without communication, administration without rules, schools without a syllabus or timetable is not possible.

The infrastructure is spread out horizontally or arranged in vertical grades or ordered to appear in succession or made to act in unison with another infrastructure or two. They underlie the structure or cumulatively act as the structure. Horizontal, vertical, sequential, and clustered placements of infrastructure are possible. Infrastructure takes the field to a wider area in space, helps extend the activity in time, relates each activity with the other, renders the results possible, delivers the results to the beneficiary, makes the effectivity of the activity greater, and helps expand the field in inherent value.

Four Levels of Infrastructure Explained

We need to distinguish the infrastructure from the component or input. Even here the same confusion sometimes arises since the infrastructure is the component or input itself. Society has four levels of existence and therefore the infrastructure of its development process also lies on four levels. So also any work exists on the same four levels. Society, work, development and man who develops the society exist at four levels and that is the rationale of infrastructures coming in four levels.

As communities, ideas, and activities relate among themselves often generating unforeseen good, infrastructures too relate among themselves. This is a fertile field of creative development. Libraries are mostly unused in Indian universities. Even in an advanced nation like USA, only 50% of the knowledge generated in the labouratories reaches the field. The interrelation is useful, productive, dynamic, and creative. Individuals, events, organisations and existence have the same structural composition. The structures rise from below or descend from above. Man, understanding an activity and creating it from his own thought, starts in the mind and provides the vital energy and physical base. In that case the structures of the mental thought create the energy structures of attitudes that rest on the physical basis of work. A new work, new to humanity, starts at the physical level, energises with enthusiasm and finally is capped with an understanding. In either case the structures contain mental ideas, vital attitudes and physical skills. Whether organised or unorganised, individual or collective, the structure is composed of these three components.

It is true infrastructures make the activity possible. Often they are the vehicles of spreading the activity. In commerce, it is the retailers who help complete the cycle of distribution and it is through the retailers the product spreads far and wide. It is not so in the school that serves a similar function.

It is obvious that the physical infrastructure cannot be so energetic as the vital infrastructure. Changes in the higher levels of infrastructure can have greater impact on the process and the result. A school having new buildings will offer greater facilities but will not affect the results of the school. A change for the better in the discipline and dedication of the pupils and teachers will certainly have a commendable effect on the results. In the 50's population was apathetic but the same population is now dynamic. The changed attitude of the population is an important cause for India's great dynamic progress now. In the 50's ports were built, road transport and education were emphasised and a host of other things very desirable in themselves were done, but the country was not astir because they were improvements in the physical infrastructure, while what is witnessed now is a change in the mental and vital infrastructure.

The importance of the infrastructure depends on the importance of the plane in which it is. It is necessary to draw the distinction between an infrastructure, a system, a component and an input. Land is infrastructure whereas fertiliser is an input; the bunds and boundaries are components of land; the method of cultivation is a system. As we said earlier, there are occasions where a system can function as an infrastructure. A system is an arrangement of work for better execution, serving as a miniature organisation and thus is self-contained. We have the system of distribution in sales, the system of gathering a stock of food grains to build up a buffer stock. The godowns that hold the food grains are the physical infrastructure; the retailers and wholesalers belong to the vital infrastructure. The system is an arrangement based on an idea different from the godowns or the distributors.

At each level the results have determinants. The physical level's efficiency is determined by the funds available. The determinant of the vital level is the discipline the society has in general. Education and information determine the efficacy of the mental infrastructure. The cultural heights of the society determine the psychological infrastructures. Funds determining the size and quality of the buildings is a known fact. Punctuality in the West is an article of faith whereas with us punctuality is a known concept, but not so well known as a practised concept. Whether it is sports or a national function or election or school, the general level of social adherence to punctuality is a determinant of their efficiency. The final results of a Planning Commission or Panchayat administration are determined by the educational attainments of that society.

Development is a whole of which infrastructures are a part. Their interdependence is inherent. As is the infrastructure, so is the development. As the part decides the whole, the whole decides the part. A very efficient, high level tourist hotel serving as an infrastructure of tourism in a backward country whose general development is low cannot flourish. The country's stage of development determines the success of the hotel. There are times when a part outshines the whole, especially when new-fangled methods are introduced. The introduction of computers in offices now puts the existence of the entire office in the shade. People forget that, after all, computers are only office machines.

The distinction between essential and non-essential components based on their determining value of the final result applies to this also. Infrastructures are only parts, but occasionally by their inherent value or their value to the final outcome they become as important as the whole or outshine the whole. A cultural event in a conference by its inherent value behaves like that. Modern machines in a factory have the character of making the people forget the company and mistake the new machines for the whole of the company. Especially in the days when machines were invented, the character of those machines carried this stamp. Ford's assembly line became very important and dominated the entire industry for a decade and we all easily forgot that it is one part by itself of a great whole.

Measurement of Infrastructure

Measuring is numerical understanding. All progress has as its foundation energy and understanding. Work done by energy and understanding leads to progress, because progress is change for the better. If we examine the point of history at which measurement arose, it will reveal itself as a point of progress. Measurement is there in a variety of fields, maybe in every field. Primarily, it is a measure of numbers. Areas, volumes and weights are also measured. Quality also lends itself to measurement. Often the quality of a thing can be reduced to a number and measured like the body temperature and blood pressure. Measurement presupposes a scale of measurement and often a device for the purpose. At bottom, measurement is a kind of organisation.

Therefore, it is an instrument of conception and further, an instrument of progress. Measurement starts with length, area, weight, quantity, size, extent, duration, number, amount and extends to all conceivable things. The science of statistics has these measurements as one of its bases. Imagine if today such measurements are no longer there or are not possible, all scientific studies and work based on them will come to a halt. Roads are measured in length and graded in quality. Population is a head count and permits its own classification. Money goes with number and number is the domain proper for money. Literacy too has its levels and numbers at each level. Natural resources like coal, oil, metals, water, forest wealth and a host of other things lend themselves to measurement of deposits or quantity when converted into refined end products, and even the period over which they will be available before coming to a point of exhaustion. The length of rivers has been measured over the ages. The quantity of flow over the differing seasons, its depth and breadth are measured too. Measurement has become a science by itself. The amount of oxygen consumed by a brain cell as well as the amount of time required for a rocket to go to the moon and return are within the reach of measurement. Alongside, measuring devices refining their previous capacity have made themselves available in the hundreds and thousands. In an age of computer, measurement rules high.

Numerical representation of time, space, volume, quantity, quality, design, and property is one of the first steps in fully grasping the entire process of development finally. The Indian development effort so far has not lent itself to such a measurement. The country's development can take further great strides if that one thing is accomplished. In a country like India where personal progress does not mainly issue out of the individual's effort, his own income is an insufficient index of his development. As the government exerts itself more in the domain of public welfare which results in individual betterment, existing statistics cannot and do not fully reflect the true state of affairs. Fresh thought must go into it and fresh scales must evolve before the development effort can have a measurable basis, if not a scientific foundation. This is true all over the world in a variety of ways. The per capita income does serve as a good measurement of the individual's economic status. This was precisely so till the components of individual progress were such that they could be measured in terms of their monetary value.

Human attitudes, and much more so, human opinions are greater determinants of one's development than human resources measurable in terms of money. Further lie values. They do not have so much relevance now as we conceive of development only as material objects and their availability. It is not an easy task. But a far better measuring scale can be evolved than is available at present in the world, if development is defined in all the terms that it comprises of and every component that goes into it is listed without fail. Fifty years ago one's development of landed property and its income entirely depended on one's own resources which meant that until he came to that point of qualifying, he could not move. And it was a crucial point in one's life. Today the lending policy of public institutions goes out of its way to bring the whole population into its net of support. It does make an enormous difference when we set about measuring one's development. Measurement is a science by itself. A part of any system is the registers. We know cases where systems were introduced at the top level and work at the bottom remained where it was. The introduction of systems requires several graded steps of implementation, of which maintenance of registers is an essential part. After the large-scale introduction of computers, we witness dozens of cases of computer systems inoperative for want of data being put in. No system can yield its expected results if the registers are not filled in regularly. Drucker's forecast fell on deaf ears except for two clients whose marked progress made everyone open their eyes. Numbers, measurements, relating them to numbers in other areas, projecting them according to a pattern have now come to stay as a part of planning.

Life has several departments. Its departments are powerfully related to one another. Some relationships are on the surface for all to see as the amount of liquor consumed and crimes committed. Many are not there on the surface, such as the level of employable skills that are determined by education. It took a World Bank study to discover that in agriculture even primary education has a good indirect effect. How can we see that there exists a relationship between consumption of sugar and the spread of media. When each of these fields is reduced to numbers, someone can examine if numbers in two columns bear any relationship at all and when they do whether it is sustained. Development in any field can be seen fully reflected in numbers. It can also be seen that numbers — quantifying — have made further development in these fields possible. The field of medical science is one instance. A man's health is measured in terms of temperature, blood pressure, level of hemoglobin and a dozen other classifications, all in numbers.

In the absence of measurement, we have to use grades like small, medium, or big in describing the audience of a speaker. 20, 200, and 25,000 if described as small, medium and big will fit very well, but will not be explanatory to the listener, since 2000 and 25,000 come under the category of big as against 20 and 200. Measurement makes precise what is otherwise vague. Measurements are numerical, unidimensional, multidimensional and can extend to areas, volumes, duration, and extension. Anything can be measured if appropriate conceptions are developed and are reduced to figurative representation. Measurement is a means where quantity reveals quality just as quality changes as quantity differs. Whether in learning or earning, as the quantity rises, the quality of the person does change.

Measurement has a maximum use value which often leads to a very precise understanding of the situation. As the normal sugar level is 130, when we measure a person's sugar level as 462, it sends a precise message to the doctor of how the treatment should be given. At its lowest, measurement shows a trend, a direction, if not more.

Absolute measurement reveals the quantitative extent of a part. It can be seen relatively as the measurement of the whole since the part, often, is a determinant of the whole. The percentage of literacy or graduates in a population can indirectly determine the wealth of the country and can even say whether it is a dictatorship or democracy. To make a part a symbol of the whole is a very effective way of measurement and issues from a comprehensive knowledge. To measure the part by the whole is not always possible. When it is possible, the knowledge always becomes integral.

Distinction between Institution and Organisation

Learning is a process that begins with the mind and ends in the body travelling through the vital. It is always the mind that learns, at best the mind in each part of the body. There is a mental part in the vital and a mental part in the physical. The process of learning goes through several stages. We can locate at least three stages of it. The three stages can be described as skill, capacity and talent. Any activity is first learnt as a skill. When the skill fully matures, it becomes capacity. In fact, the learning of several skills leaves a residual essence in man which becomes capacity and shows behind an individual skill as capacity. Skill reinforced by capacity becomes a talent in the area of that skill. Organisation is the skill of a society while Institution is the capacity of the same collectively. Rising still further, when a society reaches the level of talent with respect to that organisation, the Institution matures into the tradition of that society. We call it culture. This happens when the social acceptance is total.

An organisation has to be maintained by external human agencies. They could even be social agencies. As systems are called the skills of organisation, organisation is the skill of a society. An institution is self-existent, as no one operates it. It functions by itself. That is why it is said "institutionalise values" so that values will be self-operative.

An organisation such as an office functions through systems and individuals appointed by a central authority and it is run by rules. We cannot think of an office without an officer, staff, rules, etc. But we know that festivals and religious functions like Krishna Jayanthi are not organised by anyone. People celebrate these festivals themselves. Surely when Krishna Jayanthi was instituted, there was an organisation monitoring it. It is no longer so. Customs and usages have taken over. Individuals honour those customs. There is no central authority here. The central authority is replaced by the social tradition. The weight of people's belief constitutes the social tradition. As values are spiritual or psychological skills, we may say an institution is the system of social tradition run by the weight of beliefs. An organisation is more physical and material whereas an institution is more invisible, intangible, and psychological.

Social habits start physically and mature into psychological responses. Arranged marriages giving place to love marriages is an instance. Religious worship in its early days began as an organised activity of the community. Later the individual followed it without the society having to monitor it. An organisation exists by the work of men; an institution exists by the beliefs of the society. At the time of organising a human settlement — a village, cleaning the streets was organised by the village and enforced. As time passed, every household took upon themselves the job of cleaning the streets before their houses.

It is not as if organisations and institutions are two different sets of entities. They go together, organisation forming the foundation and institutions existing at their top. Organisational charts are the heart of an organisation. No such chart can be drawn for institutions. An administration can introduce an organisation, not an institution. We can think of the government starting a school in a town. Can we imagine someone introducing good manners or punctuality?

The best example of an institution is society while government is an organisation. As organisations mature into institutions, institutions can give birth to organisation at the next higher level. The world does not give thought to this potentiality or phenomenon. Society which is an institution gave birth to government which is an organisation. The government through its existence has given rise to a host of social behaviours as in traffic rules, tax payment, law abiding habits, etc. The existence of the police department generates good behaviour in the population. Religion is an institution. How many organisations like the church it has generated. The capacity of each institution to generate organisations at the next higher level is a potential power of development.

Work is organised; values are institutionalised. When organisations lose life or energy, they become rigid. Institutions in similar situations do not become rigid but their traditions get more entrenched. Organisation-institutions-organism-social vibration of culture are the stages of development.

Infrastructure Coming to Stay as Permanent Obstacles

Excavations in mines create deep holes and they continue to remain as holes. If life must resume there, these holes will make it impossible. People who served in the active services retain to the end the discipline the army has given them. Habits once acquired die hard. We often hear "Once a soldier, a soldier forever." This is true not only of positive endowments, but also of errors. Errors relating to infrastructure have a way of coming to stay forever. They turn into obstacles and remain as obstacles.

Any instrument of civilisation, government, society, family or individual which was once created as a help, turns in the next phase into an obstacle. This the history of change and progress. The procedures the government of India created originally as instruments of progress and change settled down in history as red tape. They have have prevented retired IAS officers, chief engineers, and sitting governors from receiving their pensions before three or four years! The most classic example is the Englishman coming from cold UK to hot South India who found the necessity to be dressed in a shirt, suit, necktie and hat. This was a dress necessary at a temperature of 10° F and not at 104° F. He could not bring himself to think that he could work as an officer without wearing those woollen clothes. Under ideal conditions, all instruments of progress must undergo the appropriate changes when the basic society that created the instruments of progress is changing. Neither life nor society functions like that. In practice, instruments once created perpetuate themselves. The greenbench is a classical example. The sacred thread of the Brahmin, the tuft and all the household rituals created once to meet the requirements of the day survived the passing centuries and changing customs. It is said the dog that sleeps on a mat goes round three times before he lies down. This is a habit the dog acquired in the forest to clear the sleeping space, but it still lingers. The human being exists in his body, by his nervous emotions and in his mind. Organisations have their counterparts. The rules laid down by the mind are different from the emotional enthusiasm with which the members work. The registers they keep are the physical part while the rules are their mental creations. Of these three things, the physical part of the organisation resists change the most, the mental rules the least. The organisations that were collecting fees in the shape of currency will not readily accept if the currency notes are replaced by cheques. It demands a change in their physical habit and the office will refuse to accept the new form of cash. Even when the physical forms part of the mental rule, it will have a way of being rigid.

In Pondicherry in the French judicial system, cases were presented by the lawyers in written form, not in the spoken form as in the British system. The French system almost made the courts silent dispensing with 95% of the spoken part of the case. After the merger, the Union Territory took to the British system. The most efficient lawyers in the previous system found themselves inefficient under the new system which eased them out. After all, we may say, what is the difficulty for the lawyer who previously wrote down the case in speaking it out to the judge? The physical habit refuses to change, even as auditors stuck to their adding habits after the arrival of the calculator.

Our idea of progress is vertical growth; but life admits of horizontal expansion that needs no psychological effort. The physical being incapable of psychological effort prefers not to change. Cooks who were used to firewood ovens shunned the gas ones when the change was coming about. At the turn of the century when the Indian took to wearing the shirt in place of his towel, he could not part with the towel and added it on to the shirt. Even over the coat he put on his towel. He could not part with it. Neither the British crown nor the Indian Rashtrapathi switched over to the motorcade from the cavalcade. It goes in the name of tradition. Truly it is not tradition that resists, but the physical habit. It is an error in the infrastructure in one form or another. The itinerary of the Prime Minister is not under his control but under the officer in charge of bandobust. When Nehru defied this protocol to go to Conjeevaram instead of Madras, the Collector stopped him on his way and requested him to go back which Nehru, true to his mettle, refused to do!

For social progress to be real, the old order should yield place to the new. That which yields place does not disappear but changes into an obstacle. The new cola was refused by the customers. Presently religious fundamentalists all over the world are a standing example of this principle. Democracy grew out of monarchy where the king was worshipped as the divine representative. His word was law, his wish was authority. Democracy outgrew monarchy, eschewed the theory of divine right. That is social evolution. The leader was elected. Having elected the leader, those who had elected him treated him as the uncrowned king. Instead of asking him to represent their wishes, they echoed his will, worshipped him, adored him, obeyed him as if he were king. The errors of the earlier system they had revolted against were made into tradition and revered.

The Negro was the slave. He was granted freedom a hundred years ago. His freedom remained on the statute book. He retained the slavish mentality in one form or another. Instead of slaving for the master, he became the slave of his lower propensities such as laziness and dissipation. A few centuries have not given him any commendable progress. In the earlier decades the farmer was fond of dumping his fields with cow dung and garbage. Later concentrated fertiliser replaced cow dung. Today he continues to retain the tendency of dumping the fields with fertiliser. The land soon becomes uncultivable.

The Vedas were esoteric doctrines. No one knew their meaning. People were asked to memorise the text. The Brahmin hails from the tradition. Now he does not read the Vedas but reads astrophysics and organic chemistry. He needs to understand them, but continues to memorise them. Radhakrishnan memorised his own speeches. V.S. Srinivasa Sastri memorised the dictionary! Memorisation remains, and remains an obstacle. It prevented Radhakrishnan from thinking. He could not bloom into a thinker because he could not outgrow the tendency to memorise whatever he read.

India ushered in development banking. The purpose was to create assets in the clients who were without assets. Banking is a field of money lending. They asked the clients for security. Programmes that are development-oriented are being implemented by an attitude that is security-oriented. When life was physical, disputes were settled by physical fights in a duel or street brawl. Rationality evolved discussion and created Parliament as its crowning body. The street brawl lingers in the Parliament. IMF is the apex body of development banks. Its founding principle is to help create the ability to earn money. It is trying to implement that policy by money value which has become an anachronism. USSR which banned the Communist party and abolished state tyranny is now implementing democracy as dictatorship. A small businessman who prospered by thrift and secrecy is unable to part with them even after becoming the chairman of a Public Limited Company. Late arrival, a habit developed when one travelled in his own cart, is carried into air travel. Flights are missed as a result.

Feudal habits are retained in modern business ruining them. The greatest obstacles to development today are the errors that related to infrastructures in earlier times.

LEVELS OF COMPREHENSION, ENJOYMENT, VALUES, ATTITUDES AND MOTIVES

In a situation that is witnessed by several people, comprehension of different people varies according to their apperceptive mass which serves as their mental background. The situation itself has several dimensions and that too influences the comprehension of the individuals. The words comprehension and understanding are used as synonyms. Still understanding is to get at the core of a thing as our mind sees it, while comprehension is to know the thing as fully as possible.

When Visweswarayya passed away at the age of 104, a poor, starving man exclaimed, "He had enough to eat." That is the view of the empty stomach. As he was a brahmachari or a grass widower, many understood his long life from that point of view. In a situation when something is lost, the first response of a guilty person is that he should prove his innocence. He understands from his point of view.

Comprehension is a mental identification with an external fact or situation or a concept. The fact, situation or concept may be in his own mind. As all knowledge is knowledge by identity in one form or another, comprehension is one such identification.

What makes for comprehension is mental energy; when organised, that energy takes the forms of understanding, idea, thought, opinion, preference, construction or habit. Fresh organisation of mental energy results in understanding. That understanding becomes an idea when it is closer to knowledge and a thought when it is closer to fact. Energy that is organised around a thought or fact becomes a thought whereas when organised around the essence of a thought. it becomes an idea. That is why we say, "I think I should move to that house. The idea is I should live within my means." Moving to a house is a thought. Living in a house whose rent is affordable is an idea.

Senses feed the comprehension. Also mind feeds itself with its own ideas as facts. Senses are the instruments of ego and its creation. Ego feels the mind with the facts gathered by senses. Thoughts that are the results really originate in the emotions, ultimately in the body. Those who try to control thoughts feel it imperative to still the bodily movements. Brain is the apex of the body or the rarefied part of the body. Therefore the higher thoughts originate from the brain. Body is external to the mind. In the stillness of mind, a yogi who tries to silence his thoughts sees in the subtle plane that thoughts enter the mind from outside. They enter from outside through the body and its senses. Three main characteristics of comprehension are organisation, clarity and strength. The volume of mental energy and its intensity determines the strength; the previous thought structure that receives the incoming energy determines its organisation. Thought turns into idea and finally into knowledge and light. Clarity expresses this process. Mind seeks light but receives only facts. It tries to convert facts into light by first converting them into thought and idea. Fact is external and gross. Thought is a mental fact. Thought losing its grossness and turning into its own essence is idea. As the fabric of thoughts is composed of facts, the fabric of ideas is composed of thoughts, rather their essence. The soul in the mind holds the light; mind itself possesses knowledge. Thought is held by memory. Idea is in the domain of imagination. Body, vital, mind, and spirit are parts of the embodied being. Each of these planes is capable of its own accomplishment. Mind accomplishes when it comprehends; the vital's accomplishment is enjoyment. Body accomplishes in the act. The instrument of mind for its accomplishment is thought; for the vital it is the nervous sensation. Body does it through physical sensation.

Mind, vital and physical each have comprehension, enjoyment and accomplishment as their sub-parts. Thinking leads to comprehension, interest to enjoyment, sensation to accomplishment. Mature mental interest generates mental enjoyment when saturated. Similarly saturated mental sensation creates mental accomplishment that is comprehension. Comprehension at the point of saturation centres itself in the physical mind. It begins as decision and finishes as determination. All parts of the being subdivide themselves as consciousness above and substance below. Mental consciousness is centred in the thinking part of the mind while brain, the expression of substance, keeps decision to itself. The substance of the vital is nerves, of the physical is the body.

It is noteworthy that the emotion is in the middle between thought and action. Emotion expresses as energy. Thought to crystallise into action or action to elevate itself into thought needs to pass through the medium of energy in the emotion. Action evolves energy of emotion and culminates as thought when mind organises it in its own plane as comprehension.

Action of the body leads to energy of the emotion and ends in comprehension of the mind. When comprehension of the mind is generated originally as comprehension, it has in it all the essence of power to accomplish in the body when saturated. As the mind is a superior plane, comprehension of the mind and the work it aims at will be more powerful than the action of the body. Primitive men worked with the body and their mental parts understood it. Over the centuries man evolved, and the body's comprehension rose to the mind as mental knowledge. Man today, while starting at this mental knowledge, can accomplish a thousand times more than the primitive man. Hence development from above is far more swift than evolution from below. As the same term is used in ascent and descent, care must be bestowed in distinguishing one from the other as the results are far different.

Comprehension, enjoyment, accomplishment are a two way process, one evolutionary and the other developmental. Each subdivides into all three, thus complicating an already complex process. Rightly understood, the complexity remains dissolving complications. The more complex it is, the richer it becomes. To know the complication as simply complexity is knowledge. To be able to see the complexity as it weaves itself into a whole is power of accomplishment. What we call DEVELOPMENT is to trace the evolution of physical accomplishment into mental comprehension and re-enact it as physical accomplishment, thus abridging it into a thousandth part of time.

Development is initiating the work at the mental level to be executed at the physical plane.

Levels of Enjoyment

Before energy is released there is no movement. Energy moves. Insufficient energy does not accomplish, nor does it work. Enough energy works. Energy in saturation can lead to enjoyment if there is no disharmony. Matter does not enjoy the saturated harmonious joy of Energy, Sri Aurobindo says.

An act is energy turning substance into result through its organisation known as skill. Result or accomplishment has two other attributes, namely, comprehension and enjoyment. Accomplishment at any level will have built into it these two other aspects. Hence enjoyment is emotional comprehension maturing in an act.

Accomplishment issues enjoyment.

Accomplishment issues comprehension.

Comprehension that enjoys accomplishes.

Enjoyment that comprehends accomplishes.

Therefore enjoyment can be a measure or index of accomplishment. Comprehension too can be a measure of accomplishment. Accomplishment can be a measure of enjoyment as well as comprehension. Accomplishment belongs to the physical, rather the substance, enjoyment to the vital, comprehension to the mental and each can be a measure or index of the other. This is so because all the three co-exist on all the planes.

We have subdivided MAN into nine parts. Enjoyment belongs to all the nine levels. Mind enjoys comprehension, comprehending the emotion of the situation or event. Poetry is mind's emotional comprehension of life's intensities as realities. In the scale of human values, the poet is placed higher than the philosopher but lower than the yogi. When the conceptual knowledge of the philosopher enriches the sentiments of man whose knowledge of life realities extends to universal scale, the Poet is born. Enjoyment belongs to the planes of quantity as well as quality. The rule is, quantity meets the needs, while quality enriches and therefore issues enjoyment. But when the quantity increases, enjoyment issues as if the quality has changed. Man earning money or acquiring power would seek to rise to knowledge to enjoy. But when man's wealth increases or power net widens, he begins to enjoy.

Enjoyment is integral, not partial. Partial conditions do not generate enjoyment. Because it is integral, it cannot hurt a part. All parts or each part falls into its place harmoniously. The question of one hurting the other does not arise. Though enjoyment belongs to all nine levels, its proper seat is the emotional vital, level No.5. We understand enjoyment is possible in expanding. True. But there can be enjoyment in giving or taking, or for that matter in any act. It does not depend on the activity but the intensity and harmony of energies in the act.

At No. 9, especially at the level of substance, there is no movement. It enjoys non-moving stability. No. 1's idea becomes a pure concept when it detaches itself from the decision of the physical mind and the sentiment of the vital mind. Each level enjoys going to the next higher level. Ascent is the primary movement that lays the foundation. Descent is the secondary movement that completes. Ascent can be likened to the discovery in the lab; descent to the commercialisation of the product. The latter is a further movement of evolution and therefore every element there will be richer. Enjoyment in the descent is richer than in the ascent. There is an expansiveness, intensity and harmony that make for enjoyment. The Ananda splits into three aspects of Love, Beauty and Joy. Ananda received by the nerves is Joy, by the mind is Beauty, by the soul is Love.

Joy is a sensation even as being is a status and consciousness is knowledge. An individual, family, organisation or nation can be culturally evaluated by the quality of its enjoyment. Austerity is enjoyment by denial. Tyranny is the enjoyment of negative intensity. Progress issues out of either experiencing enjoyment or denying it. The wider the field enjoyment reaches, the greater is its quality.

Levels of Values

Comprehension, enjoyment, values, attitudes and motives are attributes of Accomplishment. Accomplishment itself is an attribute of Accomplishment in the sense that comprehension of the physical is accomplishment. Accomplishment at the physical level is a partial accomplishment of Man's total accomplishment even as comprehension is the mental accomplishment and enjoyment is vital accomplishment. For purposes of distinction, we may call the physical faculty achievement so that it may be distinguished from the total Accomplishment. The theme of this chapter is — Man, the full man, accomplishes. His parts of being have partial accomplishment. Each uses a different faculty. The physical uses achievement, vital enjoyment, mental comprehension and the spiritual values. The total accomplishment carries all these as parts and there is an interplay or interaction.

A strategy that can be extracted from these is when one learns to do a thing from a higher plane, his effectivity is greater. To solve problems this knowledge can be very effectively used as an ACT is constituted as mechanically or methodically as a machine. It is common experience that as society advances people espouse higher values and employ higher skills and enjoy at a higher level. In any given society, the lower strata and the higher strata differ only in the fact that they chose different values.

Social organisations and institutions are born when higher comprehension arises in the society. Their effectivity depends upon the extent to which the population honours values. One basic work value is punctuality. The West has developed it and follows it as an article of faith. Their civilisation has risen high. In India neither work nor punctuality is developed. Life is low. Now that India has borrowed the Western ways at random at many levels, introduction of punctuality can raise the level of accomplishment very high. To introduce such a value or to be benefitted by such a value, a comprehensive knowledge of all these attributes and their interrelations needs to be known. This chapter is an attempt to deal with that subject. So also for systems. Cultural values can play a similar beneficial role in the West.

Introduction of punctuality without such a knowledge of all other similar attributes will be difficult, and if one succeeds it will be painful. When achieved, it will yield the practical result with a dry human personality as the product. The best way to introduce punctuality is to start with the society. It requires social planning. Punctuality as a discipline must be introduced at the level of family, small establishments, schools, etc. and be encouraged. Without accomplishment on the agenda, introduction of a value will again be dry or mechanical. Higher production in the fields and factories introduced as an aim will give the context of encouragement so that the value of punctuality is more fully accomplished. In a school where the result is 40%, if a target is to be fixed, it must take into account the potentials of pupils, teachers, the school and the community that serves it. Normally it will be realistic to aim at 50% from 40%. Bt when all the potentials are studied and the aim of full exploitation of the potentials is set, and for that purpose one work value or operational value like punctuality is seriously followed, the result will be more than 90% because at any time society taps only 5% of its potentials in an unorganised fashion. The present effort is an attempt at partial organisation. During such an effort, a host of opportunities and problems will arise. The ideas of this chapter will then be of maximum use.

Punctuality is understood in a school as punctual opening at the given hour. Then it becomes a one-time method, not a value. The school should be opened, closed, and the periods begun punctually. The lessons, the homework, the examinations, the valuation of papers etc. must be punctual in their operation. It is an overall endeavour which releases more energy of the community. Energy so released must be organised into skills at all levels. Otherwise it will be dissipated and the momentum lost. The handwriting is to be improved, manners are to be upgraded, cleanliness is to be raised, orderliness introduced as long as the energy is available.

In a practical experiment like that, each one of these 25 ideas will find ample scope for use. These ideas will help not to overdo a certain discipline or neglect a potential. The accomplishment taken at the level of the whole school will yield a very desirable result. When the unit of accomplishment is narrowed to class and then to the individual, not only results will be phenomenal but also we will know how to draw upon the potentials, to convert them into different stages of accomplishment. Incidentally, all the errors of the development policies of the nation can be seen at the level of school in full evidence. A school cannot embark on introducing punctuality without the individual class being motivated to achieve more, the handwriting of pupils improved, the silence of the teaching hour honoured.

Teachers who bring in the social attitudes that backward caste pupils cannot perform well are a bar to the school's progress. They simply cannot be told to shed that attitude. In a minor way similar attitudes in the teachers that one cannot pass an exam at an advanced age can be countered by organising self-improvement schemes for teachers. The results of such a scheme will remove the emotional foundation for the disbelief about backward castes.

In stray cases where pupils are truthful, honest, etc. they can be shown how the energy of these values can be drawn into academic results. As the energy is true, the incentive real, the strategy has a 100% chance of becoming successful. Cleanliness and orderliness coupled with punctuality can be linked with academic results, individual as well as class. This will create a very healthy atmosphere of competition and is likely to have a chain reaction.

Opinion can be a bar or help. Recognising this, one can take up in a school dozens of opinions, e.g., geometry cannot be taught, only memorisation will help; punctuality is not possible in this town; no standards can ever be achieved in a school like ours. Gathering all these opinions, one can study them and show generally where they are invalid and why. The occasion can be taken to create new right opinions. One can witness a minor miracle that these changed opinions change a school at the 141st rank in the district to the 3rd or even the 1st rank.

Development is a science. Planning will enhance the result not by a percentage but will raise the level of performance. To introduce planning one has to know the process of development thoroughly. This chapter on values contributes its mite to that whole effort. Within its own realm, each idea here will turn into a very powerful strategy inconceivable in their isolation.

Levels of Attitudes

Accomplishment is a final physical result in concrete material terms that is usable, such as food cooked, book printed, house built, a game played, an idea understood, etc. Into this goes physical work, vital energy and mental comprehension. They are the primary elements of the basic planes of life. They shape into secondary tools when energy gets organised into skills, comprehension into opinion, energy gets directed by likes. These instruments have a way of further improving themselves into various fashions of the same intensity or higher organisation and greater intensity. Comprehension is the basic endowment of mind. It shapes into opinion, preference, construction, habit, thought, idea. Energy when organised, we know, takes the further forms of skill, capacity, ability, and talent. Also energy of one plane is acted upon by another plane. Energy is organised into skill by knowledge in the physical plane. In the vital plane when the energy is acted upon by the knowledge of the mental plane, Attitude is born. Likes, dislikes, are energy directed by vital attraction primarily, though an element of the mind may often enter into its composition. Attraction, charm, affection are energies of higher intensity flowing towards another object by virtue of its vital strength, not so much directed by a mental idea. Whereas the vital energies, when endorsed and given a direction by a mental idea, channel into a given direction. And that direction is known as attitude.

In individual or social development accomplishment is a landmark to which we strive and it serves as a tool of measurement of our level of development. Considering it in both ways as a result and a measuring tool, we have to consider the various ingredients that go into its making. In a basic sense an accomplishment, being a miniature of human existence, contains all the endowments man has. In another sense, an accomplishment is traced back to its origin as a process and we study it as a result brought about by the ingredients at play in the previous stage of that succession of processes. We have now taken up, in this section, consideration of the result as brought about by its component attitude. We define attitude as the combination of mental idea and vital energy. Our theme is attitude is a determinant of result. We further say the result can be upgraded or monitored by choosing the appropriate attitude.

As we go down the line from mind to the body, we see the phenomenon of emotion of each plane shaping the knowledge of that plane and further, the knowledge of a higher plane impinging on the emotion of the lower plane. Thus, opinion arises in the mental plane, attitude in the vital and motives in the physical. Mind gives the direction, energy the force and the body the organisation. Direction from the mind, force from the vital help the physical accomplish through its organisation. Mind expresses through opinion, vital through attitudes and the physical through motives. Opinion has no energy whereas attitude is full of energy. Motive has the organisation that can shape the energy into result. In the mental plane itself mental emotion converts the mental knowledge into mental opinion. Mental organisation converts that opinion into mental decision of the mental consciousness which becomes mental determination at the level of mental substance, the brain.

We are now considering only the external results as our topic is social development. We are not discussing the inner results which belong to the domain of psychology. So our context is external, social, the situation outside man, in his circumstance or environment. That environment is like a pyramid with horizontal layers of different variety and vertical layers of different intensity. As man is a unique product down to his fingertips, where the finger print stands out as unique, so the social situations in this pyramid of myriad expressions are composed of millions of individual events each of which is unique, not to speak of the equally innumerable inner stands man can take. His response to each of the outer situations gives rise to an attitude. If the outer situations are described as facts, each fact is capable of creating an attitude in man. There are as many attitudes as there are social situations or social facts. Attitudes are the final outcome of external social situations. Therefore attitudes can be used as instruments of accomplishment. Each of the nine levels if split into three further levels of mental, vital, physical, will create 27 separate planes. Subdividing them into consciousness and substance they become 54. As a conscious movement is internal and the unconscious man is externally moved, by dividing these 54 levels into conscious and unconscious or internal and external, we land on 108 levels totally. This can be extended ad infinitum by selfish x unselfish, right x wrong, high x low, bright x darkness, if we choose. Each of these levels can have an attitude of its own.

In the unconscious process the external circumstances give us the attitude. In the conscious growth one acquires an attitude and determines the result. Attitudes, conscious or unconscious, decide the available energy to produce the result. It is obvious that one's opinion determines the scope of one's opportunity, action and accomplishment. In that sense, opinion, attitudes, skills are limiting factors when the available energy is abundant, while they are positive, helpful instruments where the available energy is not abundant. An opinion of a higher order compels the man to raise his otherwise sagging energies for action. In a person of overwhelmingly abundant actionable energy, a smaller narrow opinion is inhibiting.

In the light of the fact that knowledge has no energy and energy has no direction, we can say opinions and knowledge are factors that bring into our ken opportunities. Attitudes are the springs that unleash the energies and energise the opportunities and organisation (skill) is the instrument that brings about the result. In this view, right attitude helps opportunity take shape and appropriate skill converts the possibilities into actualities.

To draw a complete list of attitudes or their main representations and examine their capacity to determine accomplishment will cover the full scope of social development. All that is said here will apply to opinion in a lesser way and motive in a fuller way. Motive is a deep-seated centre of determination. Attitude directs energies. Motives direct accomplishment. Opinions give direction to knowledge. The physical by its constitution is a kind of the 'whole' man which is really his embodied being. The motive of the being which includes all the four parts is the real MOTIVE, but for purposes of a narrow field of social development, the attitude of the physical can be called the motive which determines the ultimate accomplishment.

Levels of Motives

Nature is Energy in motion. Of all the animate objects she has created, Man is the supreme being. Already he has a mind, a vital and a physical. Energy moving through these planes creates. Also it creates instruments in each of these planes. In the mind the moving energy creates ideas, in the vital it creates relationships, and in the body results are achieved. Further, the Energy creates an instrument in mind to create ideas and that instrument is opinion. Similarly, the instruments of attitudes and motives are created in the vital and physical.

Being a new subject, not having a developed terminology as yet, confusions may arise as to what is comprehension and sensation. For the present, let us use a terminology that is clear to us. Mind is the plane, comprehension is the faculty, opinion is the instrument. So also let us assume attitude and motives are the instruments of vital and physical.

In this section our purpose is to consider motive as an instrument. Further, to consider motive as an instrument of development is our aim. As we proceed from mind to body we move from conscious to subconscious. Hence motive is subconscious. As it is subconscious, it is carried by the physical cells from the parent to child. No man is endowed with the capacity to know his motive as, by definition, it is subconscious. He has to resort to subtle symptoms to decipher it. The whole process of civilisation is a process of becoming more conscious of our subconscious knowledge and achievement. The greatest achievements of civilisation came about when the collective had acquired a motive.

Motive properly belongs to the being, but in view of the fact that the physical, in one sense, is as comprehensive as being, we use the term motive for the physical urge. When one is subconscious he does not move by thought that is conscious but by an inner urge like hunger. So, motive is an internal force and for that reason very powerful. Mind gives direction, vital energises but the physical achieves a result by its organisation. All motives have an inbuilt organisation in them. The effectivity of the physical comes from its organisation. For the very same reason, the physical does not understand till it is able to do a thing because its understanding is organisation. Also the moment the physical understands, it cannot wait for action because organisation has an inherent dynamism. A motor either runs or not. It cannot be started and NOT run. When the organisation is energised by the electric current, it comes alive, it runs. We can as well say, the motor 'understands' when it runs. The hierarchy of opinion, attitude, motive is interlinked and each determines the other. In their formative stage, they are determined by others. After they are formed, they determine the others. Normally each of them is formed on its own. In such a situation conflict ensues. Each aspect is inclusive of the other and in that measure they are harmonious. An attitude includes an opinion. Motive includes attitudes, i.e. opinion too, indirectly. At the level of Being, the motive is most harmonious. Still, individual exclusive formation is possible which generates disharmony and conflict. One who has his own motive on his side is sure of success.

As motives are subconscious, the collective motive rarely conflicts with the individual motive. An individual motive can clash with another individual's. Such clashes are most powerful. Motives continue to grow in successive generations. When the cycle is complete, it changes, often into its very opposite. A generous man's children and grandchildren are more and more generous and at one point, the next generation becomes miserly.

Motives exist in grades. They grow horizontally and vertically. The level of motives is fixed by the level of personality. The same person can have different motives of different intensities. By extension, we can speak of mental, vital motives. An urge becomes a motive when it is irresistible or consciously effective. That is the deepest psychological force of man.

Beyond the realm of social development lies the domain of psychological growth and spiritual evolution. The world is split into mystic Asia and material Europe. No one has indicated why it is so. Beyond saying it is God's will, it is difficult to assign reasons. As the highest mountain is in Asia, one may tend to think its symbolism is a clue. Mountains are, HE said, the earth's aspiration for heaven. Whatever the truth there, the fact remains that Asia and Europe have taken on themselves opposite goals. The goals have been made possible by the motives of the populations. Material goal being the motive, it was possible for Europe to achieve it, because it was within reach. Spiritual goal being lofty, it defies achievement. Hence Asia's spiritual motive, while it is alive underneath, is covered by a life that has failed to achieve material plenty. The argument for social development in Asia is that it will surely succeed in an overwhelming measure as its deeper base is alive and strong. Only that it should awaken to its own needs.

In the individuals in whom the spiritual motive is well formed, personal development of prosperity will take on wings if they choose to exercise themselves in that direction. For that, they should appreciate the primacy of Spirit over matter.

Model of Nine Levels of Growth

Level 1

When the spirit embodied itself, it assumed a body which later developed a vital and then a mind. It may be logical that the spirit should first assume a mind and acquire the body finally. It is not so in practice. From the other end, it is logical that Mother Earth while creating would create the body first. Without going further deep into the spiritual truths of it, let us spread out our enquiry with a view to serving the theory of social development. Social development as a possible idea arose when mind knew that it could make the body work better under its hegemony. Therefore, instead of starting the study at level 9, I start at One.

Man's physical, vital, mental planes are further subdivided into mental, vital, physical in each plane, thus creating nine levels of functioning. Number One is pure mind, the pure thinker, the seat of the philosopher. Though it evolved out of the 8 previous levels, in its own perfection it stands aloof, not related to any other centre effectively. Number 2 and Number 3 are in touch with number 5 and 7 and in that measure will be influenced by them. One too is similarly in touch with 4 & 7 and is influenced as such. But One has an aloofness at the end of the cycle of evolution even as 9 has an aloofness at the beginning. Nine lives all by itself outside the reach of the rest of the centres that are yet to be developed. We cannot say the same thing about One since it issued out of the progress the other 8 levels made. Still its character of evolving out of the previous bases enables it to stand really aloof uninfluenced by any other previous levels.

Concepts are formed in One which is the seat of the philosopher. Thought at 3 is facts or is factual, i.e. related to a fact, not self-existent. At 2 they are coloured by the emotion and acquire the garb of a sentiment. Thought shedding its factual nature and weaning itself from the sentiment becomes pure thought. Pure thought seeks to be logical and rational. Thought acquires rationality when it is organised according to logic. Thus, thought acquires a structure of organised base. Its capacity to be organised leads to its growth. Systems of thought develop. Man endowed with that capacity is a thinker. Evolving from 9 he becomes a thinker traveling through the stages of work, vitality, and scholarship. Work generates energy and energy, ideas based on facts and events. One endowed with those details is the scholar. The scholar matures into thinker or philosopher. An original thinker is one whose raw materials are not work or energy or event acts. Using thoughts as his own raw material, he builds systems of thought to become an original thinker. If his thinking creates something new to the world of ideas, he becomes a creative thinker. The mind that is capable of generating ideas not based on experience in the world but based on other original ideas is a creative mind.

One, apart from being a thinker, serves as a seat of ego where ego can strike its roots deep. Ego is called the coordinating intelligence. HE also calls it reason. Sri Aurobindo equates ego and reason. Reason organises ideas around a centre. That centre is usurped by ego. One is a centre of thought, not force. But through thought, ego tries to reach the depths of one's being to draw upon its power. Ego reaching that depth through the physical will be tenacious by virtue of its physicality, but will not have the power of penetration given by the organised idea. Nor does the vital yield powers of that dimension.

Sri Aurobindo says ideas arise from the body. It is known that there are ideas of the mind, ideas of the heart and ideas of the body. When the movements of the body are energised, they seek direction for their action. That direction is the knowledge of the body. Having originated there, it reaches the mind after certain refinements. The origin of ideas is body, rather, the movements of the body.

Social development is conceived of by One and is executed by the remaining parts. The process of the social development and the process of the individual's development from 9 to 1 and further from 1 to 9 are the same. Hence One is capable of conceiving social development as an idea.

Being mind, One does not have energy or power but has only light. The only power of mind is the power of organising the ideas into a decision for action or a determination to execute. One has no power over the rest (2 to 9) except in the measure they are willing to obey.

Intrinsically One has the power to dominate all the rest as it is drawn from them, but that power accrues only when the clarity, organisation and strength of One reaches the very depth of 9. The Mind can dominate Matter if the Mind comes into its own. Presently it is Matter that dominates Mind as the Light in the Mind is not fully emerged.

Level 2

The vital in the mind is called Two, represented by feeling and sentiment in consciousness above and substance below. Sensations begin in the body, move to vital and emotion, and in the end reach mind. They are known as physical sensation, vital sensation, emotional sensation and mental sensation. Burning, itching, thirst, hunger are physical; anger, attraction, urge, impulse are vital; affection, kindness, sympathy are emotional; curiosity, memory, imagination are of the mind. The emotional sensation is fortified or organised as a thought enters it when it becomes a feeling. Sentiment is a stronger version of it when the feeling of consciousness is accepted by the mental substance. Sensitivities arise from the sentiments.

Mind is a plane of understanding, observation, comprehension, decision, imagination, conception, sympathy. Thought, emotion and action interact in each of the 3 planes of mind, vital and physical. In each plane, the action is different. In law and order problems, the action of the authorities varies from bursting tear gas shells, to firing. They move over the scale of cane charge, lathi charge, opening fire, calling in reserve police and finally the army. Each level of deterrence is meted out by a different level of officer. The same action, gaining in intensity, demands a higher officer to execute. Thought acts differently in the physical from the mind. So also emotions act in the mind very differently from the plane of body. But it retains the character of emotion in all the planes.

Viewed in this context, Sentiment and Feeling give us more views to consider. Movement of energy is both ways, from 1 to 2 and from 3 to 2. The decision of 3 is decisive as long as sympathy does not enter into its fabric. The strength of decision is watered down by the touch of emotion. Here the strength arises from its being crude. The clarity of concept loses its precision when it admits into its fold feeling or sentiment. Moving downwards from 1, sentiment is a weakening agent, weakening of a thought. Moving upwards, sentiment weakens the crudity of a decision. Sentiment is sandwiched between the refined thought and crude decision.

Action emotionalised refines the sensational thought into pure idea, re-organising it around the mental sense instead of sensational thought. Conceptual clarity is diluted by feeling to be ready to act in the medium of life. Here it loses its refined organisation for pure thinking in favour of crude organisation necessary for action.

Action issuing out of the decision of 3 will not have the benefit of ethics of feeling and will be limited to the emotions of the vital energy which belongs to society. Social emotions to be upgraded into ethical ideals need the office of feeling and sentiment.

The process of refined ideas becoming feeling is accomplished by the emotional energy in the mental plane. Its further development to decision in the descent is achieved by the energy of feeling turning into energy of action. We witness in all the planes horizontally the movements of energy of comprehension towards energy of action via energy of emotion. Vertically too, from the body to mind and vice versa, this movement retains the same character.

Personality of man is stationed or centred only at one point. To understand a man, one has to understand all his actions from this point of reference. As the 9 or 108 levels concentrate for purposes of existence of an individual and collect at one point of his most integrated centre to make it his personality, we need to discard the general discussion in favour of a given situation. This helps us evaluate his action and enables us to advise him on self-improvement.

General consideration of an individual or an individual evaluation of a general situation opens the possibilities of discussion on all sides which is the strategy by which confusion is organised.

Passion, ambition, devotion, dedication, sensibility, sensitivity, ideal, etc. emerge into clearer foci by this classification.

Two is the seat of poet as 1 is the seat of philosopher. 3 is the arsenal of the organiser. Language serves each of them differently. It supplies matter of fact phrases to the organiser, metaphor to the poet and well-defined, precise words devoid of sentiments to the scholar. Emphasizing their own version of language, the philosopher can degenerate into the doctrinaire professor, the poet into an idealist and the organiser can raise his actions to the level that demands worship or obedience.

As the descent is more powerful than the plodding ascent, we should carefully sift them out before any serious consideration.

Level 3

The mind that is seated in the brain and known to be the physical mind is 3 in our scale. This is the centre of intellectuality, decision and determination. What is decision in consciousness becomes determination in the substance. The physical substance sensitised is nerves. Its capacity to think evolves to the level of brain in the head. The physical moves and is not capable of anything other than the movement except the physical sensation. The physical movements organised by 7 become skill of a primary level. The moving physicality releases energy and generates the plane of vitality. The vital sensation going to the mind turns into thought to come back to the body to direct and dominate it. Four is the mind of the vital which gives 3 the sensational facts. Three receives the facts but not the sensation. Sensational facts when separated from the senses become pure facts. Facts are coordinated by 3 to generate thoughts. Such thoughts are organised into a system to become a decision for action. What acts in 3 is not senses but the mental sense which is the essence of senses.

This can be more fully appreciated when we consider what happens in the formation of concepts and ideas. Here it is not the mental sense that acts but the faculty of discrimination. Sense is removed from the fact so that it becomes a pure fact. Pure facts are uninfluenced even by the mental sense and lend themselves to form an idea or concept.

My friend helps me to learn the work is a sensational fact which is a rider to the work of learning. The non-sensational fact is, I am learning the work. Learning the work is a fact for the mental senses. Shorn of the mental sense, it becomes PURE when we see an unskilled part becomes skilled by the higher organised energy relating to the unorganised faculty. This is a concept, an idea.

Basically, physical moves; it creates movement and thereby generates energy. The physical movements are organised by 7 as primary skill of organised physical movements. The vital organises energy to act forcefully in a given direction. Mind organises sensational facts into decision and pure facts into ideas.

Number 3 is the organiser and every little thing achieved by civilisation so far is achieved only by 3.

Three is in direct relation with 6 & 9 that are physical too. Juxtaposed between 4 and 2, naturally it is in touch with them.

The physical mind, 3, is in direct relation to 7, the mind of the physical. Three is practical and receives only empirical facts. For this reason it can never fail. For the very same reason it cannot be creative because creativity requires imagination and must function in non-physical contexts.

No. 4 is the mind of the vital which thinks guided by the intensity of the energy and its effectivity. Psychologically it is selfish. Non-psychologically it is the thought of the energy, rather high energy. Therefore it is non-moral, cunning, shrewd, often unfailing. Morals issue out of ethics and belong to the plane of mind, not the mind of the vital. 3 receives the feed of 4 but sheds its sensation before it processes it. Shedding the sensation, 3 is enabled to decide on an issue while sensations will weaken the decision. At a further stage, the decision that is weakened by the sensation of 4, will be strengthened by the higher sensation of 2.

As 9 is the physical existence or awareness, 3 is mental existence or mental awareness. But 3 as it is not yet touched by 2 remains unemotional. Great administrators belong to 3. HE says Ford has pragmatic intelligence whose home is 3. Those in whom 3 is well developed will be successful executives.

No. 3's objectivity is less when sentiment of No. 2 colours it, but if the sentiment is one that is intense with the decision of 3, the decision is fortified.

Thought is the product of sensation in the physical part of the mind. The function of brain produces thought, one faculty of mind, contrary to the belief that mind is the result of the functioning of brain.

3 is the seat of action because it moves 7 which is the primary actor.

Level 4

The vital plane matures when it evolves the mental element in it. It is what HE calls vital mind and we have assigned 4 to it in our scale. Any plane begins with the physical, develops the vital and ends by developing mind. That is true of the mental plane too.

The development of any plane is in two dimensions. One is from physical to mental. The other is substance to consciousness. In the vital plane at 6 a beginning is made. So 6 is physical vital substance. The mere body evolving life energy evolves it as substance of life. From there horizontally 6 develops towards 4, vertically the substance develops into consciousness. Here it is the vital consciousness. The hard, inert substance releasing vital energy becomes slowly conscious of its own vitality. That is the vital consciousness. From 9 to 1 at each level substance in its upward movement towards 1 evolves consciousness, while in the downward movement consciousness develops into matter or substance. This happens at all levels.

As water expands 1700 times in becoming vapour, the upward movement is expansive in volume, while the downward movement shrinks and becomes hard. The vital power issues from this expanding volume.

If we do not consider the organisation of mind, the most efficient part of man is 4. The organisation raises the level of efficiency. As the man who has moved to 3 is not yet fully effective, No. 4 often excels him even as the graduate's earning is less than the uneducated shopkeeper. The superiority of 3 is not in question at all but till 3 comes into its own, 4 can always steal a march over him. Also, 3 being mental and rational, it is not so subtle as 4 which is entirely vital and subtle. Therefore 4 has always a penetrative insight into the weaknesses of 3 till it is fully organised. Hence the apparent superiority of 4.

3 is hampered by several aspects till it is perfectly organised when it is invulnerable. First of all, 3 is physical while 4 is mental. Therefore subtlety is greater at 4. Having come into the mental plane, 3 becomes ethical or moral while 4 is totally free of that inhibition. 4 seeks after victory at all costs while 3 is more concerned with its organisation and rightness. Victory, as anything else, pursued for its own sake, irrespective of other considerations, will certainly be more powerful and effective than result pursued under certain conditions such as ethics and systems.

Democracy made non-military civil leaders the head of a nation putting the general under them. Till then the military leader was the ruler. They were of 4. The enormous courage of 5 makes them leaders who go to victory. When that courage turns into thought, it is extremely resourceful. Sri Aurobindo says Shivaji is a vibhuti but he had no compunction to kill his opponent in a fraternal embrace, a heinous crime for a moral man. Shivaji had no moral compunctions as he was seated in No. 4.

The philosopher of 1 and the organiser of 3 are objects of ridicule for men of 4. For him, philosophy is insubstantial and the organiser is too slow and too dull-witted.

As No. 7 and No. 1 are minds too, No. 4 is in direct relationship with them. No. 7 is subconscious and No. 1 is fully conscious. The thoroughness of 7 cannot be there in 4 even as the clarity of 1 is missing. Without being thorough or clear, 4 is dynamic, fast, reaches its goal unfailingly, unfettered by ideals, ethics, sentiments.

Foresters, rustic community leaders, smugglers, mafia chieftains are of 4. They are shrewd, penetrating, disciplined and therefore unfailing. There is only one punishment among them for lack of loyalty, viz. death. Obedience and adherence are total for this reason.

In the individual who lacks courage, 4 gives superstition. His superstition arises not from outside but from his own fears and intense imagination. The intensity that creates insight in the strong creates intense fears in the weak.

4 is the seat of social security acting as social conscience. It is 4 that sets the fashions, lays down social norms, norms of public conduct, approved manners. In the ascent it processes the emotions of 5 into emotional thought. In the descent it receives the decision and determination of 3 and infuses emotional commitment to them.

In times of social degeneration, the strength of 4 determines the length of social, psychological survival. In times of social upward movement, society moves up only to the extent 4 approves. Shrewdness, insight, penetration, alertness, resourcefulness are its endowments.

Strong 4 in the head of the family will make the family a victim of tyranny, but the family will become a success though enveloped in fear and suffused by tension.

4 is the monitor of motives in consciousness and substance.

Level 5

The vital of the vital plane is pure vital even as 1 is pure mind and 9 is pure physical. In our scale it is assigned to 5. This is the seat of the warrior, the artist and all those whose emotion rises to the peak before being touched even by the mental of the vital plane 4.

The movement from below is accompanied by the phenomenon of enormous expansion of energy at the first level of physical to the vital. As energy is subtle emerging from the dense material plane, its volume expands vastly issuing power of the greatest magnitude. 5 is the peak along that path as it combines the conversion of the physical plane into the vital plane as well as No.6 into No. 5, again a conversion of the physical in the vital plane into pure vital. Next it goes to 4 when the energy becomes sensational knowledge. This conversion entails a loss of power of the vital but generates the efficacy of thought. Thought in 4 is not of the mental plane where its characteristic is ethic, logic and rationality. But it has the knowing character of thought. Knowledge unencumbered by ethical restraint, necessity of logical conversion or rational structure both of which involve considerable energy, is mercilessly powerful. Possessors of this faculty are ruthless tyrants unfailingly successful in their operations as long as their acts are in the realms outside ethics.

2, 5, and 8 are the vital parts of the various planes. Similar parts of different planes are in touch with each other. The higher inspires the lower, the lower supports the functioning of the higher. Faculties and capacities collect in each part, but will not yield results till they are saturated. When a similar part of a lower plane begins to function, the unsaturated capacities of the higher part come to its rescue. What happens in 3 cannot but influence 7 and 4 as they are similar. It is true every part influences every other part, but the mutual influence of similar parts is greater. These influences are naturally positive and negative, positive from above and negative from below. 3 is physical but mind, while 4 and 7 are mental parts. 1 directly influences 4 and 7 but 3 will influence 4 and 7 if the particular work connects them both. Such relations are a topic by themselves wide enough. 3 is mainly the organiser that organises thoughts into decision. An activity of either 4 or 7 containing an element of organisation of decision will put it in touch with 3. Suppose 8 has received a shock of fear from a fall, the great surge of courage taking place in 5 will be hampered by the resurrecting memory of 8 as it is in direct touch with it. Apart from that, as in other parts, 5 is in direct relation by sequence with 4 and 6.

In our scheme of consciousness and substance for each part we have assigned sensation and sensitivity to 5. The role of the vital is to influence the physical by bringing the mental power to bear on it. The vital organises the energies into sensations which, when reaching the mind, create thought. The body always is a docile servant to mind more than to the vital.

The five senses respond to events with their sensational energies and get coordinated as SENSATION. Mind has its own sense, better called as mental sense, which is other than the vital sensation. Mind's sense emerges when the mind separates the reports to itself from its sensational part. Power really belongs to the physical, energy to the vital, clarity to the mind. But energy too enjoys power of energy even as ideas have the mental power. Still, when the sensation seeps down to the vital substance it turns into sensitivity which has far more power than sensation. Its power comes from the fact that it goes to the substance of the vital. Really the substance in any plane is the physical of that plane. So, truly power at last comes from the physical.

Five is the pure hero, the great artist, the lover who kills himself, the patriot who sacrifices everything for his country. As 5 is untouched by mind, it has the capacity to be oblivious of the environment, consequences, commitments and will go to the target straight like an arrow.

Man was in tune with nature when 5 was the height of his evolution. At that time his faculties were pugnacity, gregariousness, survival, self-preservation, abandon of self-forgetful joy, etc.

Music is the form of sound, painting is the form of colour and lines, courage is the form of force. Hence their natural seat is 5.

Negatively 5 is the seat of fear, obsession, phobia, force of superstition.

Sensation of 5 energises the natural physiological functions with energy such as running in fear.

Great warriors like Shivaji, Alexander are of 5. Napoleon does not belong to 5 as he is pre-eminently the law giver, the organiser, but 5 was his most effective faculty while on the battlefield with bullets whizzing past him.

Level 6

Six is the physical part of the vital plane and is seated in the central nervous system, even as 3 is seated in the brain.

The physical parts of the planes have a physical organ as the seat, 3 in brain, 6 in the nerves, 9 in the body. At 6, the human personality emerge into the vital plane which means the physical movements generate vital energies. Therefore the greatest energies are witnessed at this stage. In civilisation, this is marked by the urban commercial life from rural agricultural life. Individually the blue collar worker taking to education is at 6. Any single activity can find itself at 6, for that matter at any level, irrespective of the fact that the individual is far advanced at 1 or 2 or primitive at 9 or 8. He will find himself meeting the characteristics of 6 with respect to any one activity if it is there.

An advanced thinker not used to crafts can find himself at 6 if he ever takes to it. A dud for some reason may be evolved and find himself at 6 in shooting. As faculties and parts of man have an independent existence in exceptional cases, this state of affairs is always possible. While 6 is the point where the being enters the vital plane, 5 is the point where a further expansion of 6 into 5 — physical into vital in the vital plane — is added. This is the reason for finding people of greatest vital power at 5. It is true growth in one part or growth of a faculty is generally accompanied by growth of other parts or faculties. But that growth is only in potential, not in actualities.

It is natural that 6 is in touch with 3 and 9 as they are physical parts and with 5 and 7 which are adjacent parts. The developments of 3 indirectly influence the growth of 6, while the strength or weakness of 9 lend their support to 6 and its existence. The topic of the adjacent parts and similar parts and their influence on each part is a wide one into which I do not go here.

March of civilisation finds its journey in man from 9 to 1 and from 1 to 9. Ideas, opinions, sensitivities, preferences etc. often get lodged in any part. Such opinions, etc. of the 6 cannot be removed by mental effort as there is nothing of mind in 6. Fundamentalists belong to 6. If they are to be educated, it must be vital education, not mental education. The vital is educated by sensations such as fear, attraction, not argument or explanation or reasoning. The physical cannot be educated even by sensation. It can be educated by doing a thing by itself, i.e. by direct experience only, not by other means, since it has no mind to listen to explanations nor sense centres to respond to sensations. The scientists of the world and even other social scientists have espoused the ideal of empiricism in spite of having a faculty to think and comprehend. To make a dent in their beliefs, one has to achieve in fact contrary to their beliefs. Even then, they may accept that particular achievement but in all their other fields, they will be physical with pride. The history of democracy is a standing proof of this phenomenon. After the monarch is disposed, the leader of the democracy is treated as the monarch and that attitude seeps down to the very bottom. That is the tenacity of the physical phenomenon.

During periods of calamities, man moves down to a low point. No longer the mind holds its own nor the vital. He moves down to 6 and acts only from there or from 7.

Emotion and devotion belong to consciousness and substance of 6. Devotion properly belongs to 5 but its strength and intensity reach their height only at 6.

Emotion at 4 can be coloured by some knowledge, but at 6 the scope for any tinge of knowledge is nil. Kannapan could dig out his eyes because he was a 6. Jean Valjean's emotional sense of duty to his sister rises from his being at 6. The life of a galley slave, the criminal mind, his fine emotions to Cossette all arise similarly. 6 can slave. It has no moral, ethical sense and finds it natural to be a criminal or to be a saint. To a 6, there is no difference between sainthood or a criminal life. It is simply a way of life.

6 is the point at which vital and physical sensations meet and emerge into each other in the ascent and descent. 6 is open to raw physical influence as 9 is, because it is of that type. All the power of 3 in organisation does not touch 6 because it has no idea of what it is.

Level 7

In our classification of Man into physical, vital and mental, though we have nine levels, in reality the levels are innumerable and never-ending. In each small act of ours like swallowing a mouthful of food or taking the most important decision of life, there exist strands of mental, physical, and vital intertwined. Only a general idea is attempted here, not a very minute analysis.

From such a view, 7 is the mental part of the physical which puts the physical and vital movements into an organisation that can be identified as skill. To our perception, these skills are subconscious as we are not aware of them. A subconscious skill is one that one cannot be aware of however much he tries, such as the functioning of blood circulation; but the skills acquired by 7 can be seen when we turn our attention towards them. Only they are not in our conscious perception, not so much because it cannot be known as that we do not care to take note of them. Such a subconscious skill resides in 9. When 9 is split into three parts, its mental part is subconscious which controls our involuntary organs.

Bone, flesh, nerves, tissues, ligaments, cartilage are all of different composition. Their composition varies according to their strength. Brain falls under a special category. Brain is the flesh that thinks. By thinking the flesh becomes soft, perhaps softest in the body. It is mellowed by thought. The thinking faculty of Man is carried on not only in the brain but is extended to the seat of reflexes in the spine and ends up in the cells which have a mind of their own, called by Mother "cellular mind."

For our purposes, 7 is the seat of the primary mental activity which mentalises the movements of 9 and the energies of 8. It is in touch with 4 and 1 as they too are of mind, but refuses to respond to the emotion of 4 or the ideas of 1 since it has no faculty of that description. It is just below 3, offering a constant support as foundation. Here too, the organisation, decision and determination of 3 when descending on it leaves it untouched and unmoved. As its own organisation is rudimentary, the highly complex organisation of 3 leaves it baffled. As elsewhere, 7 serves as the foundation to 3, rather offers foundational support.

The mental part turns the energies of sensation into ideas and organises them so that the idea will go back to the body to dominate it. In 7 the energies it receives are energies of physical sensation. So, the maximum possibility here is its conversion into physical ideas. Physically an idea about movement is the process of skill formation. Individual skills inside each elementary act are many. Walking, talking, drinking, driving a nail are such activities. Into any of these rudimentary acts go dozens of physical movements. For instance, in walking hundreds of muscles should learn to coordinate themselves so that the feet are firm on the ground. Walking is a willed movement. A will, a volition should arise. It is a mental movement. The body should enter locomotion if the feet are to move in steps. Blood circulation, breathing, etc. should conform to the requirements of greater energy demanded by walking. Eyes should commission themselves into seeing at a distance for clearance. A simple act of walking, before it evolved into its final shape, fashioned hundreds of individual skills as described above and then submitted them to coordination. All these are organised by 7. The organisation is there, skill formation is also there, but it is the physical skill and organisation of physical skills fashioned out of physical movements. There is no trace of thought or mind here except it is the mind of the body.

Sri Aurobindo speaks of a physical organisation that governs the world. Its organisation, the organisation of 7 and of 3 as well as the organisation of ideas into concepts at 1 have in common AN ORGANISATION. That is a physical organisation at 7 and mental organisation at 1. Sri Aurobindo speaks of discovering a higher organisation than this physical organisation to cure the disorders of Life and Mind.

Skill and capacity are its attributes in consciousness and substance. Skill converts energy by organisation into a usable tool. The essence of the effort is the process of skill formation. A great many skills forming at one level or at one point let their essences collect at that point as capacity. Skill is the process of the individual act yielding results. Capacity is the strength of their essence collected in the substance as foundation. Such a capacity can be drawn into one single skill to fortify it. That makes any skill a talent. The faculty that turns capacity to a skill for it to become a talent is ability.

The principles of formation of skills, capacity, talent, ability, etc. are the same at all levels of personality, be it physical or spiritual. The values at each point that serve as a medium are different in different planes. Coordination as in a gear plate is a physical value while fidelity to facts is a mental value at 3 where it is arriving at a decision.

Level 8

8 is the vital of the physical plane. This is the earliest of points where vitality enters human personality. Also this is the first point that is untouched by mentality. Though it is vitality, its vitality will not bear any sign of energy man knows of vitality but will be of the character of the physical, even as the mental effort of the neo-literate is education for him.

Energy and Force find their seats here in consciousness and substance. The only liveliness, freshness that can be witnessed here is the 'enormous' amount of physical energy into which the merest existence of 9 converts itself here. Movements generating energy are seen here for the first time as a phenomenon.

7 is a poor mentality and is feebly influenced by the great cunning of 4 and the brilliant ideas of 1. On a parallel, 8 is thus related to 5 and 2. Men at 8 can rise to poetry moved by the physical intensity of the occasion. At the thanksgiving function at Mother Estates, an old man moved by the emotions of the function, burst into a song that spontaneously welled up in him on the theme of the forest changing into cultivable lands. Thoughts of no description touch 8 even though primary emotion can blossom into poetry here.

Men of this type will give themselves to superstition and will not be able to question its validity. Loyalty to master, family, property, crew are too sophisticated for them. He who feels is the master, what serves is property, those who are around are kith and kin. Crew is one who happens to be around. Their emotions are still at the level of energy lacking definition of any description. Ideas of no description find an echo in them, not even mercenary gains appeal to their non-existent thoughts. Survival is right and it is their ethic. Organisation is not a concept they can identify, much less follow. Even systems do not evoke their recognition. They will find themselves identified with the plants they plant and the animals they tend. Their own families are for them extended plant and animal life. They love their soil as part of themselves and aspire to be buried where they were born.

Skills of no description can be acquired at this level, even tree climbing. As 7 is not yet born, acquiring any skill, however primary, is out of the question. Sleep is unconscious, dreams are subconscious for them. Skill in another, emotions exhibited pass them without their noticing them, as they do not have faculties to respond to them. The only endowment he has is the primary physical energy that prevents him from being condemned as a human bulk.

8 is in direct touch with 7 and 9 and in indirect touch with 2 and 5. The lives of the warrior or the poet will have in their previous generations men of 8. It receives from 5 and 2. It will be parallel to what the cream receives but will characterise the bottom.

Vitality here is still energy and no sensation. Any sensation here will be physical sensation. What does not create a physical sensation, a man in 8 will not be able to respond to. Loudspeaker, drum beating, blowing the trumpet, etc. are for men of 8. Aldous Huxley says the African drum beating and the Indian chanting will help one lose his intellectuality. "Intellectuals of the world unite. you have nothing to lose but your brains" is his description of chanting and drum beating. Chanting silences the mind, drum beating brings mind to its original physical sensations, one from above and the other from below devastatingly affecting the intellectual prowess of the brain.

Level 9

Level Nine is the pristine, pure physical, even as No. 1 is pure Mind. This is the evolutionary point at which the animal emerges into manhood. What is the bottom most point of manhood is the peak for the animal.

At this point the species has emerged into humanity but has not acquired any capacity as yet that truly belongs to man. It is just there awake. That waking state enables it to move, thus making movement possible. It is not just movement as in the stone or plant, a movement that generates outside. The animal too moves, moves by its vitality. This movement is human movement, movement of the humanised matter. In that sense, it is the greatest achievement of Nature, the evolution of Man. Its parallel now will be the appearance of the Supramental Being on earth. His own movement will not be by thought or will. It would be a self-willed movement uninitiated by thought or unexecuted by human will.

At Nine, movement and sleep are the statuses of consciousness and substance. While on the surface and awake it moves. Withdrawn into itself, the substance is in its response like a newborn baby in the womb of the mother, maybe a newly formed baby. Supramentalisation for the purpose of physical transformation takes place here at the plane of consciousness, for the purpose of the birth of Supramental being in the plane of substance.

Nine has the whole man fully in it, but in unevolved potential, not unformed potential. Nine is not in the least touched by mentality or vitality.

The physical parts of No. 3 and No. 6 are in direct touch with Nine, while it can be in direct touch only with No. 8. Nine thus is the point in man which generates vitality, the vital energies and vital sensations. For that purpose it is the first focus. The freshness of physical matter yet untainted by consciously acquired habits of even physical sensation belongs to Nine.

IN the descent, the influence of all parts from levels 1 to 8 penetrates downwards and reaches Nine too. It is really mentalised only at level 3 where even the flesh becomes sophisticated into the grey matter of the brain.

In the evolutionary scheme of things, when a species emerges, its form is fixed. It does not change later. Its maximum intelligence is given to its members at the very emergence of the species. Nine holds in full potential the maximum intelligence to which man has ever reached and its first exhibition was in the primitive man's fashioning his tools out of stone.

Except at Nine, man is conditioned by sensations of the physical and vital and thought of the mind. For purposes of further evolution, man has to decondition his parts of all the acquired habits even as 9 is fresh without those conditionings.

Supramentalisation and transformation require that unconditioned purity of the being in all parts down to this level 9.

Mother's vision of a seal had that character. SHE describes how that animal was pure, innocent, untouched by the possible perversions of the human mentality that is crooked. Buddhists, whose beliefs and training do not permit them to organise the ego have this character. When talking to them, you feel like talking to one untouched by any influence of this world of ours. Their flesh is soft to touch, carrying the softeness of unspoiled purity. The nearest version of this seen in life is the artless, guileless person incapable of shrewdness or insight. Should it be strong, it will represent the highest culture man can ever attain by purity that is strong. In such a condition, increase of purity leads to increase of strength. Maybe there, strength and purity are synonyms.

To know man in his nine parts is to know him fully. To trace his growth from level 9 to level 1 and back again from 1 to 9 is a knowledge which can hold in it in sum the entire history of man on earth.

5

Feminist Social Theory

Over the last 40 years, feminist analysis has made a major contribution to and has changed social theory, making sociologists aware of issues that were previously ignored. Feminism is also associated with changes in society – especially in North America and Western Europe, but also in other regions of the world. Many aspects of what were considered to be "private life," associated with male/female relations in household, family, and other social relationships have been transformed; many parts of society have experienced changes as a result of increased involvement of women in public life. Feminists and others argue that there is still a long road ahead before the goal of equality of males and females is achieved, but there can be no doubts that major advances have occurred toward such equality – examples include legislation and employment.

While it has been women and men, through their social actions and interaction that have changed social relationships, feminist writers and theorists have contributed to these social changes and to the development of attitudes and views more supportive of equality. As a demonstration of how social theory can be socially engaged, feminist theory has often been exemplary and, at least through the 1990s, never strayed far from practical social issues faced by women in their involvement in the social world. The feminist writers of the 1960s were part of feminist groups and political and social agitation. Currently, many feminist writers are involved in or closely associated with women's groups or social reform activities.

A section on feminist social theory would probably not have been included in a course in sociological theory a generation ago. However, feminist social theory has made major contributions not just to feminism but also to social theory in general. By focussing on the differences between biological and social, on the meaning of the social, on how a person's experience affects her understanding of the social world, and on how males and females relate to each other, feminist theory has forced sociologists to reexamine and revise their social theories. Among the issues that have entered into sociological discussion are the sociology of bodies, understandings of power, sexual violence, patriarchy, and sexuality. Each of these were ignored or were minor sociological issues – now they are often key in discussions of contemporary sociology.

Turner notes that feminists have raised radical questions about "social roles, gender identities and biological sex characteristics" so that sociologists have developed new understandings and analysis of "the relationship between society and culture, public and private, and between society and nature". Feminisms of the second wave refers to the feminist ideas and movement that emerged in the 1960s and had its greatest initial impact in the 1970s. The chapter "Feminisms Transformed" refers to the "linguistic turn" in feminism of the 1990s, and the accompanying divide between academic and grass-roots feminism. The first wave refers to the feminist movement in the late nineteenth and early twentieth centuries, the suffragettes, the struggle for the vote and for formal equality in Western Europe and North America.

Lovell's discussion examines diverse feminist approaches and contradictions within feminist theory and practice – I will attempt to explain these in conjunction with an examination of feminist approaches. In particular, we will examine the following feminist perspectives:

- Issues of equality, inequality, difference, inclusion, meanings of woman, and sex and gender. These include a discussion of "liberal" feminism.
- Marxist feminist approaches – problems with Marxian social theory from a feminist perspective and how modifications of a Marxist approach can be constructed.

- Issues related to sexuality, patriarchy, violence against women, maternal feminism, and biology and bodies. A short discussion of the linguistic turn will be included.

Lovell also examines connections of feminist theory to other sociological theory, although she concentrates too much on psychoanalytic, post-structural, and post-modern approaches. She also examines connections of feminism to the social world, although these connections are not so well explained – for example, there is little on political connections or actual studies of the situation of women. The example of young women's investment in body is insightful and reminiscent of rational choice theory. For much of these two chapters, Lovell concentrates on contradictions in and limitations for feminist approaches – in my view, a more straightforward presentation of the details of the specific feminist approaches would have been more useful. A book that I have found useful is *Feminist Political Theory* by Valerie Bryson. While Bryson concentrates on political issues, her discussion of these parallels much of social theory and her discussion of feminist theory is useful for sociologists.

PROBLEMS WITH EARLIER SOCIAL THEORY

The classical social theorists and twentieth century social theorists through the 1970s generally ignored women or had misleading analysis of issues related to women. A detailed analysis of the approach the classical social theorists took toward women and issues related to male/female relations is contained in *Natural Women, Cultured Men: A Feminist Perspective on Sociological Theory* by Rosalind Sydie of the University of Alberta. A short summary of a few of the problem areas in earlier sociological perspectives is presented here.

Women Ignored. One general line of criticism of feminists is that women are absent from the social analyses and social world of sociology. The language and analysis of classical sociologists is that of men, male activities and experiences, and the parts of society dominated by males. Marx, Weber, and Durkheim were typical of nineteenth century European writers who assumed that the social world was primarily the public world of male activities – the labour force, city life, and politics. One aspect of the long history of modern, urban, industrial society was the development of a separation between the public and private spheres. These had not always been separated in traditional societies, although there was usually a sex-based division of labour, often associated with a patriarchal system of male dominance. With the development of capitalism, cities, and industry, a public sphere dominated by men and male activities developed and expanded. Women generally became restricted to the private sphere of household and family, and had limited involvement in political, economic, or even public social life. While some women were involved in more public activities, in the nineteenth century there were movements to restrict the participation of women in public life – for example, factory legislation and the family wage.

In order to understand some of the difficulties women faced in this era, some of the details of the situation of women should be considered. First, women in late nineteenth century England were not recognized as individuals in either the legal or the liberal theoretical sense. Men still held formal power over the rest of the family, and women were mostly excluded from the public sphere. Mill and Taylor, along with some early United States feminists such as Elizabeth Cady Stanton and Susan B. Anthony, argued that the equality of women required full citizenship for women. This would include giving women enfranchisement. After 1865, when Mill was in the English Parliament, he fought for women's suffrage. He also fought "to amend the laws that gave husbands control over their wives' money and property." He also supported the campaign for birth control information to be available, and was active in other campaigns that were aimed at assisting women and children.

While there was feminist agitation in the nineteenth century, formal equality for women did not come until much later. In Canada, women did not have the right to vote in federal elections until 1918, although the franchise was extended to women two years earlier in the Prairie provinces. Quebec women did not receive the vote in provincial elections until 1940. Property ownership also rested with men through most of the nineteenth century, with changes that allowed property purchasers to become owner, regardless of sex, coming between 1872 and 1940. "By 1897 in English Canada and 1931 in Quebec, a wife employed outside the home was allowed to retain her wages". Also note that in Canada it was not until the 1969 amendments to the Criminal Code that sales of contraceptives became legal, or that abortions became legal.

In Canada, there is now formal equality in most areas of social life, with women and men having the same legal rights. The Canadian Charter of Rights and Freedoms in the 1982 Constitution Act states that "every individual is equal before and under the law and has the right to equal protection and equal benefit of the law without discrimination and, in particular, without discrimination based on race, national or ethnic origin, colour, religion, sex, age or mental or physical disability" . Section 28 states that "Notwithstanding anything in this Charter, the rights and freedoms referred to in it are guaranteed equally to male and female persons." Many feminists would argue though that this is only formal equality, not true equality.

In terms of how sociology considered public and private, recall that the classical social theories emerged in Europe as a way of explaining the society that emerged as part of the modern era. This was primarily the public sphere of social life. Since sociologists were concerned with explaining its emergence, characteristics, and forms of development, little attention was paid to the private sphere – the sphere more likely to be occupied by women. As a result, early sociological theory paid little attention to this part of social life. While the sociological analysis of the classical sociologists can be applied to both women and men, by ignoring a large part of the social world, early sociologists had little or no theory of gender relations, sexuality, or male/female inequalities – essential aspects of contemporary social theory. In addition, by not analysing the private part of the social world, early sociology may not have developed an adequate understanding of all parts of the social world.

Definitions of Sociology and the Social World

Each social theory has a definition of what is social or what is the scope of the social theory. For Goffman this was the interaction order and for Mead it was the study of the relationship among mind, self, and society. It was the classical sociologists who first defined the field of sociology. Each of these writers developed a definition of the social world, even if only implicitly, and proceeded to analyze it. For feminists and contemporary sociologists, a major problem is that the classical definitions of the social world exclude large parts of human action and interaction. Many of the excluded portions of the social world are those that were typically occupied by women and children, with classical writers showing little interest in or analysis of institutions such as the household, family, or community where women's experiences have often been centred.

The emphasis on labour and the commodity for Marx, and the division of labour for Marx and Durkheim, provide an example of this. We will examine some of the difficulties associated with Marx's approach next day – following is a short discussion of Durkheim and the division of labour.

Durkheim, concentrating on the division of labour, and its implications for social development and social solidarity, develops a similar approach. That is, it is the division of tasks in the public economy that characterizes the division of labour. Since women did not generally participate in the labour force in Durkheim's day, this eliminates women from the division of labour. To the extent that the division of labour forms the basis for morality and organic solidarity in modern society, it is primarily the activity of men that create this solidarity. It is difficult to see how women's activities contribute to organic solidarity. Since the proper study of sociology is social facts, but women are absent from the creation of social facts, women are not the proper subject of sociology.

Another way that classical sociologists define the social world is through their categories and concepts. For Marx, class and class struggle, exploitation and surplus labour, and accumulation and crises have little to do with what women experience or do, since they refer to activities in the economy and the labour force. Durkheim's social facts could include women, but they generally do not. Similarly, Weber's class, status, and party, domination, authority, bureaucracy, and rationality are all part of a public sphere in which women play little part.

Classical sociologists recognized patriarchy as a social and political system that involved the exercise of power by males over females, family, children, and household. But their conception of patriarchy was somewhat different than that of feminist analyses of patriarchy. Feminists emphasize rule by males over females but include issues such as violence, control of sexuality, and other forms of domination by males and oppression of females. Classical sociologists, especially Weber, considered it to be a part of political power and traditional authority involving control by a senior male over other males as well as females. Classical sociologists also appear to have considered it as emerging from natural differences between men and women, whereas feminists consider it more socially constructed.

In summary, the social world of the classical sociologists generally excluded the actions of women. As a result, sociology as a discipline did not have much to say about women. While each of Marx, Weber, and Durkheim did have some comments on women and family, these were generally limited comments and their sociological models would be little different if women did not exist.

CENTRAL ISSUES AND APPROACHES OF FEMINIST THEORY

Issues identified by Lovell include women's experience; equality, inequality, and difference; patriarchy and domination; bodies and biological differences between men and women; sexuality, and violence. Feminist theory examines women in the social world and addresses issues of concern to women, focussing on these from the perspective, experiences, and viewpoint of women. It cuts across conventional academic disciplines and develops ideas and approaches that are useful in a wide variety of these disciplines. Not only have feminists critiqued conventional methodological approaches, they have developed new methods – placing more emphasis on the experiences of women and new forms of knowledge. As noted earlier, feminism is closely engaged with the social world – feminist theorists tend to be women who theorize about their own experiences and interaction, it is concerned with the everyday lives and experiences of women and their social interactions, and it is often connected to women's groups, social reform, and broad social and political movements, organizations, and institutions. As a method of conducting social analysis, social research, and social theorizing, feminist theoretical perspectives provide worthwhile models and examples for sociology and other academic endeavours.

Difference

While the second wave of feminism often argued that there were common experiences of women and similar social position of women with respect to men in society, Lovell argues that there are a number of differences. Some of these sexual and gender differences; differences by race, ethnicity, and class; sexuality; and difference as a general concept. This makes it difficult to deal with issues of equality in a manner acceptable to all women, feminists may not speak for all women, and generalizations concerning all women may be trivial or false. For example, Lovell notes how feminism has sometimes been labelled as bourgeois or middle class and has been attacked as representing privilege of women in these groups.

While these attacks have sometimes been a smokescreen to discredit some feminists, these are difficult issues that feminists must address. Lovell shows how more recent feminist approaches have emphasized the importance of building alliances across difference, although this requires "genuine dialog and mutual exchange between those who are unlike". Further, some emphasize local and interpersonal issues, rather than focus exclusively on societal level political issues such as equal rights. In considering these, Lovell argues that gender, class, and race are not :discrete and cumulative forms of oppression" but are constructed in relation to each other in particular ways.

Perhaps the first concern of feminist sociology is to recognize women as full-fledged social actors in the social world. While women were always part of the social world, theoretical perspectives often did not recognize them as such. In some cases, earlier theoretical perspectives can be modified or extended so that women are recognized as such, in other cases it may not be possible to do so, thus requiring that these perspectives be rebuilt or that their limitations be recognized. For example, it would seem possible to introduce feminist theory into symbolic interaction perspectives in a way that would enrich these. Theories such as Parsons's model of the family or the instrumental and expressive appear to be much more limited and perhaps incapable of basic revision.

Sex and Gender

A second overriding concern of feminist sociology is to recognize the difference between biology and the social – the difference usually associated with sex (as biologically ascribed) and gender (as socially constructed). Lovell notes that "the distinction between sex and gender initially provided a firm plank for both Marxist and radical feminists ... the social construction of femininity". She also notes how "women's biological functions have over and over again been used to rationalize and legitimate" the social status of women. A large part of feminist theory and research has been devoted to explaining how the status, role, and position of women in the social world was socially constructed, and was not natural or unchangeable. This involved studies of the different experiences of women in different times and places, showing the great variety of ways that societies dealt with male/female relationships, resulting in the view that gender differences were much more variable and malleable than biological differences. For feminists, biological realities may be relatively unchangeable, but "what is constructed in social relations and in culture is more readily reconstructed".

Such an approach is consistent with a sociological approach – where social construction is always emphasized over biological explanations. It is also consistent with liberal or equal rights approaches to feminism. Those approaches tended to argue that the mind/body split that accorded rationality and mind to males and nature and body to females were incorrect. That is, feminists argued that both males and females have bodies that differ, but similar minds and capabilities. They argued that is was a male view that women were more connected to nature and the body, and male domination and power over females meant the relegation of females to the private sphere. But these were socially constructed views of gender by powerful males who perpetuated such differences through laws, exclusion of females, and domination of personal relationships. Feminists thus argued that females were as capable and rational as males, and there should be equality between males and females in all aspects of life, both in the public and private spheres. That is, the social construction of gender was the problem, not some inherent biological difference between men and women.

But Lovell notes that has not been easy to completely ignore biological realities and radical feminism has reintroduced the body and biological characteristics. While these are in quite different ways than in nineteenth century writings, it has become clear that the division between sex and gender is not clear-cut, nor so useful for feminist analysis as once thought. Lovell argues that there are several problems with this distinction.

First, Lovell notes that if feminists found oppression of women to be very widespread across time and place, "biology must have *something* to do with it". Anthropological and sociological evidence found great difference of experiences, role, and situation of women in different societies, so this was strong evidence for the difference between sex and gender. But feminists also made the argument that the situation of women tended to be inferior in most, if not all societies. But what does this say about social construction of gender? Does such social construction always lead to male domination and female subordination? If this is the case, then it is difficult to argue that there is not some biological aspect to this power differential. Systems of patriarchy may be a means of explaining this, but how do these systems of patriarchy emerge?

Second, while gender may be socially constructed, so are class, race, ethnicity, and sexuality, as third world women, minority women, lesbians, and others have made clear. Differences between sex and gender often did not make this apparent, and did not consider the diverse ways that these may be interconnected. As a result, a simple sex/gender distinction may not capture the variety of experiences and situations of women. Lovell notes how this meant that some women were reluctant to become feminists, or were in outright opposition to feminism. Some of these viewed feminism as an ideology of privileged, middle-class, white females.

Third, how are feminists to deal with biological realities? Lovell argues that radical feminists adopted a variety of responses. Another approach was to argue for freeing women from childbirth through "a revolution in the technology and social relations of reproduction, in which the womb would be by-passed in favor of new technologies". While this may be in the realm of science fiction, it has been argued by feminists such as Shulamith Firestone. A more conventional approach has been to argue that women should not be bound by biological realities, but participate more fully in all activities. Where these require accommodations, such as leave for childbirth, laws, policies, and organizations should restructure labour force and other activities so that full participation for women can occur. While some of this has occurred, the current structure of career and public life will require more change if this is to occur, and it may be difficult to achieve full equality with just this approach.

Fourth, Lovell argues that Marxist analysis provided an explanation of social construction of relations of reproduction, rooted in material reality. But she also notes that issues of violence against women in their personal and family life was difficult to explain within the Marxian model. While capitalism might well use women in an oppressive manner, why should "the sexual domination of women, and the extent of male violence against them" be so great and so widespread – there appears to be no explanation for this within a strictly Marxian framework of class relationships.

Finally, an argument not mentioned by Lovell is the emphasis by women and some feminists on the superior and positive characteristics of women. The alleged expressive, caring, maternal, nurturing, and conflict resolving characteristics of females are missing from instrumental, utilitarian, rational, and aggressive males. But if there is to be equality, and women and men are the same, which of these characteristics is to emerge. Would the equal female adopt the supposed male characteristics. Historically, feminists often argued that women could bring their more positive expressive characteristics to public life and social relationship, thus producing a more caring and human society. But if this is so, which of these characteristics emerges from biological sex differences and which are socially constructed gender differences? While the distinctions between sex and gender has been extremely useful from a feminist and sociological perspective, the above arguments show that it is not without its own difficulties and contradictions. The aim of the above arguments is not to abandon this conceptual distinction as to note how it may need to become more carefully used and modified in improving social theory. In terms of several of these issues, there will be changes in the social construction of gender as women participate more fully in all aspects of life, as men change their forms of participation, and as social relationships change – social theory should attempt to understand and explain these.

FEMINISM AND MARXISM

Lovell argues that Marxism emerged as a major sociological paradigm at the same time as feminism emerged. There were also strong parallels between Marxism and feminism – among these were that both were concerned with inequality, domination, and oppression, both had an emphasis on social change through group organization and political pressure, both had a methodology combining theory and practice, and both had an historical approach. Further, Marxism seemed receptive to feminism, since some Marxists had been concerned with oppression of women and both were attempting to change society.

At the same time, there were limits to these parallels and some aspects of feminism were poorly dealt with by Marxists – issues of "human reproduction and sexuality ... [were] outside the sphere of the social", Marxists often argued that forms of difference other than economic were secondary, and individually and collectively male Marxists were reluctant to change their personal lives, give up male privilege, or become more equal in personal and work relationships. The following notes survey a number of issues connected to Marxism and feminism. First are some of the reasons why the Marxist model has difficulty with feminist concepts and approaches, and this is followed with a discussion of some attempts to introduce feminist concepts and perspectives into Marxian models.

Origin of the Family

As part of its analysis, Marxism provides an historical and materialist explanation of the emergence of family, patriarchy, and the situation of women and men. *The Origin of the Family,*

Private Property and the State, published by Friedrich Engels in 1884, is the classic work dealing with these issues. Engels argued that the establishment of private property in land, tools, and livestock created the possibility for men to exercise control over the means of production. In order to ensure legitimacy of heirs and control private property, men established a patrilineal and patriarchal form of society – enforcing compulsory monogamy on women and devaluing their work and value in society. This development, which occurred in distant history, at the time of the development of agriculture, relegated women to an inferior position in society, dominated by men. This system of patriarchy maintained itself over the centuries and when capitalism emerged, capitalism found such a system useful for its new form of social organization, characterized by exploitation of workers by employers as the source of capital accumulation.

The strong point of the Marxist approach is that it provided a material explanation for the emergence and maintenance of a system of patriarchy. For many Marxists, this has made oppression on the basis of sex derivative from the development of a social surplus and the institution of private property, thus providing an economic explanation for this form of oppression. Unlike liberal feminist approaches, equality of men and women cannot be achieved within capitalism, it requires the abolition of private property and establishment of a socialist system.

The weak points of Engels's argument is that it does not appear to be historically accurate and assumes a natural division of labour between men and women. It has the implication that the elimination of private property will end patriarchy, and some Marxists use this to argue that struggles by women to achieve equality are secondary to struggles by the working class to change society, and may even divert attention from the primary contradiction between capital and labour.

Marxian Economics

Marx looks on human labour as potentially creative and this creative potential distinguishes humans from other animals. His critique of private property and capitalism is that this essence of humanity and creativity is taken away from labourers in the production process because of the existence of private property and exploitation. Marx's political economic model begins with the commodity and exchange, with the value of commodities being in direct proportion to the amount of human labour embodied in producing them. While commodities exchange at their value, surplus value emerges from extra or surplus labour, extracted from workers by employers. This occurs because the commodity labour power is a unique commodity with the capability of producing more value than the value of labour power itself. Employers purchase labour power at its value (wage paid to worker), but employ it to produce extra value, beyond that sufficient to pay the wage. This surplus value extracted from workers is ultimately turned into profits for capitalists and used to accumulate capital. This expansion of monetary and physical capital also means the extension of the exploitative capital/labour social relationships central to capitalism.

In this model, exploitation emerges as commodities are produced, and it is those workers who are employed at jobs in the production process who are exploited in that surplus labour is extracted from them. As a result, labour exercised in society but not directly engaged in production of commodities, and this includes the labour of many women and all household labour, is not exploited. Only if workers are employed and work at jobs where surplus value is extracted are exploited and become a source of capital accumulation. Since many women are not directly employed in these situations, women's labour might not be exploited or alienated in the same way as that of men's, since their labour is not subject to the forces that occur in the labour force. Marx's analysis of capitalism and the social relationships of capitalism is almost entirely that of the public economy and the creation of products – goods and services – for purposes of exchange. Commodities have value to the extent that they are exchanged, and it is only those goods and services that are exchanged on the market that form part of Marx's analysis of capitalism. From this analysis of the commodity, exploitation, surplus value, and capital accumulation, Marx explains aspects of capitalism such as class structures, cycles of expansion and contraction in the economy, the tendency toward a falling rate of profit, and other contradictions of capitalism. The central, contradictory social relationship of capitalism is the capital-labour relationship – it is this which ultimately leads toward the creation of a class-conscious proletariat. This proletariat eliminates the capitalist class and establishes socialism – common ownership of the means of production. It is under this system that workers are able to begin realizing their human potential and, according to Engels, the conditions for the creation of equality between males and females.

From a feminist perspective, there are a number of problems with this analysis. Among these are (i) the emphasis on exchange value, (ii) the claim that all value and surplus value emerge from the process of production, and (iii) the neglect of household, family, and reproduction (Lovell, pp. 306-7). These three interrelated issues are reviewed here.

Ignores use-value. Marx spends little time analysing use values, taking these for granted. Commodities must have use value in order to have exchange value (price) and be exchanged, otherwise no one would purchase them. But this does not mean that all use values are exchange values. Goods and services produced in the household for personal and family use have use value but are not ordinarily exchanged. In addition, volunteer work or work for organizations that do not sell their goods or services (churches, political parties), has the same characteristic. Given that these forms of work, and the useful goods and services that result from them do not have exchange value, there is a tendency to undervalue them in society, and this is the case for both Marxian and much conventional economic analysis. Official statistics of economic production also ignore most of the goods and services not sold on markets.

Since men tend have tended to produce exchange values and women have tended to produce goods and services with use values only, this means that much of women's labour is not valued in capitalism or in Marx's model of capitalism. For purposes of explaining exploitation, surplus value, the dynamics of capitalism, and social relationships in capitalism, it appears irrelevant. It leads to the seemingly contradictory view that those whose work is not paid are not exploited, but this is one of the implications of the Marxian model. While Marxists might consider women oppressed in their relationship with men and in the household, technically speaking they are not exploited and their work has little or nothing to do with production of surplus value.

Value from production only. A related issue is that work outside production is not recognized as creating value. While Marx recognizes human labour as creative and Marxian analysis purports to be an examination of work of humans, it is only an analysis of paid work. If it is private property and exploitation that distorts human labour, then alienation and exploitation exist only for paid labour. Most Marxian analyses of work begin with work in general but quickly become analysis of paid work in jobs, where workers are hired to produce commodities for exchange.

One issue of importance for women that emerges from this is unequal pay. In many jobs, women have been paid less than men for equivalent work. In the Marxian model, the value of labour power is the cost of production of this capacity to work. It seems difficult to argue that this cost would differ for male and female labour power. That is, the cost of producing labour power is the value of the commodities necessary for generational and daily subsistence. While it might cost a little more to maintain male than female labour, given that men tend to have larger bodies, there cannot be much difference in these costs. As a result, it is not clear why women should be paid less than men for equivalent work – but this has often been the case and the Marxian model would not appear to have an explanation for this differential.

Reproductive labour. Emerging from the last issue is a set of issues concerning the neglect of reproductive labour in the Marxian model. As noted above, the Marxian analysis initially appears to consider all human labour, but only labour exchanged for a wage is relevant to the model. Family, household, reproduction, the supply of labour, and the survival of labourers outside the formal labour market are generally taken for granted by Marx. While he devotes some discussion to the value of labour power, Marx does not have much of a theory of population or of the supply of labour. In Marx's time, women played little role in the public economy, and Marx develops no theory of how women, family, and household contribute to the value of labour power as a commodity. In essence, then, Marx's social world is the commodity, commodity exchange, the labour market, and accumulation. Lovell notes that Marx placed "human reproduction and sexuality outside the sphere of the social" and Marx argued that the reproduction of the labour force can left to the "labourer's instincts of self-preservation and of propagation". While Marxist feminists have developed analysis of the economic aspect of household and family, Lovell notes that the family is where sexual oppression, violence against women, control and regulation of sexuality, and sexual domination are located. Within the Marxian model itself, it is difficult to see how these issues could all be reduced to economic factors, so how can they be addressed.

A related implication is that aspects of the dominant and contradictory social relationship of capital and labour may be inadequately explained. Family and household activities may affect this relationship in ways that are outside the sphere of production itself. For example, class consciousness has a group aspect to it. If the working class involved the families of male workers, that is, women, children, disabled, retired, then the situation of these latter is also relevant to the forms and strength of class consciousness. This becomes clear in the history of strikes and other forms of class struggle, where having strong support of all is key to the success of workers.

Having noted the above, socialists and Marxists over the last one hundred years incorporated various struggles by women into their political programs. Trade unionists who were closely connected to socialist political movements often attempted to improve the situation of women workers.

At the same time, Marxists did not make the struggles of women central to their approach, and feminists often argue that Marxists downgraded the struggles of women, because these struggles are considered a diversion from the more important class struggle. In any case, Marxists have emphasized economic bases and solutions for women's oppression. As a result, they have generally regarded the class struggle as primary, and feminist issues as important primarily in how or whether they contribute to the class struggle. Some Marxist feminists consider sex and gender inequalities to be secondary in importance to class inequality and oppression, and contradictions related to reproduction and gender relations play a secondary role in explaining social change. Other Marxist feminists may look on class and gender inequalities as dual systems of oppression, with both being very powerful and independent systems. Marxist feminists often argue that class and gender inequalities reinforce each other and create groups that are doubly oppressed. In addition, as Tong notes, work shapes consciousness, and women's work shapes her status and self-image. Woman's position within the family may help explain the problem of developing working class consciousness. As with exchange relationships in general in capitalism, underlying these seemingly equal exchange relationships are power relationships. Various relationships, such as those between males and females, relationships in the family, prostitution, surrogate mother hood, etc. may appear to express equality, but because of the underlying unequal power relations conceal great inequalities.

Examples of Some Contemporary Marxist Feminist Approach

Out of the Marxian and the feminist tradition, there are a number of approaches to the analysis of women and of sex and gender inequalities. These are represented by various social and political movements, organizations, and theorists.

Inequality. Class structures are primary in determining the main social classes, the main forms of struggle within societies, and the life experiences of people in these classes. But secondary forms of inequality and oppression occur within each class, and these may take the form of racial and ethnic inequalities, or gender inequalities. These secondary forms could have an economic basis, where women and other oppressed groups do not have an economic basis for equality. That is, they may be prevented from owning property and do not have a means of producing a livelihood apart from their husbands or fathers. But in the economic model of Marx, at least in *Capital*, it is not clear why women would not have access to property – that is, the explanation of this comes from outside the model of capitalism.

Marxist feminists argue that "*within* any class, women are less advantaged than men in their access to material goods, power, status, and possibilities for self-actualization. The causes of this inequality lie in the organization of capitalism itself."

Bourgeois women may be wealthy, but usually are secondary to their husbands in terms of power. These women "provide emotional, social, and sexual services for the men in their class." They are well rewarded for this, often are not able to develop an independent source of livelihood or power. Middle class women may be well off, but often lack property or labour force experience, and if divorced, could find themselves in poverty.

The position of working class women is likely to be mixed, depending on whether or not they participate in the paid labour force, and then on their economic position within the labour force. If the latter is adequate to support her and her children, she may be able to have some independence. More likely though, the working class woman has little income, responsibility for household tasks, and is inferior socially and in terms of power and independence to her husband. This may allow a male wage earner to exercise "personal power, compensation for his actual powerlessness in society. She is in other words, 'the slave of a slave.'".

For women within the labour force, this work is often as alienating as that of men, or perhaps more alienating. Women are often paid less, and tend to be in subordinate positions. There are relatively few cases where women within the work force are managers or are in dominant positions within a hierarchy. For women who are not in the work force, alienation occurs in a different form, that of powerlessness, with women being required to serve others.

Family wage. Marxist feminists have attempted to develop explanations for the relatively lower pay of women than men. Throughout much of the twentieth century, the family responsibilities of women and their economic dependency on the earnings of their husband meant that their wages were depressed relative to wages of men. Many men, trade unions, and even employers argued that the wages for males needed to be living wages or family wages – sufficient to support a family. That is, the male wages should be sufficient to meet the daily and generational reproductive costs of the family and labour force. The corollary of this is that women's wages did not need to be so great, because they were at least partially supported by their husbands. Single females were expected to work only temporarily, until marriage, so did not need high wages either. As a result, the dependency of women on men, and the attempt to pursue a high wage strategy for men, may have led to relatively low wages for women. To some extent, this may have been a byproduct of trade union approaches to male wages.

Reserve army of labour. Marx argued that the reserve army of unemployed workers was always replenished by capitalism, thus exercising downward pressure on the wages of workers in the labour force. It was the maintenance and reconstruction of this reserve army that prevented workers from gaining wages exceeding the value of their labour power. If workers were able to boost wages during a time of economic expansion, one of the effects of this was to slow capital accumulation, thus causing an economic slowdown, unemployment, and replenishment of the reserve army.

One part of the reserve army is women – for much of the late nineteenth and early twentieth centuries, most women were in the home and worked in the labour force only periodically. Of course, poor women and women from disadvantaged groups had to work in the labour force to provide a minimal level of income for themselves and their families. In wartime, or in other periods or places of labour shortages, women could be drawn into the labour force as needed. Since the primary attachment of these women was to the home and family, not paid labour, these women did not need to be paid as much as men. In addition, having these women available meant that they could be used to prevent male wages from rising too much.

While the reserve army of labour argument may have explained some of the operations of the labour force through the 1950s, following that women entered the labour force in large numbers and have not left the labour force. This was one of the great social changes of the latter part of the twentieth century – altering the structure of the labour force, family, home, and male/female relationships. One part of the reserve army of labour is the latent reserve – people who have not yet been drawn into the paid labour force. One Marxist argument is that women formed a part of the latent labour reserve, one that could be drawn into the labour force as needed. This may help explain some of the inequality and lower pay of women in the labour force.

Household and Family. Some Marxists view the household as an institution that functions to support capitalism – permitting or even encouraging exploitation. That is, by creating and recreating sexual inequalities, and keeping women in the home with responsibility for family subsistence, emotional support and reproduction, the family is an institution used by capitalism to assist in the exploitation of labour and maintenance of stability within a system of class oppression and inequality. As noted earlier, it can be argued that since women are concerned with maintenance of household and family, they act as a conservative force on the development of working class consciousness. Some other aspects of this are as follows.

Consumers. Households and families are good consuming units within modern capitalism. Each household is a separate consuming units, with separate needs. While these consuming units need not be organized on a family basis, or with sexual inequalities, in order to perform this role in society, in fact they are very well adapted to maintaining and expanding purchases.

In social and political terms, this role can also play a conservatizing force with respect to class struggles. Women's lower wages and the difficulty of supporting a family, can be used by employers as a means of undermining trade union struggles. Since the responsibility of women is to maintain the household, this can have a conservatizing effect. Where there is a need for change, women are often isolated by separation into private households, and organizing to create change can be difficult.

Labour Force. So long as women have primary responsibility for reproduction (physical and socialization) and household and family maintenance, women constitute a cheap form of labour, a reserve army of labour. They have been a latent reserve over the last forty years, some are a short term reserve over the economic cycle, and women are a labour reserve in a generational sense. That is, the expectation that women will not be as committed to many jobs as men, with time taken off for childbearing, child care, care of elderly parents, etc., allows employers to pay women less than men. And this also presents both employers and men with an argument that women should be paid somewhat less, or advance somewhat less quickly in their careers. The lower status of women within society also allows women to be paid less, since some wages and salaries are structured on status considerations.

Surplus Value. Household and family act to create cheap labour that can be used in the expansion of surplus value. That is, much of the necessary labour required by society to maintain and reproduce the population and labour force is carried out as unpaid labour by women working in the home. Workers come to the labour force at no cost to employers, and if employers had to pay the full cost of reproducing their work force, wages would be considerably greater than they currently are. Where wages are family wages, so that the male wage is large enough to support the whole family, there is still much unpaid work in the home, and if employers payed for this, there would be a considerable redistribution of income from males to females. As a result, there is indirect exploitation of female labour. The work of women in the household permits the extraction of surplus value and while men are directly exploited, women are exploited in an indirect manner by not being paid for the value of the labour that produces surplus value.

Unproductive Labour and Exploitation. The unpaid labour performed by women for men can really be regarded as unpaid labour performed for capitalists. In the classical Marxian framework, such labour is unproductive. Marxist feminists argue that reproductive and household labour is productive of surplus value, and should be compensated in some manner. This has led some to argue that women should be paid wages for housework, rather than arguing that male/female inequalities are overcome only through women entering the paid labour force.

Others have argued that men exploit women in an economic sense, and men extract surplus value from women. Some Marxists argue that the family must be abolished and that paying wages for housework will just preserve the traditional inequalities. What is necessary is more socialization of household work, with women being fully able to participate in the public sphere. Potentially, under communism, the division between public and private would disappear, and this could form the basis for sex and gender equalities.

Women as Class. Another line of argument that some feminists have adopted is that women are a class, or a sexual class as opposed to the common Marxist view of a social or economic class. Eisenstein considers women as a sexual class because they "constitute the basic and necessary activities of society: reproduction, child rearing, nurturing, consuming, domestic labouring, *and* wage-earning. Women are a sexual class because *what they do as women* – the activities they are responsible for in society, the labour that they perform – is essential and necessary to the operation of society as it presently exists.". This consideration of women as a sexual class is based on a common position within the mode of production and reproduction, and a common position with respect to another sexual class, that is, males. This means a different set of interests, and also at least some opposed interests to those of males. Eisenstein argues that patriarchy is somewhat different than capitalism as a system, where the bourgeoisie is organized and must be opposed. Rather than struggling against men, the struggle of women is against patriarchy, and its expressions. The latter may be found in the market, in the state, in the family, etc. For Eisenstein, sexual class consciousness must be formed through social movements like the suffrage movement or feminist movements. The manner in which feminist struggles over the last thirty years have proceeded has develop this sexual class consciousness.

This argument was paralled by French materialist feminism on women as class. Christine Delphy, a French feminist, argues that women are a class relative to the relations of production (and reproduction). "Because they perform unpaid housework all women share a common economic position" and "as a category of human beings *destined by birth* to become a member of this class, they constitute a caste". Delphy argues that men exploit women's labour through the labour/marriage contract. This "domestic exploitation takes place outside the capitalist mode of production ... this is not simply derived from class struggle and capitalism, but it has an independent material basis in women's unpaid domestic labour". Lovell notes how this leads to men exploiting women, not just in economic terms, but "also the sexual and reproductive bodies of women". It is the gender differentiated system of power that produces this.

From this, some Marxist and other feminists have argued there are dual systems or a capitalist patriarchy. Modern society is clearly characterized by capitalism as an economic and material force; it is also characterized by patriarchy, a system of domination of women by men. While some argue that one of these can be reduced to the other, a dual systems approach argues that each of these are "dynamic forces at work in history, which must therefore be understood in terms of both class and gender struggle". Hartmann argues that the two may build on each other but they may be in conflict with each other – for example, the past fifty years where patriarchal privileges for males may have been undercut by the strong growth in demand for women's work in the paid labour force. Each of the two systems has a certain autonomy and set of forces and structures that maintain the system. Marx outlined the forces that maintained and expanded capitalism. Feminists have presented various arguments concerning the causes and forces associated with patriarchy. Marxist and socialist feminist solutions embody a wide range of changes. Some would argue that the end of capitalism is sufficient, but the record of the socialist countries was not encouraging in this respect. More likely this approach would argue for an end of the nuclear family, at least as it is currently structured. But really ending patriarchy and inequality may require changes at all levels, in the economy, in attitudes, in institutions, etc.

CONTEMPORARY FEMINIST THEORY: THEORETICAL ORIENTATION

Feminist theory is distinct from other theoretical perspectives in that it is woman-centered and interdisciplinary, and it actively promotes ways to achieve social justice. Three core questions inform feminist theory: (1) "What about the women?" (2) "Why is the social world as it is?" and (3) "How can we change and improve the social world so as to make it a more just place for women and for all people?"

Feminist theorists have also started to question the differences between women, including how race, class, ethnicity, and age intersect with gender. In sum, feminist theory is most concerned with giving a voice to women and highlighting the various ways women have contributed to society.

The Historical Roots of Feminist Theory

Historically, feminist activity has paralleled liberation events, including the American and French Revolutions, the abolitionist movement in the 1830s, the mobilization for suffrage in the early 1900s, and the civil rights movement in the 1960s and 1970s. These historical movements of feminism are referred to as *waves*. First-wave feminism-including the first women's rights convention, which was held in Seneca Falls, NY, in 1848, and the passage of the 19th Amendment, which gave women the right to vote in 1920-is characterized by women's struggle for political rights. Second-wave feminism of the 1960s and 1970s and the third-wave feminism of today emphasize a variety of issues, including the growth of feminist organizations and publications and the increasing numbers of feminists in government, the educational system, and other professions.

Varieties of Contemporary Feminist Theory

Four varieties of feminist theory attempt to answer the question "What about the women?" The *gender difference perspective* tries to answer this question by examining how women's location in, and experience of, social situations differ from men's. Cultural feminists look to the different values associated with womanhood and femininity (e.g., caring, cooperation, and pacifism) as a reason why men and women experience the social world differently. Other feminist theorists believe that the different roles assigned to women and men within institutions better explain gender difference, including the sexual division of labour in the household. Existential and phenomenological feminists focus on how women have been marginalized and defined as the *Other* in patriarchal societies. Women are thus seen as objects and are denied the opportunity for self-realization.

Gender-inequality theories look to answer the question "What about the women?" by recognizing that women's location in, and experience of, social situations are not only different but also *unequal* to men's. Liberal feminists argue that women have the same capacity as men for moral reasoning and agency, but that patriarchy, particularly the sexist patterning of the division of labour, has historically denied women the opportunity to express and practice this reasoning. Women have been isolated to the private sphere of the household and, thus, left without a voice in the public sphere. Even after women enter the public sphere, they are still expected to manage the private sphere and take care of household duties and child rearing. Liberal feminists point out that marriage is a site of gender inequality and that women do not benefit from being married as men do. Indeed, married women have higher levels of stress than unmarried women and married men. According to liberal feminists, the sexual division of labour in both the public and private spheres needs to be altered in order for women to achieve equality.

Theories of gender oppression go further than theories of gender difference and gender inequality by arguing that not only are women different from or unequal to men, but that they are actively oppressed, subordinated, and even abused by men. Power is the key variable in the two main theories of gender oppression: *psychoanalytic feminism* and *radical feminism*. Psychoanalytic feminists attempt to explain power relations between men and women by reformulating Freud's theories of the subconscious and unconscious, human emotions, and childhood development. They feel that conscious calculation cannot fully explain the production and reproduction of patriarchy. For example, the unconscious fear that men have towards their own mortality may account for why men are driven to control women. Radical feminists argue that being a woman is a positive thing in and of itself, but that this is not acknowledged in patriarchal societies where women are oppressed. They identify physical violence as being at the base of patriarchy, but they think that patriarchy can be defeated if women come recognize their own value and strength, establish a sisterhood of trust with other women, confront oppression critically, and form female separatist networks in the private and public spheres.

Structural oppression theories posit that women's oppression and inequality are a result of capitalism, patriarchy, and racism. *Socialist feminism* combines Marxian class analysis with feminist social protest in an attempt to answer the question "What about the women?" They agree with Marx and Engels that the working class is exploited as a consequence of the capitalist mode of production, but they seek to extend this exploitation not just to class but also to gender. *Intersectionality theorists* seek to explain oppression and inequality across a variety of variables, including class, gender, race, ethnicity, and age. They make the important insight that not all women experience oppression in the same way. White women and black women, for example, face different forms of discrimination in the workplace. Thus, different groups of women come to view the world through a shared standpoint of "heterogeneous commonality."

Feminism and Postmodernism

During the 1990s some feminists began to incorporate postmodern ideas and vocabulary into their theoretical work. The oppositional epistemology of postmodernism complemented feminism, particularly in questioning the relation of power to knowledge. However, feministtheorists are cautious of the postmodern turn in social theory for several reasons. They view postmodernism as too removed from political struggles. Postmodernism may lead people away from collective action and towards a radical individualism. Furthermore, feminists argue that postmodernism is too divorced from material reality-its focus on discourse, representation, and texts ignores material inequality, injustice, and oppression.

TOWARDS A FEMINIST SOCIOLOGICAL THEORY

Feminist sociological theory combines the various types of feminism discussed thus far to focus on five major areas: the sociology of knowledge, the macro-social order, the micro-social order, subjectivity, and theory integration. A feminist sociology of knowledge emphasizes standpoint theory and intersectionality theory in relation to knowledge production and power relations. Feminist sociologists who study the macro-social order seek to expand Marx's analysis of economic production to social production more generally, including the household, the state, religion, and sexuality. One main topic of concern for these theorists is the production and reproduction of gender ideology. Feminist sociologists who study the micro-social order emphasize the role of gender in everyday interactions and the different meanings that men and women have regarding specific situations. Subjectivity occupies a special place in feminist sociological theory as it seeks to understand how women are socialized to see themselves through the eyes of men. When women learn to internalize the generalized other, or the perspective of society, it is a male-centered other that they must relate to. In other words, women, like other subordinate groups in society, develop a bifurcated consciousness where they live with both the reality of actual experience and the reality of social typifications. Other feminist theorists question the reasons why a male-dominated sociology has categorized and divided the world into micro or macro. Feminist sociologists seek to integrate macro-and micro-level social phenomena. For example, Dorothy E. Smith (1926-) discusses "relations of ruling," "generalized, anonymous, impersonal texts," and "local actualities of lived experiences."

FEMINIST SOCIOLOGY

Feminist sociology is a conflict theory and theoretical perspective which observes gender in its relation to power, both at the level of face-to-face interaction and reflexivity within a social structure at large. Focuses include sexual orientation, race, economic status, and nationality. At the core of feminist sociology is the idea of the systematic oppression of women and the historical dominance of men within most societies: 'patriarchy'. Feminist thought has a rich history, however, which may be categorised into three 'waves'. The current, 'third wave', emphasizes the concepts of globalization, postcolonialism, post-structuralism and postmodernism. Contemporary feminist thought has frequently tended to do-away with all generalizations regarding sex and gender, closely linked with antihumanism, posthumanism, queer theory and the work of Michel Foucault.

Heterosexism

Heterosexism is a system of attitudes, bias, and discrimination in favor of opposite-sex sexuality and relationships. At one point, heterosexual marriage was the only lawful union between two people that was recognized and given full benefits in the United States.This clearly put homosexual couples of both sexes at a disadvantage, making their relationships less valid in the eyes of the government than that of a relationship between a man and a woman.

Feminism and Race

Women who suffer from oppression due to race may find themselves in a double bind. The relationship between feminism and race was largely overlooked until the second wave of feminists produced greater literature on the topic of 'black feminism'.

Feminist Critiques of Multiculturalism

Debates within ethnic relations, particularly regarding the opposing perspectives of assimilationism and multiculturalism, have led to the accusation that feminism is incompatible with multiculturalist policy. The remit of multiculturalism is to allow distinct cultures to reside in Western societies, or separate societies in general, and one possible consequence is that certain religious or traditional practices may negate Western feminist ideals. Central debates include the topics of arranged marriage and female genital mutilation. Others have argued that these debates stem from Western orientalism and general political reluctance to accept foreign migrants.

FEMINIST THEORY

Feminist theory is the extension of feminism into theoretical, or philosophical discourse, it aims to understand the nature of gender inequality. It examines women's social roles and lived experience, and feminist politics in a variety of fields, such as anthropology and sociology, psychoanalysis, economics, literary criticism, and philosophy. While generally providing a critique of social relations, much of feminist theory also focuses on analysing gender inequality and the promotion of women's rights, interests, and issues. Themes explored in feminism include art history and contemporary art, aesthetics, discrimination, stereotyping, objectification (especially sexual objectification), oppression, and patriarchy.

History of Feminist Theory

Feminist theories have emerged as early as 1792 (– 1920s) in such publications as "The Changing Woman", "Ain't I a Woman", "Speech after Arrest for Illegal Voting", and so on. "The Changing Woman" is a Navajo Myth that gave credit to a woman who, in the end, populated the world. Footnote with citation. In 1851, Sojourner Truth addressed women's rights issues through her publication, "Ain't I a Woman." Sojourner Truth addressed the issues surrounding limited rights to women based on the flawed perceptions that men held of women. Truth argued that if a woman of colour can perform tasks that were supposedly limited to men, then any woman of any colour could perform those same tasks. After her arrest for illegally voting, Susan B. Anthony gave a speech within court in which she addressed the issues of language within the constitution documented in her publication, "Speech after Arrest for Illegal voting" in 1872. Anthony questioned the authoritative principles of the constitution and its male gendered language. She raised the question of why women should be punished under law but they cannot use the law for their own protection (women could not vote, own property, nor themselves in marriage). She also critiqued the constitution for its male gendered language and questioned why women should have to abide by laws that do not specify women. Although there were not any feminist terminologies based on their arguments, all of these women have founded a lexicon of debates that contribute to feminist theory. For example, Sojourner Truth raised the issue of the intersectionality debate and Susan B. Anthony raised the issue of the language debate. Nancy Cott makes a distinction between *modern feminism* and its antecedents, particularly the struggle for suffrage. In the United States she places the turning point in the decades before and after women obtained the vote in 1920 (1910–1930). She argues that the prior *woman movement* was primarily about woman as a *universal* entity, whereas over this 20 year period it transformed itself into one primarily concerned with social differentiation, attentive to *individuality* and diversity. New issues dealt more with woman's condition as a social construct, gender identity, and relationships within and between genders. Politically this represented a shift from an ideological alignment comfortable with the right, to one more radically associated with the left.

Susan Kingsley Kent says that Freudian patriarchy was responsible for the diminished profile of feminism in the inter-war years, others such as Juliet Mitchell consider this to be overly simplistic since Freudian theory is not wholly incompatible with feminism. Some feminist scholarship shifted away from the need to establish the origins of family, and towards analysing the process of patriarchy. In the immediate postwar period, Simone de Beauvoir stood in opposition to an image of "the woman in the home". De Beauvoir provided an existentialist dimension to feminism with the publication of *Le Deuxième Sexe* (The Second Sex) in 1949. As the title implies, the starting point is the implicit inferiority of women, and the first question de Beauvoir asks is "what is a woman"?. Woman she realizes is always perceived of as "other", "*she is defined and differentiated with reference to man and not he with reference to her*". In this book and her essay, "*Woman: Myth & Reality*", de Beauvoir anticipates Betty Friedan in seeking to demythologise the male concept of woman. "*A myth invented by men to confine women to their oppressed`state. For women it is not a question of asserting themselves as women, but of becoming full-scale human beings.*" "One is not born, but rather becomes, a woman", or as Toril Moi puts it "a woman defines herself through the way she lives her embodied situation in the world, or in other words, through the way in which she makes something of what the world makes of her". Therefore, woman must regain subject, to escape her defined role as "other", as a Cartesian point of departure. In her examination of myth, she appears as one who does not accept any special privileges for women. Ironically, feminist philosophers have had to extract de Beauvoir herself from out of the shadow of Jean-Paul Sartre to fully appreciate her. While more philosopher and novelist than activist, she did sign one of the *Mouvement de Liberation des Femmes* manifestos.

The resurgence of feminist activism in the late 1960s was accompanied by an emerging literature of what might be considered female associated issues, such as concerns for the earth and spirituality, and environmental activism. This in turn created an atmosphere conducive to reigniting the study of and debate on matricentricity, as a rejection of determinism, such as Adrienne Rich and Marilyn French while for socialist feminists like Evelyn Reed, patriarchy held the properties of capitalism.

Elaine Showalter describes the development of Feminist theory as having a number of phases. The first she calls "feminist critique"-where the feminist reader examines the ideologies behind literary phenomena. The second Showalter calls

"Gynocritics"-where the "woman is producer of textual meaning" including "the psychodynamics of female creativity; linguistics and the problem of a female language; the trajectory of the individual or collective female literary career and literary history". The last phase she calls "gender theory"-where the "ideological inscription and the literary effects of the sex/gender system" are explored." This model has been criticized by Toril Moi who sees it as an essentialist and deterministic model for female subjectivity. She also criticized it for not taking account of the situation for women outside the west. From the 1970s onwards, psychoanalytical ideas that has been arising in the field of French feminism has gained a decisive influence on feminist theory. Feminist psychoanalysis deconstructed the phallic hypotheses regarding the Unconscious. Julia Kristeva, Bracha Ettinger and Luce Irigaray developed specific notions concerning unconscious sexual difference, the feminine and motherhood, with wide implications for film and literature analysis.

Disciplines

There are a number of distinct feminist disciplines, in which experts in other areas apply feminist techniques and principles to their own fields. Additionally, these are also debates in which shape feminist theory and they can be applied interchangeably in the arguments of feminist theorists.

Bodies

In western thought bodies have been historically associated solely with women whereas men have been associated with the mind. The notion of the body (and not the mind) being associated with women has served as a justification to deem women as property, objects, and exchangeable commodities (among men). For example, women's bodies have been objectified throughout history through the changing ideologies of fashion, diets, exercise programs, cosmetic surgery, etc. The race and class of women can be a determinate of whether one body will be treated as decoration and protected which is associated with middle or upper-class women's bodies. On the other hand, the other body is recognized for its use in labour and exploitation which is generally associated with women's bodies in the working-class or with women of colour. Second-wave feminist activism has argued for reproductive rights and choice, women's health (movement), and lesbian rights (movement) which are also associated with this Bodies debate.

Epistemologies

The generation and production of knowledge has been an important part of feminist theory. This debate proposes such questions as "Are there 'women's ways of knowing' and 'women's knowledge'? And "How does the knowledge women produce about themselves differ from that produced by patriarchy?" Feminist theorists have also proposed the "feminist standpoint knowledge" which attempts to replace "the view from nowhere" with the model of knowing that expels the "view from women's lives". Central to feminism is that women are systematically subordinated, and bad faith exists when women surrender their agency to this subordination, e.g., acceptance of religious beliefs that a man is the dominant party in a marriage by the will of God; Simone de Beauvir labels such women "mutilated" and "immanent".

Love

A life's project to be in love may result in bad faith; love is an example of bad faith given by both Simone de Beuvoir and Jean Paul Sartre. A woman in love may in bad faith allow herself to be subjugated by her lover, who has created a dependency of the woman on him, allowed by the woman in bad faith.

Intersections of Race, Class, and Gender

This debate can also be termed as intersectionality. This debate raises the issue of understanding the oppressive lives of women that are not only shaped by gender alone but by other elements as racism, classism, ageism, heterosexism, etc. One example of the concept of intersectionality can be seen through the Mary Ann Weathers' publication, "An Argument for Black Women's Liberation as a Revolutionary Force." Mary Ann Weathers states that "black women, at least the Black women I have come in contact with in the movement, have been expending all their energies in "liberating" Black men " Women of colour were put in a position of choosing sides. White women wanted women of colour and working-class women to become a part of the women's movement over struggling with their men (working-class, poor, and men of colour) against class oppression and racism in the Civil Rights Movement. This was a conflict for women of colour and working-class women who had to decide whether to fight against racism or classism versus sexism—or prioritize and participate in the hierarchy. It did not help that the women's movement was shaped primarily by white women during the first and second feminist waves and the issues surrounding women of colour were not addressed. Contemporary feminist theory addresses such issues of intersectionality in such publications as "Age, Race, Sex, and Class" by Kimberlee Crenshaw.

Language

In this debate, women writers have addressed the issues of masculinized writing through male gendered language that may not serve to accommodate the literary understanding of women's lives. Such masculinized language that feminist theorists address is the use of, for example, "God the Father" which is looked upon as a way of designating the sacred as solely men (or, in other words, biblical language glorifies men through all of the masculine pronouns like "he" and "him" and addressing God as a "He"). Feminist theorists attempt to reclaim and redefine women through re-structuring language. For example, feminist theorists have used the term "womyn" instead of "women." Some feminist theorists find solace in changing titles of unisex jobs (for example, police officer versus policeman or mail carrier versus mailman). Some feminist theorists have reclaimed and redefined such words as "dyke" and "bitch"—and others have invested redefining knowledge into feminist dictionaries.

Psychoanalysis

Psychoanalytic feminism is based on Freud and his psychoanalytic theories. It maintains that gender is not biological but is based on the psycho-sexual development of the individual. Psychoanalytical feminists believe that gender inequality comes from early childhood experiences, which lead men to believe themselves to be masculine, and women to believe themselves feminine. It is further maintained that gender leads to a social system that is dominated by males, which in turn influences the individual psycho-sexual development. As a solution it was suggested to avoid the gender-specific structuring of the society by male-female coeducation. In the last 30 years, the contemporary French psychoanalytical theories concerning the feminine, that refer to sexual difference rather than to gender, with psychoanalysts like Julia Kristeva, Maud Mannoni, Luce Irigaray, and Bracha Ettinger has largely influenced not only feminist theory but also the understanding of the subject in philosophy and the general field of psychoanalysis itself. Other feminist psychoanalysts whose contribution enriched the field are Jessica Benjamin and Jacqueline Rose.

Literary Theory

Feminist literary criticism is literary criticism informed by feminist theories or politics. Its history has been varied, from classic works of female authors such as George Eliot, Virginia Woolf, and Margaret Fuller to cutting-edge theoretical work in women's studies and gender studies by "third-wave" authors. In the most general, feminist literary criticism before the 1970s was concerned with the politics of women's authorship and the representation of women's condition within literature. Since the arrival of more complex conceptions of gender and subjectivity, feminist literary criticism has taken a variety of new routes. It has considered gender in the terms of Freudian and Lacanian psychoanalysis, as part of the deconstruction of existing power relations.

Film Theory

Feminists have taken many different approaches to the analysis of cinema. These include discussions of the function of women characters in particular film narratives or in particular genres, such as film noir, where a woman character can often be seen to embody a subversive sexuality that is dangerous to men and is ultimately punished with death. In considering the way that films are put together, many feminist film critics, such as Laura Mulvey, have pointed to the "male gaze" that predominates in classical Hollywood film making. Through the use of various film techniques, such as shot reverse shot, the viewer is led to align themself with the point of view of a male protagonist. Notably, women function as objects of this gaze far more often than as proxies for the spectator. Feminist film theory of the last twenty years is heavily influenced by the general transformation in the field of aesthetics, including the new options of articulating the gaze, offered by psychoanalytical French feminism.

Art History

Linda Nochlin and Griselda Pollock are prominent art historians writing on contemporary and modern artists and articulating Art history from a feminist perspective since the 1970s. Pollock works with French psychoanalysis, and in particular with Kristeva's and Ettinger's theories, to offer new insights into art history and contemporary art with special regard to questions of trauma and trans-generation memory in the works of women artists.

History

Feminist history refers to the re-reading and re-interpretation of history from a feminist perspective. It is not the same as the history of feminism, which outlines the origins and evolution of the feminist movement. It also differs from women's history, which focuses on the role of women in historical events. The goal of feminist history is to explore and illuminate the female viewpoint of history through rediscovery of female writers, artists, philosophers, etc., in order to recover and demonstrate the significance of women's voices and choices in the past.

Geography

Feminist geography is often considered part of a broader postmodern approach to the subject which is not primarily concerned with the development of conceptual theory in itself but rather focuses on the real experiences of individuals and groups in their own localities, upon the geographies that they live in within their own communities. In addition to its analysis of the real world, it also critiques existing geographical and social studies, arguing that academic traditions are delineated by patriarchy, and that contemporary studies which do not confront the nature of previous work reinforce the male bias of academic study.

Philosophy

The Feminist philosophy refers to a philosophy approached from a feminist perspective. Feminist philosophy involves attempts to use methods of philosophy to further the cause of the feminist movements, it also tries to criticize and/or reevaluate the ideas of traditional philosophy from within a feminist view. There really is not a specific school for feminist philosophy like there have been in regard to other theories. Meaning, Feminist philosophers are just philosophers after all and can be found in the analytic and continental traditions, and the different viewpoints taken on philosophical issues with those traditions. Feminist philosophers, also have many different viewpoints taken on philosophical issues within those traditions. Feminist philosophers who are feminists can belong to many different varieties of feminism. The writings of Judith Butler, Rosi Braidotti, and Donna Haraway are most significant psychoanalytically informed influences on contemporary feminist philosophy. These women have been the main driving force behind the Feminism philosophy.

Politics

Feminist political theory is a recently emerging field in political science focusing on gender and feminist themes within the state, intitutions and policies. It questions the "modern political theory, dominated by universalistic liberalist thought, which claims indifference to gender or other identity differences and has therefore taken its time to open up to such concerns".

Economics

Feminist economics broadly refers to a developing branch of economics that applies feminist insights and critiques to economics. Research under this heading is often interdisciplinary, critical, or heterodox. It encompasses debates about the relationship between feminism and economics on many levels: from applying mainstream economic methods to under-researched "women's" areas, to questioning how mainstream economics values the reproductive sector, to deeply philosophical critiques of economic epistemology and methodology. One prominent issue that feminist economists investigate is how the Gross Domestic Product (GDP) does not adequately measure unpaid labour predominantly performed by women, such as housework, childcare, and eldercare. Feminist economists have also challenged and exposed the rhetorical approach of mainstream economics. They have made critiques of many basic assumptions of mainstream economics, including the Homo economicus model. In the Houseworker's Handbook Betsy Warrior presents a cogent argument that the reproduction and domestic labour of women form the foundation of economic survival; although, unremunerated and not included in the GDP. Warrior also notes that the unacknowledged income of men from illegal activities like arms, drugs and human trafficking, political graft, religious emollients and various other undisclosed activities provide a rich revenue stream to men, which further invalidates GDP figures. They have been instrumental in creating alternative models, such as the Capability Approach and incorporating gender into the analysis of economic data. Marilyn Power suggests that feminist economic methodology can be broken down into five categories.

Legal Theory

The study of feminist legal theory is a school thought based on the feminist view that law's treatment of women in relation to men has not been equal or fair. The goals of feminist legal theory as defined by leading theorist Claire Dalton, consist of understanding and exploring the female experience, figuring out if law and institutions oppose females, and figuring out what changes can be committed to. This is to be accomplished through studying the connections between the law and gender as well as applying feminist analysis to concrete areas of law.

6

Classical Sociological Theory

SOCIAL CLASS THEORY

Social class analysis was the first major attempt to explain political life in terms of sociological variables, so it is reasonable to consider the class model first. This is especially true because the other two models to be considered in this chapter were developed partly as counters to the social class model. Karl Marx was the first major social theorist to base his work primarily on a class model, although many of his ideas can be traced back to one or another of the earlier writers. It is the Marxian formulation of class analysis which has had the greatest influence on political sociology and which will be dealt with here. Marx's work was not limited to political sociology; indeed, much of the genius of his work lay in his attempt to comprehend the entire course of human history. Since he concluded that the basic dynamic of history could be found in economic life, his most detailed work was in economics. But his ultimate goal was to develop a theory of social change, and his model of social change was the basis of all his work. We will begin by summarizing that theory, following closely a well-known summary that Marx himself made in the introduction to one of his works.

Marx argued that men enter into social relationships independently of their wills and that their beliefs and behaviors are largely determined by the social conditions in which they find themselves. The most important of these conditions are those which are directly related to economic production, and these relationships tend to determine other aspects of social behaviour and beliefs. Only in a highly affluent, technologically advanced society could men and women choose to be free. The economic conditions which determine people's social relationships vary from epoch to epoch, as economic conditions change. However, in all previous history (excepting prehistoric tribes) there has been a polarization between oppressor and oppressed. As the oppressors become better organized and more efficient, they change the economic system to make it even more exploitative. They must do this, otherwise they themselves would be destroyed by others who would. This increase in the efficiency of exploitation is the source of progress. It brings about increases in wealth and economic productivity, as well as financing advances in science and culture. However, there is a negative side as well. Social tensions increase because the noneconomic organization of society fails to change rapidly enough to fit the new economic conditions. Classes which are no longer economically useful, such as feudal lords or small businessmen or craftsmen, fight against progress in order to defend their privileged position. When these social tensions become sufficiently acute, an era of social revolution ensues and the society is changed to a more modern form. In this way the transition was made from a feudal to a capitalist society in France with the revolution of 1789. Marx expected that when economic conditions advanced fully enough there would be a similar revolutionary period and capitalist societies would be transformed into socialist societies.

Marxist theory differs on a very basic level from sociological theories-such as functionalism-which consider social order to be self-sustaining and disorder to be unusual and undesirable. Marxist theory expects tension, conflict, and change as necessary for human progress. Conflict between social classes, in particular, is viewed by the Marxist as the basic source of social evolution. Marx viewed political life as a reflection of the class struggle. When he analyzed political struggles, he viewed each of the participating parties and leaders as representatives of social classes, and he explained their behaviour as resulting from their class interests. In its basic form Marxist theory has an elegant simplicity and grandeur, similar to many religious doctrines. It can be readily understood by people who are not professional social scientists. Indeed, Marx and his comrade

Friedrich Engels wrote The Communist Manifesto precisely to communicate their theory to factory workers. This simplicity is often criticized by academics who are preoccupied with the subtleties and complexities of the world and mistrust any theory which seems to be guilty of "oversimplification." Marx was not concerned with the objections of these academicians, indeed he felt that their devotion to pedantic details often served to obscure basic truths about society. While the simplicity of popular versions of Marxism may have made it appeal to some people who were seeking simple answers to complex problems, Marx himself was quite capable of doing highly insightful analyses of the details of complex situations when he felt that these were called for. Indeed, many of the points which later political critics have made, in refuting a simplistic version of "vulgar Marxism," were actually anticipated by Marx in some of his own work:

On a general level, Marxism is often criticized for placing too much emphasis on economic factors and not recognizing the complex interconnectedness of the world. This, however, does not recognize the sophistication which Marx brought to his analyses of specific historical events. Any theory draws generalizations about reality and in doing so reality must be "simplified."

More meaningful criticism goes beyond simply citing the complexity of the universe and specifies ways in which the generalizations drawn by the class theorists are inadequate. Much of this more serious criticism has been made by authors who are sympathetic with the Marxist approach. Marxist theory was developed in the nineteenth century and dealt with the social situation at that time. Marx tried to avoid making explicit predictions about the future, since he felt that our understanding of future conditions would come only after we had experienced those conditions (this is a consequence of his assumption that material conditions determine ideas). Social change has proceeded rapidly since Marx's time, however, and many of the problems with social class analysis today come from resistance on the part of some of its political supporters to modifying the model in keeping with recent changes. Perhaps the most marked change since Marx's time is the tremendous growth in the economic productivity of the developed capitalist countries.

Marx anticipated this increase in productivity, but underestimated the ability of capitalists to use this wealth to buy off the working classes by giving them higher and higher wages. Marx, along with other economists of his time, based his theories on a competitive model of capitalism, and did not fully anticipate the role of monopolistic corporations. He expected that capitalists would be forced to compete with each other, and consequently to maintain their workers at a minimal level of pay. He did not anticipate the development of Keynesian economics and of effective government policies aimed at regulating the economy and avoiding crises. It is not hard to understand why Marx failed to anticipate these things. He wrote at a time, for example, when there were maximum wage laws, not minimum wage laws as there are today. The growth of the new middle class is another phenomenon which cannot be readily dealt with in classic Marxist theory.

Marxist theory is generally weak in dealing with intermediate classes or strata. Marx noted the economic decline of the craftsmen and small businessmen who made up the middle class in the early days of capitalism, and he predicted that as these groups diminished as an economic force their political role would also decline. He felt that the technological advances made under capitalism would lead to an increased polarization between a relatively unskilled factory labour force and a class of wealthy capitalists. Only in scattered references in his later work did he begin to note a new development-the growth of the new middle class. Members of this class are still part of the working class in the strict economic sense since they earn their living by selling their labour power, but their level of education permits them to earn higher wages and maintain a style of life intermediate between that of the manual working class and that of the upper class. The role of intermediate classes or strata in political life is not easily explained by economic factors. While it has often been assumed that these classes will play a moderating role, seeking compromise between the upper class and the proletariat, this is not necessarily so. Further social changes may weaken the position of the middle class making their position more equivalent to that of manual workers. The recent surplus of college-educated workers in the United States has stimulated a growth of unionism among white-collar employees in many fields. Many white-collar employees are finding that despite their professional training they are working for large, impersonal bureaucracies where their economic position can be improved only through united action. The working-class pattern that these white-collar workers are assuming, however, is not the revolutionary one that Marx hoped for, and predicted, but a class conflict which has been legalized, regulated, and made a part of the existing social system.

Rather than being resolved through major confrontations, conflicts are regularized and accepted as part of the normal course of events. Means of dealing with them are developed which contribute to a more stable social order than one in which the dominant group simply imposes its will on the weaker. Conflicts are never ultimately resolved in this way, but neither do they lead to revolutionary upheavals. Marx, of course, was aware of the possibilities of conflicts being handled in this way, but he felt that such solutions could only be temporary. Today, theorists in the Marxist tradition such as Marcuse are grappling with the possibility that advanced industrial societies will be able to contain indefinitely the conflicts which Marx thought would lead to revolutionary change. The great increase in international inequality is another historical change which requires modifications in classical Marxist theory. In today's world inequality is often more pronounced between countries than it is between social strata in the same country. While Marx did not deal extensively with this topic, it has been thoroughly studied by liberal writers such as Hobson, and their findings have been incorporated into Marxist theory by Lenin and others.

DEFINITION OF SOCIOLOGY

Sociology (in the sense in which this highly ambiguous word is used here) is a science which attempts the interpretive understanding of social action in order thereby to arrive at a causal explanation of its course and effects. In "action" is included all human behaviour when and insofar as the acting individual attaches a subjective meaning to it. Action in this sense may be either overt or purely inward or subjective; it may consist of positive intervention in a situation, or of deliberately refraining from such intervention or passively acquiescing in the situation. Action is social insofar as, by virtue of the subjective meaning attached to it by the acting individual (or individuals), it takes account of the behaviour of others and is thereby oriented in its course.

METHODOLOGICAL FOUNDATIONS OF SOCIOLOGY

"Meaning" may be of two kinds. The term may refer first to the actual existing meaning in the given concrete case of a particular actor, or to the average or approximate meaning attributable to a given plurality of actors; or secondly to the theoretically conceived pure type of subjective meaning attributed to the hypothetical actor or actors in a given type of action. In no case does it refer to an objectively "correct" meaning or one which is "true" in some metaphysical sense. It is this which distinguishes the empirical sciences of action, such as sociology and history, from the dogmatic disciplines in that area, such as jurisprudence, logic, ethics, and aesthetics, which seek to ascertain the "true" and "valid" meanings associated with the objects of their investigation.

The line between meaningful action and merely reactive behaviour to which no subjective meaning is attached, cannot be sharply drawn empirically. A very considerable part of all sociologically relevant behaviour, especially purely traditional behaviour, is marginal between the two. In the case of many psychophysical processes, meaningful (i.e., subjectively understandable) action is not to be found at all; in others it is discernible only by the expert psychologist. Many mystical experiences which cannot be adequately communicated in words are, for a person who is not susceptible to such experiences, not fully understandable. At the same time the ability to imagine one's self performing a similar action is not a necessary prerequisite to understanding; "one need not have been Caesar in order to understand Caesar." For the verifiable accuracy of interpretation of the meaning of a phenomenon, it is a great help to be able to put one's self imaginatively in the place of the actor and thus sympathetically to participate in his experiences, but this is not an essential condition of meaningful interpretation. Understandable and non-understandable components of a process are often intermingled and bound up together. All interpretation of meaning, like all scientific observation, strives for clarity and verifiable accuracy of insight and comprehension.

The basis for certainty in understanding can be either rational, which can be further subdivided into logical and mathematical, or it can be of an emotionally empathic or artistically appreciative quality. In the sphere of action things are rationally evident chiefly when we attain a completely clear intellectual grasp of the action-elements in their intended context of meaning. Empathic or appreciative accuracy is attained when, through sympathetic participation, we can adequately grasp the emotional context in which the action took place. The highest degree of rational understanding is attained in cases involving the meanings of logically or mathematically related propositions; their meaning may be immediately and unambiguously intelligible. We have a perfectly clear understanding of what it means when somebody employs the proposition $2 \times 2 = 4$ or the Pythagorean theorem in reasoning or argument, or when someone correctly carries out a logical train of reasoning according to our accepted modes of thinking. In the same way we also understand what a person is doing when he tries to achieve certain ends by choosing appropriate means on the basis of the facts of the situation as experience has accustomed us to interpret them. Such an interpretation of this type of rationally purposeful action possesses, for the understanding of the choice of means, the highest degree of verifiable certainty. With a lower degree of certainty, which is, however, adequate for most purposes of explanation, we are able to understand errors, including confusion of problems of the sort that we ourselves are liable to, or the origin of which we can detect by sympathetic self-analysis.

On the other hand, many ultimate ends or values toward which experience shows that human action may be oriented, often cannot be understood completely, though sometimes we are able to grasp them intellectually. The more radically they differ from our own ultimate values, however, the more difficult it is for us to make them understandable by imaginatively participating in them. Depending upon the circumstances of the particular case we must be content either with a purely intellectual understanding of such values or when even that fails, sometimes we must simply accept them as given data. Then we can try to understand the action motivated by them on the basis of whatever opportunities for approximate emotional and intellectual interpretation seem to be available at different points in its course. These difficulties apply, for instance, for people not susceptible to the relevant values, to many unusual acts of religious and charitable zeal; also certain kinds of extreme rationalistic fanaticism of the type involved in some forms of the ideology of the "rights of man" are in a similar position for people who radically repudiate such points of view.

The more we ourselves are susceptible to them the more readily can we imaginatively participate in such emotional reactions as anxiety, anger, ambition, envy, jealousy, love, enthusiasm, pride, vengefulness, loyalty, devotion, and appetites of all sorts, and thereby understand the irrational conduct which grows out of them. Such conduct is "irrational," that is, from the point of view of the rational pursuit of a given end. Even when such emotions are found in a degree of intensity of which the observer himself is completely incapable, he can still have a significant degree of emotional understanding of their meaning and can interpret intellectually their influence on the course of action and the selection of means.

For the purposes of a typological scientific analysis it is convenient to treat all irrational, affectually determined elements of behaviour as factors of deviation from a conceptually pure type of rational action. For example, a panic on the stock exchange can be most conveniently analysed by attempting to determine first what the course of action would have been if it had not been influenced by irrational affects; it is then possible to introduce the irrational components as accounting for the observed deviations from this hypothetical course. Similarly, in analysing a political or military campaign it is convenient to determine in the first place what would have been a rational course, given the ends of the participants and adequate knowledge of all the circumstances. Only in this way is it possible to assess the causal significance of irrational factors as accounting for the deviations from this type. The construction of a purely rational course of action in such cases serves the sociologist as a type ("ideal type") which has the merit of clear understandability and lack of ambiguity. By comparison with this it is possible to understand the ways in which actual action is influenced by irrational factors of all sorts, such as affects and errors, in that they account for the deviation from the line of conduct which would be expected on the hypothesis that the action were purely rational.

Only in this respect and for these reasons of methodological convenience, is the method of sociology "rationalistic." It is naturally not legitimate to interpret this procedure as involving a "rationalistic bias" of sociology, but only as a methodological device. It certainly does not involve a belief in the actual predominance of rational elements in human life, for on the question of how far this predominance does or does not exist, nothing whatever has been said. That there is, however, a danger of rationalistic interpretations where they are out of place naturally cannot be denied. All experience unfortunately confirms the existence of this danger.

In all the sciences of human action, account must be taken of processes and phenomena which are devoid of subjective meaning, in the role of stimuli, results, favouring or hindering circumstances. To be devoid of meaning is not identical with being lifeless or non-human; every artefact, such as for example a machine, can be understood only in terms of the meaning which its production and use have had or will have for human action; a meaning which may derive from a relation to exceedingly various purposes. Without reference to this meaning such an object remains wholly unintelligible. That which is intelligible or understandable about it is thus its relation to human action in the role either of means or of end; a relation of which the actor or actors can be said to have been aware and to which their action has been oriented. Only in terms of such categories is it possible to "understand" objects of this kind. On the other hand, processes or conditions, whether they are animate or inanimate, human or non-human, are in the present sense devoid of meaning insofar as they cannot be related to an intended purpose. That is to say they are devoid of meaning if they cannot be related to action in the role of means or ends but constitute only the stimulus, the favouring or hindering circumstances. It may be that the incursion of the Dollart at the beginning of the twelfth century had historical significance as a stimulus to the beginning of certain migrations of considerable importance. Human mortality, indeed the organic life cycle generally from the helplessness of infancy to that of old age, is naturally of the very greatest sociological importance through the various ways in which human action has been oriented to these facts. To still another category of facts devoid of meaning belong certain psychic or psycho-physical phenomena such as fatigue, habituation, memory, etc.; also certain typical states of euphoria under some conditions of ascetic mortification; finally, typical variations in the reactions of individuals according to reaction-time, precision, and other modes. But in the last analysis the same principle applies to these as to other phenomena which are devoid of meaning. Both the actor and the sociologist must accept them as data to be taken into account.

It is altogether possible that future research may be able to discover non-understandable uniformities underlying what has appeared to be specifically meaningful action, though little has been accomplished in this direction thus far. Thus, for example, differences in hereditary biological constitution, as of "races," would have to be treated by sociology as given data in the same way as the physiological facts of the need of nutrition or the effect of senescence on action. This would be the case if, and insofar as, we had statistically conclusive proof of their influence on sociologically relevant behaviour. The recognition of the causal significance of such factors would naturally not in the least alter the specific task of sociological analysis or of that of the other sciences of action, which is the interpretation of action in terms of its subjective meaning. The effect would be only to introduce certain non-understandable data of the same order as others which, it has been noted above, are already present, into the complex of subjectively understandable motivation at certain points. Thus it may come to be known that there are typical relations between the frequency of certain types of teleological orientation of action or of the degree of certain kinds of rationality and the cephalic index or skin colour or any other biologically inherited characteristic.

Understanding may be of two kinds: the first is the direct observational understanding of the subjective meaning of a given act as such, including verbal utterances. We thus understand by direct observation, in this sense, the meaning of the proposition 2 × 2 =4 when we hear or read it. This is a case of the direct rational understanding of ideas. We also understand an outbreak of anger as manifested by facial expression, exclamations or irrational movements. This is direct observational understanding of irrational emotional reactions. We can understand in a similar observational way the action of a woodcutter or of somebody who reaches for the knob to shut a door or who aims a gun at an animal. This is rational observational understanding of actions.

Understanding may, however, be of another sort, namely explanatory understanding. Thus we understand in terms of motive the meaning an actor attaches to the proposition twice two equals four, when he states it or writes it down, in that we understand what makes him do this at precisely this moment and in these circumstances. Understanding in this sense is attained if we know that he is engaged in balancing a ledger or in making a scientific demonstration, or is engaged in some other task of which this particular act would be an appropriate part. This is rational understanding of motivation, which consists in placing the act in an intelligible and more inclusive context of meaning. Thus we understand the chopping of wood or aiming of a gun in terms of motive in addition to direct observation if we know that the wood-chopper is working for a wage, or is chopping a supply of firewood for his own use, or possibly is doing it for recreation. But he might also be "working off" a fit of rage, an irrational case. Similarly we understand the motive of a person aiming a gun if we know that he has been commanded to shoot as a member of a firing squad, that he is fighting against an enemy, or that he is doing it for revenge. The last is affectually determined and thus in a certain sense irrational. Finally we have a motivational understanding of the outburst of anger if we know that it has been provoked by jealousy, injured pride, or an insult. The last examples are all affectually determined and hence derived from irrational motives. In all the above cases the particular act has been placed in an understandable sequence of motivation, the understanding of which can be treated as an explanation of the actual course of behaviour. Thus for a science which is concerned with the subjective meaning of action, explanation requires a grasp of the complex of meaning in which an actual course of understandable action thus interpreted belongs. In all such cases, even where the processes are largely affectual, the subjective meaning of the action, including that also of the relevant meaning complexes, will be called the "intended" meaning. This involves a departure from ordinary usage, which speaks of intention in this sense only in the case of rationally purposive action.

In all these cases understanding involves the interpretive grasp of the meaning present in one of the following contexts: (a) as in the historical approach, the actually intended meaning for concrete individual action; or (b) as in cases of sociological mass phenomena the average of, or an approximation to, the actually intended meaning; or (c) the meaning appropriate to a scientifically formulated pure type (an ideal type) of a common phenomenon. The concepts and "laws" of pure economic theory are examples of this kind of ideal type. They state what course a given type of human action would take if it were strictly rational, unaffected by errors or emotional factors and if, furthermore, it were completely and unequivocally directed to a single end, the maximisation of economic advantage. In reality, action takes exactly this course only in unusual cases, as sometimes on the stock exchange; and even then there is usually only an approximation to the ideal type.

Every interpretation attempts to attain clarity and certainty, but no matter how clear an interpretation as such appears to be from the point of view of meaning, it cannot on this account alone claim to be the causally valid interpretation. On this level it must remain only a peculiarly plausible hypothesis. In the first place the "conscious motives" may well, even to the actor himself, conceal the various "motives" and "repressions" which constitute the real driving force of his action. Thus in such cases even subjectively honest self-analysis has only a relative value. Then it is the task of the sociologist to be aware of this motivational situation and to describe and analyse it, even though it has not actually been concretely part of the conscious "intention" of the actor; possibly not at all, at least not fully. This is a borderline case of the interpretation of meaning. Secondly, processes of action which seem to an observer to be the same or similar may fit into exceedingly various complexes of motive in the case of the actual actor. Then even though the situations appear superficially to be very similar we must actually understand them or interpret them as very different; perhaps, in terms of meaning, directly opposed. Third, the actors in any given situation are often subject to opposing and conflicting impulses, all of which we are able to understand. In a large number of cases we know from experience it is not possible to arrive at even an approximate estimate of the relative strength of conflicting motives and very often we cannot be certain of our interpretation. Only the actual outcome of the conflict gives a solid basis of judgment.

More generally, verification of subjective interpretation by comparison with the concrete course of events is, as in the case of all hypotheses, indispensable. Unfortunately this type of verification is feasible with relative accuracy only in the few very special cases susceptible of psychological experimentation. The approach to a satisfactory degree of accuracy is exceedingly various, even in the limited number of cases of mass phenomena which can be statistically described and unambiguously interpreted. For the rest there remains only the possibility of comparing the largest possible number of historical or contemporary processes which, while otherwise similar, differ in the one decisive point of their relation to the particular motive or factor the role of which is being investigated. This is a fundamental task of comparative sociology. Often, unfortunately there is available only the dangerous and uncertain procedure of the "imaginary experiment" which consists in thinking away certain elements of a chain of motivation and working out the course of action which would then probably ensue, thus arriving at a causal judgment.

For example, the generalisation called Gresham's Law is a rationally clear interpretation of human action under certain conditions and under the assumption that it will follow a purely rational course. How far any actual course of action corresponds to this can be verified only by the available statistical evidence for the actual disappearance of undervalued monetary units from circulation. In this case our information serves to demonstrate a high degree of accuracy. The facts of experience were known before the generalisation, which was formulated afterward; but without this successful interpretation our need for causal understanding would evidently be left unsatisfied. On the other hand, without the demonstration that what can here be assumed to be a theoretically adequate interpretation also is in some degree relevant to an actual course of action, a "law," no matter how fully demonstrated theoretically, would be worthless for the understanding of action in the real world. In this case the correspondence between the theoretical interpretation of motivation and its empirical verification is entirely satisfactory and the cases are numerous enough so that verification can be considered established. But to take another example, Eduard Meyer has advanced an ingenious theory of the causal significance of the battles of Marathon, Salamis, and Platea for the development of the cultural peculiarities of Greek, and hence, more generally, Western, civilisation. This is derived from a meaningful interpretation of certain symptomatic facts having to do with the attitudes of the Greek oracles and prophets toward the Persians. It can only be directly verified by reference to the examples of the conduct of the Persians in cases where they were victorious, as in Jerusalem, Egypt, and Asia Minor, and even this verification must necessarily remain unsatisfactory in certain respects. The striking rational plausibility of the hypothesis must here necessarily be relied on as a support. In very many cases of historical interpretation which seem highly plausible, however, there is not even a possibility of the order of verification which was feasible in this case. Where this is true the interpretation must necessarily remain a hypothesis.

A motive is a complex of subjective meaning which seems to the actor himself or to the observer an adequate ground for the conduct in question. We apply the term "adequacy on the level of meaning" to the subjective interpretation of a coherent course of conduct when and insofar as, according to our habitual modes of thought and feeling, its component parts taken in their mutual relation are recognised to constitute a "typical" complex of meaning. It is more common to say "correct." The interpretation of a sequence of events will on the other hand be called causally adequate insofar as, according to established generalisations from experience, there is a probability that it will always actually occur in the same way. An example of adequacy on the level of meaning in this sense is what is, according to our current norms of calculation or thinking, the correct solution of an arithmetical problem. On the other hand, a causally adequate interpretation of the same phenomenon would concern the statistical probability that, according to verified generalisations from experience, there would be a correct or an erroneous solution of the same problem. This also refers to currently accepted norms but includes taking account of typical errors or of typical confusions. Thus causal explanation depends on being able to determine that there is a probability, which in the rare ideal case can be numerically stated, but is always in some sense calculable, that a given observable event (overt or subjective) will be followed or accompanied by another event.

A correct causal interpretation of a concrete course of action is arrived at when the overt action and the motives have both been correctly apprehended and at the same time their relation has become meaningfully comprehensible. A correct causal interpretation of typical action means that the process which is claimed to be typical is shown to be both adequately grasped on the level of meaning and at the same time the interpretation is to some degree causally adequate. If adequacy in respect to meaning is lacking, then no matter how high the degree of uniformity and how precisely its probability can be numerically determined, it is still an incomprehensible statistical probability, whether dealing with overt or subjective processes. On the other hand, even the most perfect adequacy on the level of meaning has causal significance from a sociological point of view only insofar as there is some kind of proof for the existence of a probability that action in fact normally takes the course which has been held to be meaningful. For this there must be some degree of determinable frequency of approximation to an average or a pure type.

Statistical uniformities constitute understandable types of action in the sense of this discussion, and thus constitute "sociological generalisations," only when they can be regarded as manifestations of the understandable subjective meaning of a course of social action. Conversely, formulations of a rational course of subjectively understandable action constitute sociological types of empirical process only when they can be empirically observed with a significant degree of approximation.

It is unfortunately by no means the case that the actual likelihood of the occurrence of a given course of overt action is always directly proportional to the clarity of subjective interpretation. There are statistics of processes devoid of meaning such as death rates, phenomena of fatigue, the production rate of machines, the amount of rainfall, in exactly the same sense as there are statistics of meaningful phenomena. But only when the phenomena are meaningful is it convenient to speak of sociological statistics. Examples are such cases as crime rates, occupational distributions, price statistics, and statistics of crop acreage. Naturally there are many cases where both components are involved, as in crop statistics.

Processes and uniformities which it has here seemed convenient not to designate as (in the present case) sociological phenomena or uniformities because they are not "understandable," are naturally not on that account any the less important. This is true even for sociology in the present sense which restricts it to subjectively understandable phenomena – a usage which there is no intention of attempting to impose on anyone else. Such phenomena, however important, are simply treated by a different method from the others; they become conditions, stimuli, furthering or hindering circumstances of action.

Action in the sense of a subjectively understandable orientation of behaviour exists only as the behaviour of one or more individual human beings. For other cognitive purposes it may be convenient or necessary to consider the individual, for instance, as a collection of cells, as a complex of biochemical reactions, or to conceive his "psychic" life as made up of a variety of different elements, however these may be defined. Undoubtedly such procedures yield valuable knowledge of causal relationships. But the behaviour of these elements, as expressed in such uniformities, is not subjectively understandable. This is true even of psychic elements because the more precisely they are formulated from a point of view of natural science, the less they are accessible to subjective understanding. This is never the road to interpretation in terms of subjective meaning. On the contrary, both for sociology in the present sense, and for history, the object of cognition is the subjective meaning-complex of action. The behaviour of physiological entities such as cells, or of any sort of psychic elements may at least in principle be observed and an attempt made to derive uniformities from such observations. It is further possible to attempt, with their help, to obtain a causal explanation of individual phenomena; that is, to subsume them under uniformities. But the subjective understanding of action takes the same account of this type of fact and uniformity as of any others not capable of subjective interpretation. This is true, for example, of physical, astronomical, geological, meteorological, geographical, botanical, zoological, and anatomical facts and of such facts as those aspects of psychopathology which are devoid of subjective meaning or the facts of the natural conditions of technological processes.

For still other cognitive purposes as, for instance, juristic, or for practical ends, it may on the other hand be convenient or even indispensable to treat social collectivities, such as states, associations, business corporations, foundations, as if they were individual persons. Thus they may be treated as the subjects of rights and duties or as the performers of legally significant actions. But for the subjective interpretation of action in sociological work these collectivities must be treated as solely the resultants and modes of organisation of the particular acts of individual persons, since these alone can be treated as agents in a course of subjectively understandable action. Nevertheless, the sociologist cannot for his purposes afford to ignore these collective concepts derived from other disciplines. For the subjective interpretation of action has at least two important relations to these concepts. In the first place it is often necessary to employ very similar collective concepts, indeed often using the same terms, in order to obtain an understandable terminology. Thus both in legal terminology and in everyday speech the term "state" is used both for the legal concept of the state and for the phenomena of social action to which its legal rules are relevant. For sociological purposes, however, the phenomenon "the state" does not consist necessarily or even primarily of the elements which are relevant to legal analysis; and for sociological purposes there is no such thing as a collective personality which "acts." When reference is made in a sociological context to a "state," a "nation," a "corporation," a "family," or an "army corps," or to similar collectivities, what is meant is, on the contrary, only a certain kind of development of actual or possible social actions of individual persons. Both because of its precision and because it is established in general usage the juristic concept is taken over, but is used in an entirely different meaning.

Secondly, the subjective interpretation of action must take account of a fundamentally important fact. These concepts of collective entities which are found both in common sense and in juristic and other technical forms of thought, have a meaning in the minds of individual persons, partly as of something actually existing, partly as something with normative authority. This is true not only of judges and officials, but of ordinary private individuals as well. Actors thus in part orient their action to them, and in this role such ideas have a powerful, often a decisive, causal influence on the course of action of real individuals. This is above all true where the ideas concern a recognised positive or negative normative pattern. Thus, for instance, one of the important aspects of the "existence" of a modern state, precisely as a complex of social interaction of individual persons, consists in the fact that the action of various individuals is oriented to the belief that it exists or should exist, thus that its acts and laws are valid in the legal sense. This will be further discussed below. Though extremely pedantic and cumbersome it would be possible, if purposes of sociological terminology alone were involved, to eliminate such terms entirely, and substitute newly-coined words. This would be possible even though the word "state" is used ordinarily not only to designate the legal concept but also the real process of action. But in the above important connection, at least, this would naturally be impossible.

Thirdly, it is the method of the so-called "organic" school of sociology to attempt to understand social interaction by using as a point of departure the "whole" within which the individual acts. His action and behaviour are then interpreted somewhat in the way that a physiologist would treat the role of an organ of the body in the "economy" of the organism, that is from the point of view of the survival of the latter. How far in other disciplines this type of functional analysis of the relation of "parts" to a "whole" can be regarded as definitive, cannot be discussed here; but it is well known that the biochemical and biophysical modes of analysis of the organism are in principle opposed to stopping there. For purposes of sociological analysis two things can be said. First, this functional frame of reference is convenient for purposes of practical illustration and for provisional orientation. In these respects it is not only useful but indispensable. But at the same time if its cognitive value is overestimated and its concepts illegitimately "reified," it can be highly dangerous. Secondly, in certain circumstances this is the only available way of determining just what processes of social action it is important to understand in order to explain a given phenomenon. But this is only the beginning of sociological analysis as here understood. In the case of social collectivities, precisely as distinguished from organisms, we are in a position to go beyond merely demonstrating functional relationships and uniformities. We can accomplish something which is never attainable in the natural sciences, namely the subjective understanding of the action of the component individuals. The natural sciences on the other hand cannot do this, being limited to the formulation of causal uniformities in objects and events, and the explanation of individual facts by applying them. We do not "understand" the behaviour of cells, but can only observe the relevant functional relationships and generalise on the basis of these observations. This additional achievement of explanation by interpretive understanding, as distinguished from external observation, is of course attained only at a price-the more hypothetical and fragmentary character of its results. Nevertheless, subjective understanding is the specific characteristic of sociological knowledge.

It would lead too far afield even to attempt to discuss how far the behaviour of animals is subjectively understandable to us and vice versa; in both cases the meaning of the term understanding and its extent of application would be highly problematical. But insofar as such understanding existed it would be theoretically possible to formulate a sociology of the relations of men to animals, both domestic and wild. Thus many animals "understand" commands, anger, love, hostility, and react to them in ways which are evidently often by no means purely instinctive and mechanical and in some sense both consciously meaningful and affected by experience. There is no *a priori* reason to suppose that our ability to share the feelings of primitive men is very much greater. Unfortunately we either do not have any reliable means of determining the subjective state of mind of an animal or what we have is at best very unsatisfactory. It is well known that the problems of animal psychology, however interesting, are very thorny ones. There are in particular various forms of social organisation among animals: "monogamous and polygamous families," herds, flocks, and finally "state," with a functional division of labour. The extent of functional differentiation found in these animal societies is by no means, however, entirely a matter of the degree of organic or morphological differentiation of the individual members of the species. Thus, the functional differentiation found among the termites, and in consequence that of the products of their social activities, is much more advanced than in the case of the bees and ants. In this field it goes without saying that a purely functional point of view is often the best that can, at least for the present, be attained, and the investigator must be content with it. Thus it is possible to study the ways in which the species provides for its survival; that is, for nutrition, defence, reproduction, and reconstruction of the social units. As the principal bearers of these functions, differentiated types of individuals can be identified: "kings," "queens," "workers," "soldiers," "drones," "propagators," "queen's substitutes," and so on. Anything more than that was for a long time merely a matter of speculation or of an attempt to determine the extent to which heredity on the one hand and environment on the other would be involved in the development of these "social" proclivities. This was particularly true of the controversies between Gotte and Weisman. The latter's conception of the omnipotence of natural selection was largely based on wholly non-empirical deductions. But all serious authorities are naturally fully agreed that the limitation of analysis to the functional level is only a necessity imposed by our present ignorance which it is hoped will only be temporary.

It is relatively easy to grasp the significance of the functions of these various differentiated types for survival. It is also not difficult to work out the bearing of the hypothesis of the inheritance of acquired characteristics or its reverse on the problem of explaining how these differentiations have come about, and further, what is the bearing of different variants of the theory of heredity. But this is not enough. We would like especially to know first what factors account for the original differentiation of specialised types from the still neutral undifferentiated species-type. Secondly, it would be important to know what leads the differentiated individual in the typical case to behave in a way which actually serves the survival value of the organised group. Wherever research has made any progress in the solution of these problems it has been through the experimental demonstration of the probability or possibility of the role of chemical stimuli or physiological processes, such as nutritional states, the effects of parasitic castration, etc., in the case of the individual organism.

How far there is even a hope that the existence of "subjective" or "meaningful" orientation could be made experimentally probable, even the specialist today would hardly be in a position to say. A verifiable conception of the state of mind of these social animals, accessible to meaningful understanding, would seem to be attainable even as an ideal goal only within narrow limits. However that may be, a contribution to the understanding of human social action is hardly to be expected from this quarter. On the contrary, in the field of animal psychology, human analogies are and must be continually employed. The most that can be hoped for is, then, that these biological analogies may some day be useful in suggesting significant problems.

For instance they may throw light on the question of the relative role in the early stages of human social differentiation of mechanical and instinctive factors, as compared with that of the factors which are accessible to subjective interpretation generally, and more particularly to the role of consciously rational action. It is necessary for the sociologist to be thoroughly aware of the fact that in the early stages even of human development, the first set of factors is completely predominant. Even in the later stages he must take account of their continual interaction with the others in a role which is often of decisive importance. This is particularly true of all "traditional" action and of many aspects of charisma. In the latter field of phenomena lie the seeds of certain types of psychic "contagion" and it is thus the bearer of many dynamic tendencies of social processes. These types of action are very closely related to phenomena which are understandable either only in biological terms or are subject to interpretation in terms of subjective motives only in fragments and with an almost imperceptible transition to the biological. But all these facts do not discharge sociology from the obligation, in full awareness of the narrow limits to which it is confined, to accomplish what it alone can do.

The various works of Othmar Spann are often full of suggestive ideas, though at the same time he is guilty of occasional misunderstandings, and above all, of arguing on the basis of pure value judgments which have no place in an empirical investigation. But he is undoubtedly correct in doing something to which, however, no one seriously objects, namely, emphasising the sociological significance of the functional point of view for preliminary orientation to problems. This is what he calls the "universalistic method." We certainly need to know what kind of action is functionally necessary for "survival," but further and above all for the maintenance of a cultural type and the continuity of the corresponding modes of social action, before it is possible even to inquire how this action has come about and what motives determine it. It is necessary to know what a "king," an "official," an "entrepreneur," a "procurer," or a "magician" does; that is, what kind of typical action, which justifies classifying an individual in one of these categories, is important and relevant for an analysis, before it is possible to undertake the analysis itself. But it is only this analysis itself which can achieve the sociological understanding of the actions of typically differentiated human (and only human) individuals, and which hence constitutes the specific function of sociology. It is a monstrous misunderstanding to think that an "individualistic" method should involve what is in any conceivable sense an individualistic system of values. It is as important to avoid this error as the related one which confuses the unavoidable tendency of sociological concepts to assume a rationalistic character with a belief in the predominance of rational motives, or even a positive valuation of "rationalism." Even a socialistic economy would have to be understood sociologically in exactly the same kind of "individualistic" terms; that is, in terms of the action of individuals, the types of "officials" found in it, as would be the case with a system of free exchange analysed in terms of the theory of marginal utility. It might be possible to find a better method, but in this respect it would be similar. The real empirical sociological investigation begins with the question: What motives determine and lead the individual members and participants in this socialistic community to behave in such a way that the community came into being in the first place, and that it continues to exist? Any form of functional analysis which proceeds from the whole to the parts can accomplish only a preliminary preparation for this investigation – a preparation, the utility and indispensability of which, if properly carried out, is naturally beyond question.

It is customary to designate various sociological generalisations, as for example "Gresham's Law," as scientific "laws." These are in fact typical probabilities confirmed by observation to the effect that under certain given conditions an expected course of social action will occur, which is understandable in terms of the typical motives and typical subjective intentions of the actors. These generalisations are both understandable and define in the highest degree insofar as the typically observed course of action can be understood in terms of the purely rational pursuit of an end, or where for reasons of methodological convenience such a theoretical type can be heuristically employed. In such cases the relations of means and end will be clearly understandable on grounds of experience, particularly where the choice of means was "inevitable." In such cases it is legitimate to assert that insofar as the action was rigorously rational it could not have taken any other course because for technical reasons, given their clearly defined ends, no other means were available to the actors. This very case demonstrates how erroneous it is to regard any kind of "psychology" as the ultimate foundation of the sociological interpretation of action. The term "psychology," to be sure, is today understood in a wide variety of senses. For certain quite specific methodological purposes the type of treatment which attempts to follow the procedures of the natural sciences employs a distinction between "physical" and "psychic" phenomena which is entirely foreign to the disciplines concerned with human action, at least in the present sense. The results of a type of psychological investigation which employs the methods of the natural sciences in any one of various possible ways may naturally, like the results of any other science, have, in specific contexts, outstanding significance for sociological problems; indeed this has often happened. But this use of the results of psychology is something quite different from the investigation of human behaviour in terms of its subjective meaning. Hence sociology has no closer logical relationship on a general analytical level to this type of psychology than to any other science. The source of error lies in the concept of the "psychic." It is held that everything which is not physical is *ipso facto* psychic, but that the meaning of a train of mathematical reasoning which a person carries out is not in the relevant sense "psychic." Similarly the rational deliberation of an actor as to whether the results of a given proposed course of action will or will not promote certain specific interests, and the corresponding decision, do not become one bit more understandable by taking "psychological" considerations into account. But it is precisely on the basis of such rational assumptions that most of the laws of sociology, including those of economics, are built up. On the other hand, in explaining the irrationalities of action sociologically, that form of psychology which employs the method of subjective understanding undoubtedly can make decisively important contributions. But this does not alter the fundamental methodological situation.

It has continually been assumed as obvious that the science of sociology seeks to formulate type concepts and generalised uniformities of empirical process. This distinguishes it from history, which is oriented to the causal analysis and explanation of individual actions, structures, and personalities possessing cultural significance. The empirical material which underlies the concepts of sociology consists to a very large extent, though by no means exclusively, of the same concrete processes of action which are dealt with by historians. Among the various bases on which its concepts are formulated and its generalisations worked out, is an attempt to justify its important claim to be able to make a contribution to the causal explanation of some historically and culturally important phenomenon. As in the case of every generalising science, the abstract character of the concepts of sociology is responsible for the fact that, compared with actual historical reality, they are relatively lacking in fullness of concrete content. To compensate for this disadvantage, sociological analysis can offer a greater precision of concepts. This precision is obtained by striving for the highest possible degree of adequacy on the level of meaning in accordance with the definition of that concept put forward above. It has already been repeatedly stressed that this aim can be realised in a particularly high degree in the case of concepts and generalisations which formulate rational processes. But sociological investigation attempts to include in its scope various irrational phenomena, as well as prophetic, mystic, and affectual modes of action, formulated in terms of theoretical concepts which are adequate on the level of meaning. In all cases, rational or irrational, sociological analysis both abstracts from reality and at the same time helps us to understand it, in that it shows with what degree of approximation a concrete historical phenomenon can be subsumed under one or more of these concepts. For example, the same historical phenomenon may be in one aspect "feudal," in another "patrimonial," in another "bureaucratic," and in still another "charismatic." In order to give a precise meaning to these terms, it is necessary for the sociologist to formulate pure ideal types of the corresponding forms of action which in each case involve the highest possible degree of logical integration by virtue of their complete adequacy on the level of meaning. But precisely because this is true, it is probably seldom if ever that a real phenomenon can be found which corresponds exactly to one of these ideally constructed pure types. The case is similar to a physical reaction which has been calculated on the assumption of an absolute vacuum. Theoretical analysis in the field of sociology is possible only in terms of such pure types. It goes without saying that in addition it is convenient for the sociologist from time to time to employ average types of an empirical statistical character. These are concepts which do not require methodological discussion at this point. But when reference is made to "typical" cases, the term should always be understood, unless otherwise stated, as meaning ideal-types, which may in turn be rational or irrational as the case may be (thus in economic theory they are always rational), but in any case are always constructed with a view to adequacy on the level of meaning.

It is important to realise that in the sociological field as elsewhere, averages, and hence average types, can be formulated with a relative degree of precision only where they are concerned with differences of degree in respect to action which remains qualitatively the same. Such cases do occur, but in the majority of cases of action important to history or sociology the motives which determine it are qualitatively heterogeneous. Then it is quite impossible to speak of an "average" in the true sense. The ideal-types of social action which for instance are used in economic theory are thus "unrealistic" or abstract in that they always ask what course of action would take place if it were purely rational and oriented to economic ends alone. But this construction can be used to aid in the understanding of action not purely economically determined but which involves deviations arising from traditional restraints, affects, errors, and the intrusion of other than economic purposes or considerations.

This can take place in two ways. First, in analysing the extent to which in the concrete case, or on the average for a class of cases, the action was in part economically determined along with the other factors. Secondly, by throwing the discrepancy between the actual course of events and the ideal-type into relief, the analysis of the non-economic motives actually involved is facilitated. The procedure would be very similar in employing an ideal-type of mystical orientation with its appropriate attitude of indifference to worldly things, as a tool for analysing its consequences for the actor's relation to ordinary life; for instance, to political or economic affairs. The more sharply and precisely the ideal-type has been constructed, thus the more abstract and unrealistic in this sense it is, the better it is able to perform its methodological functions in formulating the clarification of terminology, and in the formulation of classifications, and of hypotheses. In working out a concrete causal explanation of individual events, the procedure of the historian is essentially the same. Thus in attempting to explain the campaign of 1866, it is indispensable both in the case of Moltke and of Benedek to attempt to construct imaginatively how each, given fully adequate knowledge both of his own situation and of that of his opponent, would have acted. Then it is possible to compare with this the actual course of action and to arrive at a causal explanation of the observed deviations, which will be attributed to such factors as misinformation, strategical errors, logical fallacies, personal temperament, or considerations outside the realm of strategy. Here, too, an ideal-typical construction of rational action is actually employed even though it is not made explicit.

The theoretical concepts of sociology are ideal-types not only from the objective point of view, but also in their application to subjective processes. In the great majority of cases actual action goes on in a state of inarticulate half-consciousness or actual unconsciousness of its subjective meaning. The actor is more likely to "be aware" of it in a vague sense than he is to "know" what he is doing or be explicitly self-conscious about it. In most cases his action is governed by impulse or habit. Only occasionally and, in the uniform action of large numbers often only in the case of a few individuals, is the subjective meaning of the action, whether rational or irrational, brought clearly into consciousness.

The ideal-type of meaningful action where the meaning is fully conscious and explicit is a marginal case. Every sociological or historical investigation, in applying its analysis to the empirical facts, must take this fact into account. But the difficulty need not prevent the sociologist from systematising his concepts by the classification of possible types of subjective meaning. That is, he may reason as if action actually proceeded on the basis of clearly self-conscious meaning. The resulting deviation from the concrete facts must continually be kept in mind whenever it is a question of this level of concreteness, and must be carefully studied with reference both to degree and kind. It is often necessary to choose between terms which are either clear or unclear. Those which are clear will, to be sure, have the abstractness of ideal types, but they are nonetheless preferable for scientific purposes.

"OBJECTIVITY" IN SOCIAL SCIENCE

There is no absolutely "objective" scientific analysis of culture – or put perhaps more narrowly but certainly not essentially differently for our purposes – of "social phenomena" independent of special and "one-sided" viewpoints according to which – expressly or tacitly, consciously or unconsciously – they are selected, analysed and organised for expository purposes. The reasons for this lie in the character of the cognitive goal of all research in social science which seeks to transcend the purely formal treatment of the legal or conventional norms regulating social life.

The type of social science in which we are interested is an empirical science of concrete reality. Our aim is the understanding of the characteristic uniqueness of the reality in which we move. We wish to understand on the one hand the relationships and the cultural significance of individual events in their contemporary manifestations and on the other the causes of their being historically so and not otherwise. Now, as soon as we attempt to reflect about the way in which life confronts us in immediate concrete situations, it presents an infinite multiplicity of successively and coexistently emerging and disappearing events, both "within" and "outside" ourselves. The absolute infinitude of this multiplicity is seen to remain undiminished even when our attention is focused on a single "object," for instance, a concrete act of exchange, as soon as we seriously attempt an exhaustive description of all the individual components of this "individual phenomenon," to say nothing of explaining it causally. All the analysis of infinite reality which the finite human mind can conduct rests on the tacit assumption that only a finite portion of this reality constitutes the object of scientific investigation, and that only it is "important" in the sense of being "worthy of being known." But what are the criteria by which this segment is selected? It has often been thought that the decisive criterion in the cultural sciences, too, was in the last analysis, the "regular" recurrence of certain causal relationships. The "laws" which we are able to perceive in the infinitely manifold stream of events must – according to this conception – contain the scientifically "essential" aspect of reality. As soon as we have shown some causal relationship to be a "law," (i.e., if we have shown it to be universally valid by means of comprehensive historical induction, or have made it immediately and tangibly plausible according to our subjective experience), a great number of similar cases order themselves under the formula thus attained. Those elements in each individual event which are left unaccounted for by the selection of their elements subsumable under the "law" are considered as scientifically unintegrated residues which will be taken care of in the further perfection of the system of "laws." Alternatively they will be viewed as "accidental" and therefore scientifically unimportant because they do not fit into the structure of the "law;" in other words, they are not typical of the event and hence can only be the objects of "idle curiosity." Accordingly, even among the followers of the Historical School we continually find the attitude which declares that the ideal, which all the sciences, including the cultural sciences, serve and toward which they should strive even in the remote future, is a system of propositions from which reality can be "deduced." As is well known, a leading natural scientist believed that he could designate the (factually unattainable) ideal goal of such a treatment of cultural reality as a sort of "astronomical" knowledge.

Let us not, for our part, spare ourselves the trouble of examining these matters more closely – however often they have already been discussed. The first thing that impresses one is that the "astronomical" knowledge which was referred to is not a system of laws at all. On the contrary, the laws which it presupposes have been taken from other disciplines like mechanics. But it too concerns itself with the question of the individual consequence which the working of these laws in a unique configuration produces, since it is these individual configurations which are significant for us. Every individual constellation which it "explains" or predicts is causally explicable only as the consequence of another equally individual constellation which has preceded it. As far back as we may go into the grey mist of the far-off past, the reality to which the laws apply always remains equally individual, equally undeducible from laws. A cosmic "primeval state" which had no individual character or less individual character than the cosmic reality of the present would naturally be a meaningless notion. But is there not some trace of similar ideas in our field in those propositions sometimes derived from natural law and sometimes verified by the observation of "primitives," concerning an economic-social "primeval state" free from historical "accidents," and characterised by phenomena such as "primitive agrarian communism," sexual "promiscuity," etc., from which individual historical development emerges by a sort of fall from grace into concreteness?

The social-scientific interest has its point of departure, of course, in the real, i.e., concrete, individually-structured configuration of our cultural life in its universal relationships which are themselves no less individually structured, and in its development out of other social cultural conditions, which themselves are obviously likewise individually structured. It is clear here that the situation which we illustrated by reference to astronomy as a limiting case (which is regularly drawn on by logicians for the same purpose) appears in a more accentuated form. Whereas in astronomy, the heavenly bodies are of interest to us only in their quantitative and exact aspects, the qualitative aspect of phenomena concerns us in the social sciences. To this should be added that in the social sciences we are concerned with psychological and intellectual phenomena the empathic understanding of which is naturally a problem of a specifically different type from those which the schemes of the exact natural sciences in general can or seek to solve.

Despite that, this distinction in itself is not a distinction in principle, as it seems at first glance. Aside from pure mechanics, even the exact natural sciences do not proceed without qualitative categories. Furthermore, in our own field we encounter the idea (which is obviously distorted) that at least the phenomena characteristic of a money-economy – which are basic to our culture – are quantifiable and on that account subject to formulation as "laws." Finally it depends on the breadth or narrowness of one's definition of "law" as to whether one will also include regularities which because they are not quantifiable are not subject to numerical analysis. Especially insofar as the influence of psychological and intellectual factors is concerned, it does not in any case exclude the establishment of rules governing rational conduct. Above all, the point of view still persists which claims that the task of psychology is to play a role comparable to mathematics for the *Geisteswissenschaften* in the sense that it analyses the complicated phenomena of social life into their psychic conditions and effects, reduces them to their most elementary possible psychic factors and then analyses their functional interdependences. Thereby a sort of "chemistry," if not "mechanics," of the psychic foundations of social life would be created. Whether such investigations can produce valuable and – what is something else – useful results for the cultural sciences, we cannot decide here. But this would be irrelevant to the question as to whether the aim of socioeconomic knowledge in our sense, i.e., knowledge of reality with respect to its cultural significance and its causal relationships, can be attained through the quest for recurrent sequences. Let us assume that we have succeeded by means of psychology or otherwise in analysing all the observed and imaginable relationships, of social phenomena into some ultimate elementary "factors," that we have made an exhaustive analysis and classification of them and then formulated rigorously exact laws covering their behaviour. – What would be the significance of these results for our knowledge of the historically given culture or any individual phase thereof, such as capitalism, in its development and cultural significance? As an analytical tool, it would be as useful as a textbook of organic chemical combinations would be for our knowledge of the biogenetic aspect of the animal and plant world. In each case, certainly an important and useful preliminary step would have been taken. In neither case can concrete reality be deduced from "laws" and "factors." This is not because some higher mysterious powers reside in living phenomena (such as "dominants," "entelechies," or whatever they might be called). This, however, presents a problem in its own right. The real reason is that the analysis of reality is concerned with the configuration into which those (hypothetical!) "factors" are arranged to form a cultural phenomenon which is historically significant to us. Furthermore, if we wish to "explain" this individual configuration "causally" we must invoke other equally individual configurations on the basis of which we will explain it with the aid of those (hypothetical!) "laws."

The determination of those (hypothetical) "laws" and "factors" would in any case only be the first of the many operations which would lead us to the desired type of knowledge. The analysis of the historically given individual configuration of those "factors" and their significant concrete interaction, conditioned by their historical context and especially the rendering intelligible of the basis and type of this significance would be the next task to be achieved. This task must be achieved, it is true, by the utilisation of the preliminary analysis, but it is nonetheless an entirely new and distinct task. The tracing as far into the past as possible of the individual features of these historically evolved configurations which are contemporaneously significant, and their historical explanation by antecedent and equally individual configurations would be the third task. Finally the prediction of possible future constellations would be a conceivable fourth task.

For all these purposes, clear concepts and the knowledge of those (hypothetical) "laws" are obviously of great value as heuristic means – but only as such. Indeed they are quite indispensable for this purpose. But even in this function their limitations become evident at a decisive point. In stating this, we arrive at the decisive feature of the method of the cultural sciences. We have designated as "cultural sciences" those disciplines which analyse the phenomena of life in terms of their cultural significance. The significance of a configuration of cultural phenomena and the basis of this significance cannot however be derived and rendered intelligible by a system of analytical laws, however perfect it may be, since the significance of cultural events presupposes a value-orientation toward these events. The concept of culture is a value-concept. Empirical reality becomes "culture" to us because and insofar as we relate it to value ideas. It includes those segments and only those segments of reality which have become significant to us because of this value-relevance. Only a small portion of existing concrete reality is coloured by our value-conditioned interest and it alone is significant to us. It is significant because it reveals relationships which are important to us due to their connection with our values. Only because and to the extent that this is the case is it worthwhile for us to know it in its individual features. We cannot discover, however, what is meaningful to us by means of a "presuppositionless" investigation of empirical data. Rather, perception of its meaningfulness to us is the presupposition of its becoming an object of investigation. Meaningfulness naturally does not coincide with laws as such, and the more general the law the less the coincidence. For the specific meaning which a phenomenon has for us is naturally not to be found in those relationships which it shares with many other phenomena.

The focus of attention on reality under the guidance of values which lend it significance and the selection and ordering of the phenomena which are thus affected in the light of their cultural significance is entirely different from the analysis of reality in terms of laws and general concepts. Neither of these two types of the analysis of reality has any necessary logical relationship with the other. They can coincide in individual instances but it would be most disastrous if their occasional coincidence caused us to think that they were not distinct in principle. The cultural significance of a phenomenon, e.g., the significance of exchange in a money economy, can be the fact that it exists on a mass scale as a fundamental component of modern culture.

But the historical fact that it plays this role must be causally explained in order to render its cultural significance understandable. The analysis of the general aspects of exchange and the technique of the market is a – highly important and indispensable – preliminary task. For not only does this type of analysis leave unanswered the question as to how exchange historically acquired its fundamental significance in the modern world; but above all else, the fact with which we are primarily concerned, namely, the cultural significance of the money-economy – for the sake of which we are interested in the description of exchange technique, and for the sake of which alone a science exists which deals with that technique – is not derivable from any "law." The generic features of exchange, purchase, etc., interest the jurist – but we are concerned with the analysis of the cultural significance of the concrete historical fact that today exchange exists on a mass scale.

When we require an explanation, when we wish to understand what distinguishes the social-economic aspects of our culture, for instance, from that of Antiquity, in which exchange showed precisely the same generic traits as it does today, and when we raise the question as to where the significance of "money economy" lies, logical principles of quite heterogenous derivation enter into the investigation. We will apply those concepts with which we are provided by the investigation of the general features of economic mass phenomena – indeed, insofar as they are relevant to the meaningful aspects of our culture, we shall use them as means of exposition. The goal of our investigation is not reached through the exposition of those laws and concepts, precise as it may be. The question as to what should be the object of universal conceptualisation cannot be decided "presuppositionlessly" but only with reference to the significance which certain segments of that infinite multiplicity which we call "commerce" have for culture. We seek knowledge of an historical phenomenon, meaning by historical: significant in its individuality. And the decisive element in this is that only through the presupposition that a finite part alone of the infinite variety of phenomena is significant, does the knowledge of an individual phenomenon become logically meaningful. Even with the widest imaginable knowledge of "laws," we are helpless in the face of the question: how is the causal explanation of an individual fact possible – since a description of even the smallest slice of reality can never be exhaustive? The number and type of causes which have influenced any given event are always infinite and there is nothing in the things themselves to set some of them apart as alone meriting attention.

A chaos of "existential judgments" about countless individual events would be the only result of a serious attempt to analyse reality "without presuppositions." And even this result is only seemingly possible, since every single perception discloses on closer examination an infinite number of constituent perceptions which can never be exhaustively expressed in a judgment. Order is brought into this chaos only on the condition that in every case only a part of concrete reality is interesting and significant to us, because only it is related to the cultural values with which we approach reality. Only certain sides of the infinitely complex concrete phenomenon, namely those to which we attribute a general cultural significance, are therefore worthwhile knowing. They alone are objects of causal explanation. And even this causal explanation evinces the same character; an exhaustive causal investigation of any concrete phenomena in its full reality is not only practically impossible – it is simply nonsense. We select only those causes to which are to be imputed in the individual case, the "essential" feature of an event. Where the individuality of a phenomenon is concerned, the question of causality is not a question of laws but of concrete causal relationships; it is not a question of the subsumption of the event under some general rubric as a representative case but of its imputation as a consequence of some constellation. It is in brief a question of imputation. Wherever the causal explanation of a "cultural phenomenon"

– a "historical individual" is under consideration, the knowledge of causal laws is not the end of the investigation but only a means. It facilitates and renders possible the causal imputation to their concrete causes of those components of a phenomenon the individuality of which is culturally significant. So far and only so far as it achieves this, is it valuable for our knowledge of concrete relationships. And the more "general" (i.e., the more abstract) the laws, the less they can contribute to the causal imputation of individual phenomena and, more indirectly, to the understanding of the significance of cultural events.

What is the Consequence of all This?

Naturally, it does not imply that the knowledge of universal propositions, the construction of abstract concepts, the knowledge of regularities and the attempt to formulate "laws" have no scientific justification in the cultural sciences. Quite the contrary, if the causal knowledge of the historians consists of the imputation of concrete effects to concrete causes, a valid imputation of any individual effect without the application of "nomological" knowledge – i.e., the knowledge of recurrent causal sequences-would in general be impossible. Whether a single individual component of a relationship is, in a concrete case, to be assigned causal responsibility for an effect, the causal explanation of which is at issue, can in doubtful cases be determined only by estimating the effects which we generally expect from it and from the other components of the same complex which are relevant to the explanation. In other words, the "adequate" effects of the causal elements involved must be considered in arriving at any such conclusion. The extent to which the historian (in the widest sense of the word) can perform this imputation in a reasonably certain manner, with his imagination sharpened by personal experience and trained in analytic methods, and the extent to which he must have recourse to the aid of special disciplines which make it possible, varies with the individual case. Everywhere, however, and hence also in the sphere of complicated economic processes, the more certain and the more comprehensive our general knowledge the greater is the certainty of imputation. This proposition is not in the least affected by the fact that even in the case of all so-called "economic laws" without exception, we are concerned here not with "laws" in the narrower exact natural-science sense, but with adequate causal relationships expressed in rules and with the application of the category of "objective possibility." The establishment of such regularities is not the end but rather the means of knowledge. It is entirely a question of expediency, to be settled separately for each individual case, whether a regularly recurrent causal relationship of everyday experience should be formulated into a "law." Laws are important and valuable in the exact natural sciences, in the measure that those sciences are universally valid. For the knowledge of historical phenomena in their concreteness, the most general laws, because they are most devoid of content, are also the least valuable. The more comprehensive the validity – or scope – of a term, the more it leads us away from the richness of reality since in order to include the common elements of the largest possible number of phenomena, it must necessarily be as abstract as possible and hence devoid of content. In the cultural sciences, the knowledge of the universal or general is never valuable in itself.

The conclusion which follows from the above is that an "objective" analysis of cultural events, which proceeds according to the thesis that the ideal of science is the reduction of empirical reality to "laws," is meaningless. It is not meaningless, as is often maintained, because cultural or psychic events for instance are "objectively" less governed by laws. It is meaningless for a number of other reasons. Firstly, because the knowledge of social laws is not knowledge of social reality but is rather one of the various aids used by our minds for attaining this end; secondly, because knowledge of cultural events is inconceivable except on a basis of the significance which the concrete constellations of reality have for us in certain individual concrete situations. In which sense and in which situations this is the case is not revealed to us by any law; it is decided according to the value-ideas in the light of which we view "culture" in each individual case. "Culture" is a finite segment of the meaningless infinity of the world process, a segment on which human beings confer meaning and significance. This is true even for the human being who views a particular culture as a mortal enemy and who seeks to "return to nature." He can attain this point of view only after viewing the culture in which he lives from the standpoint of his values, and finding it "too soft." This is the purely logical-formal fact which is involved when we speak of the logically necessary rootedness of all historical entities in "evaluative ideas." The transcendental presupposition of every cultural science lies not in our finding a certain culture or any "culture" in general to be valuable but rather in the fact that we are cultural beings, endowed with the capacity and the will to take a deliberate attitude toward the world and to lend it significance. Whatever this significance may be, it will lead us to judge certain phenomena of human existence in its light and to respond to them as being (positively or negatively) meaningful. Whatever may be the content of this attitude, these phenomena have cultural significance for us and on this significance alone rests its scientific interest. Thus when we speak here of the conditioning of cultural knowledge through evaluative ideas (following the terminology of modern logic), it is done in the hope that we will not be subject to crude misunderstandings such as the opinion that cultural significance should be attributed only to valuable phenomena. Prostitution is a cultural phenomenon just as much as religion or money. All three are cultural phenomena only because, and only insofar as, their existence and the form which they historically assume touch directly or indirectly on our cultural interests and arouse our striving for knowledge concerning problems brought into focus by the evaluative ideas which give significance to the fragment of reality analysed by those concepts.

All knowledge of cultural reality, as may be seen, is always knowledge from particular points of view. When we require from the historian and social research worker as an elementary presupposition that they distinguish the important from the trivial and that they should have the necessary "point of view" for this distinction, we mean that they must understand how to relate the events of the real world consciously or unconsciously to universal "cultural values," and to select out those relationships which are significant for us. If the notion that those standpoints can be derived from the "facts themselves" continually recurs, it is due to the naive self-deception of the specialist, who is unaware that it is due to the evaluative ideas with which he unconsciously approaches his subject matter, that he has selected from an absolute infinity a tiny portion with the study of which he concerns himself In connection with this selection of individual special "aspects" of the event, which always and everywhere occurs, consciously or unconsciously, there also occurs that element of cultural-scientific work which is referred to by the often-heard assertion that the "personal" element of a scientific work is what is really valuable in it, and that personality must be expressed in every work if its existence is to be justified. To be sure, without the investigator's evaluative ideas, there would be no principle of selection of subject-matter and no meaningful knowledge of the concrete reality. Just as without the investigator's conviction regarding the significance of particular cultural facts, every attempt to analyse concrete reality is absolutely meaningless, so the direction of his personal belief, the refraction of values in the prism of his mind, gives direction to his work. And the values to which the scientific genius relates the object of his inquiry may determine (i.e., decide) the "conception" of a whole epoch, not only concerning what is regarded as "valuable," but also concerning what is significant or insignificant, "important" or "unimportant" in the phenomena.

Accordingly, cultural science in our sense involves "subjective" presuppositions insofar as it concerns itself only with those components of reality which have some relationship, however indirect, to events to which we attach cultural significance. Nonetheless, it is entirely causal knowledge exactly in the same sense as the knowledge of significant concrete natural events which have a qualitative character. Among the many confusions which the overreaching tendency of a formal-juristic outlook has brought about in the cultural sciences, there has recently appeared the attempt to "refute" the "materialistic conception of history" by a series of clever but fallacious arguments which state that since all economic life must take place in legally or conventionally regulated forms, all economic "development" must take the form of striving for the creation of new legal forms. Hence it is said to be intelligible only through ethical maxims, and is on this account essentially different from every type of "natural" development. Accordingly the knowledge of economic development is said to be "teleological" in character. Without wishing to discuss the meaning of the ambiguous term "development," or the logically no-less-ambiguous term "teleology" in the social sciences, it should be stated that such knowledge need not be "teleological" in the sense assumed by this point of view. The cultural significance of normatively regulated legal relations and even norms themselves can undergo fundamental revolutionary changes even under conditions of the formal identity of the prevailing legal norms. Indeed, if one wishes to lose one's self for a moment in fantasies about the future, one might theoretically imagine, let us say, the "socialisation of the means of production" unaccompanied by any conscious "striving" toward this result, and without even the disappearance or addition of a single paragraph of our legal code; the statistical frequency of certain legally regulated relationships might be changed fundamentally, and in many cases, even disappear entirely; a great number of legal norms might become practically meaningless and their whole cultural significance changed beyond identification. *De lege ferenda* discussions may be justifiably disregarded by the "materialistic conception of history," since its central proposition is the indeed inevitable change in the significance of legal institutions. Those who view the painstaking labour of causally understanding historical reality as of secondary importance can disregard it, but it is impossible to supplant it by any type of a "teleology." From our viewpoint, "purpose" is the conception of an effect which becomes a cause of an action. Since we take into account every cause which produces or can produce a significant effect, we also consider this one. Its specific significance consists only in the fact that we not only observe human conduct but can and desire to understand it.

Undoubtedly, all evaluative ideas are "subjective." Between the "historical" interest in a family chronicle and that in the development of the greatest conceivable cultural phenomena which were and are common to a nation or to mankind over long epochs, there exists an infinite gradation of "significance" arranged into an order which differs for each of us. And they are, naturally, historically variable in accordance with the character of the culture and the ideas which rule men's minds. But it obviously does not follow from this that research in the cultural sciences can only have results which are "subjective" in the sense that they are valid for one person and not for others. Only the degree to which they interest different persons varies. In other words, the choice of the object of investigation and the extent or depth to which this investigation attempts to penetrate into the infinite causal web, are determined by the evaluative ideas which dominate the investigator and his age. In the method of investigation, the guiding "point of view" is of great importance for the construction of the conceptual scheme which will be used in the investigation. In the mode of their use, however, the investigator is obviously bound by the norms of our thought just as much here as elsewhere. For scientific truth is precisely what is valid for all who seek the truth.

MARX THEORY OF HISTORY

Marx did not set out his theory of history in great detail. Accordingly it has to be constructed from a variety of texts, both those where he attempts to apply a theoretical analysis to past and future historical events, and those of a more purely theoretical nature. Of the latter, the 1859 Preface to A Critique of Political Economy has achieved canonical status. However The German Ideology, co-written with Engels in 1845, is a vital early source in which Marx first sets out the basics of the outlook of historical materialism. We shall briefly outline both texts, and then look at the reconstruction of Marx's theory of history in the hands of his philosophically most influential recent exponent, G.A. Cohen.

The German Ideology

In The German Ideology Marx and Engels contrast their new materialist method with the idealism which had characterised previous German thought. Accordingly they take pains to set out the 'premises of the materialist method'. They start, they say, from 'real human beings', emphasising that human beings are essentially productive, in that they must produce their means of subsistence in order to satisfy their material needs. The satisfaction of needs engenders new needs of both a material and social kind, and forms of society arise corresponding to the state of development of human productive forces. Material life determines, or at least 'conditions' social life, and so the primary direction of social explanation is from material production to social forms, and thence to forms of consciousness. As the material means of production develop, 'modes of co-operation' or economic structures rise and fall, and eventually communism will become a real possibility once the plight of the workers and their awareness of an alternative motivates them sufficiently to become revolutionaries.

1859 PREFACE

In the sketch of The German Ideology, all the key elements of historical materialism are present, even if the terminology is not yet that of Marx's more mature writings. Marx's statement in 1859 Preface renders much the same view in sharper form. Cohen's reconstruction of Marx's view in the Preface begins from what Cohen calls the Development Thesis, which is presupposed, rather than explicitly stated in the Preface. This is the thesis that the productive forces tend to develop, in the sense of becoming more powerful, over time.

This states not that they always do develop, but that there is a tendency for them to do this. The productive forces are the means of production, together with productively applicable knowledge: technology, in other words. The next thesis is the primacy thesis, which has two aspects. The first states that the nature of the economic structure is explained by the level of development of the productive forces, and the second that the nature of the superstructure-the political and legal institutions of society-is explained by the nature of the economic structure. The nature of a society's ideology is also explained in terms of its economic structure, although this receives less emphasis in Cohen's interpretation.

Revolution and epoch change is understood as the consequence of an economic structure no longer being able to continue to develop the forces of production. At this point the development of the productive forces is said to be fettered, and, according to the theory once an economic structure fetters development it will be revolutionised-'burst asunder'-and eventually replaced with an economic structure better suited to preside over the continued development of the forces of production. In outline, then, the theory has a pleasing simplicity and power. It seems plausible that human productive power develops over time, and plausible too that economic structures exist for as long as they develop the productive forces, but will be replaced when they are no longer capable of doing this. Yet severe problems emerge when we attempt to put more flesh on these bones.

FUNCTIONAL EXPLANATION

Prior to Cohen's work, historical materialism had not been regarded as a coherent view within English-language political philosophy. The antipathy is well summed up with the closing words of H.B. Acton's The Illusion of the Epoch 'Marxism is a philosophical farrago'. One difficulty taken particularly seriously by Cohen is an alleged inconsistency between the explanatory primacy of the forces of production, and certain claims made elsewhere by Marx which appear to give the economic structure primacy in explaining the development of the productive forces. For example, in The Communist Manifesto Marx states that: 'The bourgeoisie cannot exist without constantly revolutionising the instruments of production.' This appears to give causal and explanatory primacy to the economic structure-capitalism-which brings about the development of the forces of production. Cohen accepts that, on the surface at least, this generates a contradiction. Both the economic structure and the development of the productive forces seem to have explanatory priority over each other.

Unsatisfied by such vague resolutions such as 'determination in the last instance', or the idea of 'dialectical' connections, Cohen self-consciously attempts to apply the standards of clarity and rigour of analytic philosophy to provide a reconstructed version of historical materialism. The key theoretical innovation is to appeal to the notion of functional explanation (also sometimes called 'consequence explanation'). The essential move is cheerfully to admit that the economic structure does indeed develop the productive forces, but to add that this, according to the theory, is precisely why we have capitalism (when we do). That is, if capitalism failed to develop the productive forces it would disappear. And, indeed, this fits beautifully with historical materialism. For Marx asserts that when an economic structure fails to develop the productive forces-when it 'fetters' the productive forces-it will be revolutionised and the epoch will change. So the idea of 'fettering' becomes the counterpart to the theory of functional explanation. Essentially fettering is what happens when the economic structure becomes dysfunctional. Now it is apparent that this renders historical materialism consistent. Yet there is a question as to whether it is at too high a price.

For we must ask whether functional explanation is a coherent methodological device. The problem is that we can ask what it is that makes it the case that an economic structure will only persist for as long as it develops the productive forces. Jon Elster has pressed this criticism against Cohen very hard. If we were to argue that there is an agent guiding history who has the purpose that the productive forces should be developed as much as possible then it would make sense that such an agent would intervene in history to carry out this purpose by selecting the economic structures which do the best job. However it is clear that Marx makes no such metaphysical assumptions. Elster is very critical-sometimes of Marx, sometimes of Cohen-of the idea of appealling to 'purposes' in history without those being the purpose of anyone.

Cohen is well aware of this difficulty, but defends the use of functional explanation by comparing its use in historical materialism with its use in evolutionary biology. In contemporary biology it is commonplace to explain the existence of the stripes of a tiger, or the hollow bones of a bird, by pointing to the function of these features. Here we have apparent purposes which are not the purposes of anyone. The obvious counter, however, is that in evolutionary biology we can provide a causal story to underpin these functional explanations; a story involving chance variation and survival of the fittest. Therefore these functional explanations are sustained by a complex causal feedback loop in which dysfunctional elements tend to be filtered out in competition with better functioning elements. Cohen calls such background accounts 'elabourations' and he concedes that functional explanations are in need of elabourations. But he points out that standard causal explanations are equally in need of elabourations.

We might, for example, be satisfied with the explanation that the vase broke because it was dropped on the floor, but a great deal of further information is needed to explain why this explanation works. Consequently Cohen claims that we can be justified in offering a functional explanation even when we are in ignorance of its elabouration. Indeed even in biology we have had detailed causal elabourations of functional explanations only relatively recently. Prior to Darwin, or arguably Lamark, the only candidate causal elabouration was to appeal to God's purposes. Darwin outlined a very plausible mechanism, but having no genetic theory was not able to elabourate it into a detailed account. Our knowledge remains incomplete to this day. Nevertheless it seems perfectly reasonable to say that birds have hollow bones in order to facilitate flight. Cohen's point is that the weight of evidence that organisms are adapted to their environment would permit even a pre-Darwinian atheist to assert this functional explanation with justification. Hence one can be justified in offering a functional explanation even in absence of a candidate elabouration: if there is sufficient weight of inductive evidence.

At this point the issue, then, divides into a theoretical question and an empirical one. The empirical question is whether or not there is evidence that forms of society exist only for as long as they advance productive power, and are replaced by revolution when they fail. Here, one must admit, the empirical record is patchy at best, and there appear to have been long periods of stagnation, even regression, when dysfunctional economic structures were not revolutionised.

The theoretical issue is whether a plausible elabourating explanation is available to underpin Marxist functional explanations. Here there is something of a dilemma. In the first instance it is tempting to try to mimic the elaboration given in the Darwinian story, and appeal to chance variations and survival of the fittest. In this case 'fittest' would mean 'most able to preside over the development of the productive forces'. Chance variation would be a matter of people trying out new types of economic relations. On this account new economic structures begin through experiment, but thrive and persist through their success in developing the productive forces.

However the problem is that this would seem to introduce a larger element of contingency than Marx seeks, for it is essential to Marx's thought that one should be able to predict the eventual arrival of communism. Within Darwinian theory there is no warrant for long-term predictions, for everything depends on the contingencies of particular situations. A similar heavy element of contingency would be inherited by a form of historical materialism developed by analogy with evolutionary biology. The dilemma, then, is that the best model for developing the theory makes predictions based on the theory unsound, yet the whole point of the theory is predictive. Hence one must either look for an alternative means of producing elabourating explanation, or give up the predictive ambitions of the theory.

Rationality

The driving force of history, in Cohen's reconstruction of Marx, is the development of the productive forces, the most important of which is technology. But what is it that drives this? Ultimately, in Cohen's account, it is human rationality. Human beings have the ingenuity to apply themselves to develop means to address the scarcity they find. This on the face of it seems very reasonable.

Yet there are difficulties. As Cohen himself acknowledges, societies do not always do what would be rational for an individual to do. Co-ordination problems may stand in our way, and there may be structural barriers. Furthermore it is relatively rare for those who introduce new technologies to be motivated by the need to address scarcity. Rather, under capitalism, the profit motive is the key. Of course it might be argued that this is the social form that the material need to address scarcity takes under capitalism.

But still one may raise the question whether the need to address scarcity always has the influence that it appears to have taken on in modern times. For example, a ruling class's absolute determination to hold on to power may have led to economically stagnant societies.

Alternatively it might be thought that a society may put religion or the protection of traditional ways of life ahead of economic needs. This goes to the heart of Marx's theory that man is an essentially productive being and that the locus of interaction with the world is industry. As Cohen himself later argued in his essays such as 'Reconsidering Historical Materialism' this may appear one-sided, and ignore other powerful elements in human nature. This criticism chimes with a criticism from the previous section; that the historical record may not, in fact, display the tendency to growth in the productive forces assumed by the theory.

MORALITY

The issue of Marx and morality poses a conundrum. On reading Marx's works at all periods of his life, there appears to be the strongest possible distaste towards bourgeois capitalist society, and an undoubted endorsement of future communist society. Yet the terms of this antipathy and endorsement are far from clear. Despite expectations, Marx never says that capitalism is unjust to the workers. Neither does he say that communism would be a just form of society. In fact he takes pains to distance himself from those who engage in a discourse of justice, and makes a conscious attempt to exclude direct moral commentary in his own works. The puzzle is why this should be, given the weight of indirect moral commentary one finds. There are, initially, separate questions, concerning Marx's attitude to capitalism and to communism. There are also separate questions concerning his attitude to ideas of justice, and to ideas of morality more broadly concerned. This, then, generates four questions: (1) Did Marx think capitalism unjust?; (2) did he think that capitalism could be morally criticised on other grounds?; (3) did he think that communism would be just? (4) did he think it could be morally approved of on other grounds? These are the questions we shall consider in this section.

The initial argument that Marx must have thought that capitalism is unjust is based on the observation that Marx argued that all capitalist profit is ultimately derived from the exploitation of the worker. Capitalism's dirty secret is that it is not a realm of harmony and mutual benefit but a system in which one class systematically extracts profit from another. How could this fail to be unjust? Yet it is notable that Marx never concludes this, and in Capital he goes as far as to say that such exchange is 'by no means an injustice'.

Allen Wood has argued that Marx took this approach because his general theoretical standpoint excludes any trans-epochal standpoint from which one can comment on the justice of an economic system. Even though one can criticize particular behaviour from within an economic structure as unjust (and theft under capitalism would be an example of this) it is not possible to criticise capitalism as a whole. This is a consequence of Marx's analysis of the role of ideas of justice from within historical materialism. That is to say, juridicial institutions are part of the superstructure, and ideas of justice are ideological, and the role of both the superstructure and ideology, in the functionalist reading of historical materialism adopted here, is to stabilise the economic structure. Consequently to state that something is just under capitalism is simply a judgement applied to those elements of the system that will tend to have the effect of advancing capitalism. This is further explained through Marx's dictum that in any society the ruling ideas are those of the ruling class; the core of the theory of ideology.

Ziyad Husami, however, argues that Wood is mistaken, ignoring the fact that for Marx ideas undergo a double determination in that the ideas of the non-ruling class may be very different from those of the ruling class. Of course it is the ideas of the ruling class that receive attention and implementation, but this does not mean that other ideas do not exist. Husami goes as far as to argue that members of the proletariat under capitalism have an account of justice which matches communism. From this privileged standpoint of the proletariat, which is also Marx's standpoint, capitalism is unjust, and so it follows that Marx thought capitalism unjust.

Plausible though it may sound, Husami's argument fails to account for two related points. First, it cannot explain why Marx never described capitalism as unjust, and second it does not account for the distance Marx wanted to place between his own scientific socialism, and that of the utopian socialists who argued for the injustice of capitalism. Hence one cannot avoid the conclusion that the 'official' view of Marx is that capitalism is not unjust.

Nevertheless, this leaves us with a puzzle. Much of Marx's description of capitalism-his use of the words 'embezzlement', 'robbery' and 'exploitation' &mdash belie the official account. In my view the only satisfactory way of understanding this issue is, once more, from G.A. Cohen who proposes that Marx believed that capitalism was unjust, but did not believe that he believed it was unjust. In other words Marx, like so many of us, did not have perfect knowledge of his own mind. In his explicit reflections on the justice of capitalism he was able to maintain his official view. But in less guarded moments his real view slips out, even if never in explicit language. Such an interpretation is bound to be controversial, but it makes good sense of the texts.Whatever one concludes on the question of whether Marx thought capitalism unjust, it is, nevertheless, obvious that Marx thought that capitalism was not the best way for human beings to live. Here points made in his early writings remain present throughout his writings, if no longer connected to an explicit theory of alientation. The worker finds work a torment, suffers poverty, overwork and lack of fulfilment and freedom. People do not relate to each as humans should.

Does this amount to a moral criticism of capitalism or not? In the absence of any special reason to argue otherwise, it simply seems obvious that Marx's critique is a moral one. Capitalism impedes human flourishing. Marx, though, once more refrained from making this explicit; he seemed to show no interest in locating his criticism of capitalism in any of the traditions of moral philosophy, or explaining how he was generating a new tradition. There may have been two reasons for his caution. The first was that while there were bad things about capitalism there is, from a world historical point of view, much good about it too. For without capitalism communism would not be possible. Capitalism is to be transcended, not abolished, and this may be difficult to convey in the terms of moral philosophy.

Second, and perhaps more importantly, we need to return to the contrast between scientific and utopian socialism. The utopians appealled to universal ideas of truth and justice to defend their proposed schemes, and their theory of transition was based on the idea that appealing to moral sensibilities would be the best, perhaps only, way of bringing about the new chosen society. Marx wanted to distance himself from this tradition of utopian thought, and the key point of distinction was to argue that the route to understanding the possibilities of human emancipation lay in the analysis of historical and social forces, not in morality. Hence, for Marx, any appeal to morality was theoretically a backward step.

This leads us now to Marx's assessment of communism. Would communism be a just society? In considering Marx's attitude to communism and justice there are really only two viable possibilities: either he thought that communism would be a just society or he thought that the concept of justice would not apply: that communism would transcend justice. Communism is described by Marx, in the Critique of the Gotha Programme, as a society in which each person should contribute according to their ability and receive according to their need. This certainly sounds like a theory of justice, and could be adopted as such. However it is possibly truer to Marx's thought to say that this is part of an account in which communism transcends justice, as Lukes has argued.

If we start with the idea that the point of ideas of justice is to resolve disputes, then a society without disputes would have no need or place for justice. We can see this by reflecting upon Hume's idea of the circumstances of justice. Hume argued that if there was enormous material abundance-if everyone could have whatever they wanted without invading another's share-we would never have devised rules of justice. And, of course, Marx often suggested that communism would be a society of such abundance.

But Hume also suggested that justice would not be needed in other circumstances; if there were complete fellow-feeling between all human beings. Again there would be no conflict and no need for justice. Of course one can argue whether either material abundance or human fellow-feeling to this degree would be possible, but the point is that both arguments give a clear sense in which communism transcends justice.

Nevertheless we remain with the question of whether Marx thought that communism could be commended on other moral grounds. One compelling argument is that Marx's career simply makes no sense unless we can attribute this belief to him. But beyond this we can be brief in that the considerations adduced in section 2 above apply again. Communism clearly advances human flourishing, in Marx's view. The only reason for denying that, in Marx's vision, it would amount to a good society is a theoretical antipathy to the word 'good'. And here the main point is that, in Marx's view, communism would not be brought about by high-minded benefactors of humanity. Quite possibly his determination to retain this point of difference between himself and the Utopian socialists led him to disparage the importance of morality to a degree that goes beyond the call of theoretical necessity. Karl Marx and Friedrich Engels strove to put into practical effect the humanitarian concept of

Feuerbach. In so doing, they founded a new economic movement called Socialism. According to Marx, the supreme end of man is an immanent and material one, and consists in happiness. This material happiness must be obtained through organized collectivism. In fact, according to Marx, reality is governed by economic needs (historical materialism). Economic reality develops according to Hegel's dialectical principles; that is, reality must deny itself in order to reach a higher degree of being.

In application, this principle means that the present organization of society must be destroyed (even through violent revolution, if necessary, because only through such destruction can a better political, economic, and social organization be achieved. To establish this new format of society, working men (the proletariat) must be organized and take up the struggle against the capitalists who defraud them. Thus the actors in this drama are the social classes--the proletariat is arrayed against capitalism. This struggle, according to Marx and Engels, will end in victory for the proletariat, that is, in the triumph of universal Socialism.

LIFE AND WORKS

Karl Marx (picture) was born on May 5, 1818 and died on March 14, 1883. He was a German economist, philosopher, and revolutionist whose writings form the basis of the body of ideas known as Marxism. With the aid of Friedrich Engels (picture) he produced much of the theory of modern socialism and communism. Marx's father, Heinrich, was a Jewish lawyer who had converted his family to Christianity partly in order to preserve his job in the Prussian state. Karl himself was baptized in the Evangelical church. As a student at the University of Berlin, young Marx was strongly influenced by the philosophy of Georg Hegel and by a radical group called Young Hegelians, who attempted to apply Hegelian ideas to the movement against organized religion and the Prussian autocracy. In 1841, Marx received a doctorate in philosophy.

In 1842, Marx became editor of the Rheinische Zeitung in Cologne, a liberal democratic newspaper for which he wrote increasingly radical editorials on social and economic issues. The newspaper was banned by the Prussian government in

1843, and Marx left for Paris with his bride, Jenny von Westphalen. There he went further in his criticism of society, building on the Young Hegelian criticism of religion. Ludwig Feuerbach had written a book called The Essence of Christianity, arguing that God had been invented by humans as a projection of their own ideals. Feuerbach wrote that man, however, in creating God in his own image, had "alienated himself from himself." He had created another being in contrast to himself, reducing himself to a lowly, evil creature who needed both church and government to guide and control him. If religion were abolished, Feuerbach claimed, human beings would overcome their alienation.

Marx applied this idea of alienation to private property, which he said caused humans to work only for themselves, not for the good of their species. In his papers of this period, published as Economic and Philosophic Manuscripts of 1844, he elabourated on the idea that alienation had an economic base. He called for a communist society to overcome the dehumanizing effect of private property. In 1845, Marx moved to Brussels, and in 1847 he went to London. He had previously made friends with Friedrich Engels, the son of a wealthy textile manufacturer who, like himself, had been a Young Hegelian. They collabourated on a book which was a criticism of some of their Young Hegelian friends for their stress on alienation.

In 1845, Marx jotted down some notes, Theses on Feuerbach, which he and Engels enlarged into a book, The German Ideology, in which they developed their materialistic conception of history. They argued that human thought was determined by social and economic forces, particularly those related to the means of production. They developed a method of analysis they called dialectical materialism, in which the clash of historical forces leads to changes in society. In 1847 a London organization of workers invited Marx and Engels to prepare a program for them. It appeared in 1848 as The Communist Manifesto. In it they declared that all history was the history of class struggles. Under capitalism, the struggle between the working class and the business class would end in a new society, a communist one. The outbreak of the Revolutions of 1848 in Europe led Marx to return to Cologne, where he began publication of the Neue Rheinische Zeitung, but with the failure of the German liberal democratic movement he moved permanently, in 1849, to London. For many years he and his family lived in poverty, aided by small subventions from Engels and by bequests from the relatives of Marx's wife. From 1851 to 1862 he contributed articles and editorials to The New York Tribune, then edited by Horace Greeley. Most of his time, however, was spent in the British Museum, studying economic and social history and developing his theories. Marx's ideas began to influence a group of workers and German emigres in London, who established the International Workingmen's Association in 1864, later known as the First International. By the time of the brief Commune of Paris in 1871, Marx's name had begun to be well known in European political circles. A struggle developed within the International between Marx and the Russian anarchist Mikhail Bakunin, whom Marx eventually defeated and expelled, at the cost of destroying the International.

In 1867, Marx published the first volume of Das Kapital. The next two volumes, edited by Engels, were published after Marx's death. The fourth volume was edited by Karl Kautsky. Marx's last years were marked by illness and depression. Marx continued to write treatises on socialism, urging that his followers disdain softhearted bourgeois tendencies. At Marx's funeral in Highgate Cemetery in London, Engels spoke of him as "the best-hated and most-calumniated man of his time." The importance of Marx's thought, however, extends far beyond the revolutionary movements whose prophet he became. His writings on economics and sociology are still influential in academic circles and among many who do not share his political views. The main philosophical works of Karl Marx that are of interest to most students are the Communist Manifesto and Das Kapital.

ECONOMIC SOCIOLOGY

Economic sociology studies the social effects of economic phenomena, particularly with respect to the concept of modernity and its constituent aspects (rationalisation, secularisation, urbanisation, and so on). The term “economic sociology” was first coined by William Stanley Jevons in 1879, later to be used in the works of Emile Durkheim, Max Weber and Georg Simmel between 1890 and 1920.

Theory

Economic sociology arose as a new approach to the analysis of economic phenomena; emphasising particularly the role economic structures and institutions play upon society, and the influence a society holds over the nature of economic structures and institutions. The relationship between capitalism and modernity is a salient issue, perhaps best demonstrated in Weber's *The Protestant Ethic and the Spirit of Capitalism* (1905) and Simmel's *The Philosophy of Money* (1900). Economic sociology may be said to have begun with Tocqueville's *Democracy in America* (1835-40) and *The Old Regime and the Revolution* (1856). Marx's historical materialism would attempt to demonstrate how economic forces influence the structure of society on a fundamental level. Emile Durkheim's *The Division of Labour in Society* was published in 1922, whilst Max Weber's *Economy and Society* was released in the same year.

Contemporary economic sociology focuses particularly on the social consequences of economic exchanges, the social meanings they involve and the social interactions they facilitate or obstruct. Influential figures in modern economic sociology include Fred L. Block, James S. Coleman, Mark Granovetter, Harrison White, Paul DiMaggio, Joel M. Podolny, Richard Swedberg and Viviana Zelizer in the United States, as well as Luc Boltanski, Laurent Thevenot, or Jens Beckert in Europe. To this may be added Amitai Etzioni, who has popularised the idea of socioeconomics, and Chuck Sabel and Wolfgang Streeck, who work in the tradition of political economy/sociology.

The focus on mathematical analysis and utility maximisation during the 20th century has led some to see economics as a discipline moving away from its roots in the social sciences. Many critiques of economics or economic policy begin from the accusation that abstract modelling is missing some key social phenomenon that needs to be addressed. In reply, many mainstream economists point out that such cultural and social arguments often seem to favour the interests of local monopolists and the already powerful.

Economic sociology is an attempt by sociologists to redefine in sociological terms questions traditionally addressed by economists. It is also an answer to attempts by economists (such as Gary Becker) to bring economic approaches-in particular utility maximisation and game theory-to the analysis of social situations that are not obviously related to production or trade. Karl Polanyi, in his book *The Great Transformation*, was the first theorist to come up with the idea of the "embeddedness", meaning that the economy is "embedded" in social institutions which is vital so that the market does not destroy other aspects of human life.

Marxist Sociology

Modern Marxist thought has focused on the social implications of consumerism (or "commodity fetishism") and economic development within the system of economic relations that produce them. Important theorists include Georg Lukács, Theodor Adorno, Max Horkheimer, Walter Benjamin, Guy Debord, Louis Althusser, Nicos Poulantzas, Ralph Miliband, Jürgen Habermas, Raymond Williams, Fredric Jameson, Antonio Negri, and Stuart Hall.

7

Rise of Sociology as an Intellectual Tradition

Since ancient times man has been interested in issues of his own living among other people. Why do people try to join living with other people, not without? What makes them fix borders, form separate states and struggle with each other? Why do some people possess all benefits, others are deprived of them? Searching for answers to these questions forced ancient thinkers to focus their attention on man and the society where he lives in. Emergence of sociology is obliged to the concept "society", its theoretical development and use in practice. Attempts to comprehend optimal ways of governing, social order, people's effective activities were first made by ancient Chinese and Indian philosophers.

Antique philosophers made their contribution by suggesting new ideas which are now considered fundamentals of sociology. For instance, Plato and Aristotle developed a doctrine of human and the society; their works initiated studies of certain social institutions such as the state, family and law.

Following the principle of social division of labour, *Plato* (427-347 BC) created a first in the world theory of stratification according to which the society is divided into three classes: higher class consisting of wise men who govern the state; middle class or warriors who defend the society from disorder, and lower class consisting of craftsmen and peasants. Anyway, in his theory there was no place for slaves whose destiny was hard work considered as unworthy by free citizens.

Aristotle considered middle class a foot-hold of order. To his mind, the state is better governed if egoistic interests of the rich are limited, the poor are not excluded from government, and middle class is greater and stronger than the rich and the poor.

Traditionally the origins of sociology are seen in European philosophy of the XVIII century, a period that is referred to as the Age of Enlightenment or the Age of Reason. This movement advocated rationality as a means to establish an authoritative system of ethics, aesthetics, and knowledge. The intellectual leaders of this movement regarded themselves as courageous and elite, and saw their purpose as leading the world toward progress and out of a long period of doubtful tradition, full of irrationality, superstition and tyranny. The Enlightenment also provided a framework for the American and French Revolutions, as well as leading to the rise of capitalism and birth of socialism. The XVIII century also saw a continued rise of empirical philosophical ideas, and their application to political economy, government and sciences such as physics, chemistry and biology. However, investigations of this age were far from being systemic and integral. Lots of important issues were not paid attention to, that's why achievements in learning social phenomena were less considerable as compared to other sciences.

Of utmost interest of the period became study of social communities and processes of their development and functioning. The study was caused by two factors. The first factor was industrial development of European countries; the second one was that all spheres of human activities became more complicated that raised problems of people's interactions and their government, creation of social order in the society etc. When problems were realized and sounded, prerequisites for developing a new science appeared, science which could study groups of people and their behaviour in groups, human interactions and their results.

As origins of sociology are seen in spiritual and political ideas of the Enlightenment and reaction to the French Revolution, French thinkers, English and German philosophers who worked and created in that period are considered direct predecessors of sociological knowledge.

Of German philosophers *Immanuel Kant* (1724-1804) is more often recollected due to his contribution to development of social problems, in particular problems of personality. Kant believed that man is an ambivalent being by his nature: he is both good and bad, honest and dishonest, fair and unfair, free and dependent. To his mind, man's natural negative character is hidden and displayed in those living conditions which make man reveal his vices. But man is striving for self-perfection and his ally is reason that helps man to overcome his negative qualities. Kant considered that harmony between human and the society is achieved if man overcomes his vices by obeying laws and moral norms.

Georg Hegel (1770-1831) made this dialectics more generalized. His aim was to define basic determinants of historic development so that he could examine peculiarities of its realization in different historic periods and show correlation of historic necessity and people's conscious activities. He drew a picture of social reality all parts of which (objective and subjective, dynamic and static, material and ideal) are interrelated by a dialectic method.

Of French philosophers one can mention *Charles Montesquieu, Jean-Jacques Rousseau, Saint-Simon* and others. *Ch. Montesquieu* (1689-1755) underlined importance of comparative research of social phenomena. *J.-J. Rousseau* (1712-1778) distinguished classes in the society and believed that man's nature is good but man is "spoilt" by the society. Into the basis of harmonic arrangement of the society he put social agreement, i.e. consensus of people as reflection of their common will which is expressed in laws.

Saint-Simon (1760-1825) was possibly the first to suggest planning as a way to run economy. To his mind, social problems could be solved by moral and religious reforming, based on employers' good will to better the working conditions. In the book the thinkers suggested an idea of developing a new science of the society which, by analogy with physics, should be based on observation, experiment and other methods of natural sciences. Initially, the science was given the name of *social physics*.

By that time a social theory presented a mixed spectrum of various views in which both basic and additional motives were combined; basic motives bore rational and irrational character while economic, political, legal and moral interests constituted the entity of additional ones. Those views reflected thinkers and researchers' outlook, their ideological positions and ways of studying social problems.

In this context legacy by *A. Comte* (1798-1857), the initiator of sociology, was not an exception. There are two reasons why A. Comte is acknowledged as the founding father of sociology. First, he developed a systematic and hierarchical classification of all sciences and by including sociology into them, he gave grounds for establishing its autonomy as a discipline; second, in 1839 he changed the name of social physics into sociology. His fundamental works are *Cours de philosophie positive* in 6 volumes (1830-1842), *Système de politique positive* (1850-1854).

A. Comte's legacy includes the law of three phases, his contribution to further development of the theory of an industrial society started by Saint-Simon. It is by his statement of this law that he is best known in the English-speaking world. The law says that the society has gone through three phases:

1. theological, or military authority;
2. metaphysical, or feudal authority;
3. scientific, or positive phase seen as an industrial civilization.

In the theological phase man's place in the society and the society's restrictions upon man were referred to God. The metaphysic phase involved justification of universal rights as something on a higher plane than the authority of any human ruler could countermand. The scientific phase is that one in which people could find solutions to social problems and bring them into force despite of the proclamations of human rights or prophecy of the will of God. For its time, the idea of a scientific phase was considered up-to-date.

A. Comte also formulated the law of three phases: human development (social progress) progresses from a theological stage, in which nature was mythically conceived and man sought the explanation of natural phenomena from supernatural beings, through a metaphysical stage in which nature was conceived of as a result of obscure forces and man sought the explanation of natural phenomena from them to the final positive stage in which all abstract and obscure forces are discarded, and natural phenomena are explained by their constant relationship. This progress is forced through the development of human mind and increasing application of thought, reasoning and logic to the understanding of world. Due to it, A. Comte thought that industrialization is the result of a scientific way of thinking spread out in all spheres of human life but not of technical and economic progress.

However, he rejected the role of general theory in sociology: instead of theoretic generalization of empiric data to make up a whole of them, he presented the society as a simple entity of interconnected facts. He didn't clearly determine the subject of a new science; either he didn't find its scientific method to learn laws of social development.

A great contribution to establishing the methodological basis of sociology, mostly its empiric basis, was made by *Lambert Ketle* (1796-1874), a French and Belgian mathematician and statistician. He brought in new theoretic and methodological ideas and a new sample of research aimed at solving certain applied problems. His achievements in sociology are as follows:

- discovery of statistical laws;
- understanding a social law as a stable tendency of changing means;
- methodical recommendations how to formulate questions in forms and questionnaires.

Herbert Spencer (1820-1903), a British philosopher, is also acknowledged as one of the founders of sociology as he published a number of works devoted to different domains, such as *Principles of Sociology* and *Principles of Ethics*. They included his ideas on evolution, that's why H. Spencer is seen as the originator of the scientific perspective called Social Darwinism. Furthermore, his major works predated those of Charles Darwin. H. Spencer's book, *First Principles*, is an exposition of the evolutionary principles underlying all domains of reality. It was H. Spencer, *not* Ch. Darwin who coined the phrase "survival of the fittest", as well as popularizing of the term "evolution".

H. Spencer considered the society as an organism made up of systems subdivided into smaller ones. The inner system performs the function of preserving the organism by adaptation to the conditions of "subsistence"; the external system performs the function of regulation and control between the subsystems and milieu; the intermediate system is in charge of distribution, transit and communication. By this approach to the study of the society H. Spencer marked the basic elements of functionalism, later developed by other researchers: a systemic character of the society as a totality of actions which are not reduced to the actions of individuals; the conception of the system's structure that is built due differentiation and stabilized through integration.

H. Spencer used the criterion of comparative meaning to classify societies as military and industrial ones. Military societies have common systems of belief, people interact due to violence and compulsion, in other words, people exist for the state. Industrial societies, in which the economic system dominates, are characterized by democratic principles, diversity of belief systems, people's interactions are voluntary: the state is for people. Human development progresses from military societies to industrial ones, although a return to military forms can't be excluded. Besides, H. Spencer believed that social order in industrial societies could not be adequately explained as an outcome of contractual agreements between people motivated by self-interests.

Criticizing H. Spencer's conceptions, modern sociologists agree that alongside with Marxism it was the first experience of combining a historical-evolutionary approach to analyze social phenomena with a structural-functional one.

Classical Tradition in Sociology

A classical tradition in any science is often connected with institutionalization of its knowledge. And sociology was not an exception. Its classical tradition started with the theories worked out by E. Durkheim, K. Marx, M. Weber, G. Simmel and other celebrities.

A French thinker *Emile Durkheim* (1858-1917) is widely acknowledged as a founding father of modern sociology, who helped to define the subject-matter of sociology and establish its autonomy as a discipline.

In his doctrine of *social realism* E. Durkheim saw the domain of sociology as the study of social facts, not individuals.

He believed that societies had their own realities which could not simply be reduced to the actions and motives of people, and peopele were molded and constrained by their social settings. In his work, *The Rules of Sociological Method* (1895), he demonstrated that law was a social fact, embodied in formal, codified rules and not dependent on humans or on any particular act of law enforcement for its existence. He came to see social norms as regulating people's behaviour by means of institutionalized values which the human internalized, rather than the society simply acting as an external constraint.

In another work, *The Division of Labour in Society* (1893), E. Durkheim argued against H. Spencer's understanding of social order in industrial societies. To his mind, a pursuit of self-interest would lead to social instability, as manifest in various forms of social deviance such as suicide. He distinguished two forms of social order found in primitive and modern societies. In primitive societies he identified mechanical solidarity which was based on common beliefs and consensus found in collective consciousness.

As societies become industrialized and more complex, the increasing division of labour destroys mechanical solidarity and moral integration, thus rendering social order problematic. E. Durkheim was well aware that industrial societies exhibited many conflicts and that force was an important factor in preventing social disruption. He believed, however, that in advanced societies a new form of order would arise on the basis of organic solidarity. It would comprise the interdependence of economic ties arising out of differentiation and specialization within modern economy, a new network of occupational associations such as guilds that would link people to the state, and the emergence of collectively created moral restraints on egoism within these associations.

Anyway, the main idea of his work may be expressed in the following statements:

- division of labour leads to cohesion;
- division of labour gradually replaces religion as the basis of social cohesion. This process of change gives rise to social difficulties that result in anomie, or feeling of aimlessness or despair.

In *Suicide* (1897), which represents the most influential sociological contribution to this issue, E. Durkheim explained how even apparently individual decisions to commit a suicide could be understood as being affected by different forms of social solidarity in different social settings. In identifying types of suicide he used the suicide statistics of different societies and different groups within them.

Karl Marx (1818-1883) is generally viewed as political scientist, economist and sociologist although he was not of high opinion about the sociology of A. Comte that expressed interests and consciousness of the bourgeoisie. *Marxist sociology* is materialistic interpretation of history (which F. Engels adapted as dialectical materialism) which was certainly influenced by G. Hegel's claim that reality (and history) should be viewed dialectically, through a clash of opposing forces. K. Marx asserted that "philosophers have only interpreted the world in various ways; the point however is to change it", and he clearly dedicated himself to trying to change the world. The researcher believed that he could study history and the society scientifically and discern tendencies of history and the resulting outcome of social conflicts.

Marxist analysis of history is based on a distinction between means of production, or land, natural resources, and technology that are necessary for the production of material goods, and social relations of production, i.e. social relationships people enter into as they acquire and use means of production. Together these comprise the mode of production. For K. Marx, the society is a system of social relations (economic, political, legal etc.) where the subjects of social relations are groups of people, or classes and individuals. He asserted that the economy determines the social structure in the statement about the economic basis and superstructure, i.e. social, cultural and political phenomena are determined by the mode of production. To his mind, economic, cultural, and political changes go together in coherent patterns, and they are linked because economic and technological changes determine political and cultural changes.

K. Marx observed that within any given society the mode of production changes, and European societies had progressed from a feudal mode of production to a capitalist one. In general, he believed that the means of production change more rapidly than the relations of production. A proof is that we develop a new technology, such as the Internet, and only later laws to regulate that technology are developed. For K. Marx, the mismatch between the basis and superstructure, or between economic and social, is a major source of social disruption and conflict. As for social conflict, it was Karl Marx who provided extensive work on conflict theory relating to the economic basis of the society in relation to social classes. He basically highlighted class struggle and supported the working class for a healthy society.

However, K. Marx was rather pessimistic about capitalism because he witnessed ruin of peasantry and rapid enrichment of the bourgeoisie, growth of poverty and crime in towns etc. That's why he put forward a new approach to social development, that of destroying the old society and substituting it with a new one, more fair. In other words, advocating revolutionary change of the society K. Marx used the conflict perspective, that's why he is regarded an initiator of the theory of social conflict.

An Italian scientist *Vilfredo Pareto* (1848-1923) made several important contributions to economics, sociology and moral philosophy, especially in the study of income distribution and in the analysis of individuals' choices. He introduced the concept of Pareto efficiency and helped to develop the field of microeconomics with ideas such as indifference curves. He is well known for the observation that 20% of the population owned 80% of the property in Italy, later generalized (by Joseph Juran and others) into the Pareto principle, and generalized further to the concept of a Pareto distribution. The Pareto index is a measure of inequality of income distribution.

Pareto's social policies were put on paper in his work, *Mind and Society*, in which he discussed questions of elites and elitism. *Elite* is a selected group of people whose personal abilities, specialized training or other attributes place them at the top of any field. *Elitism* is a belief or attitude that elite are the people whose views on a matter are to be taken most seriously, or who are alone fit to govern. Thus, elite is seen as occupying a special position of authority or privilege in a group, set apart from the majority of people who do not match up with their abilities or attributes. Members of inherited elite are called aristocrats.

Abilities or attributes that identify elite vary. They include:

- high level of academic qualifications,
- high level of experience in a given field,
- high intelligence,
- high natural abilities such as athletic abilities,
- high creativity,
- good taste,
- claimed God-given qualities, abilities, or status.

Commonly, large amount of personal wealth, often assessed as a reward of elite qualities by those who are impressed by it, are insufficient on their own, as every nouveau riche can attest. Elitism takes many forms, some of which are positive and some negative. Positive forms of elitism are formed in situations in which members of a community with special abilities or special qualifications are afforded greater respect in honour of their abilities or qualifications. Their position in the top of their field is used in order to benefit everybody.

Negative forms of elitism are formed when a group of people with high abilities or attributes conspire to give themselves extra privileges at the expense of all other people. This form of elitism may be described as discrimination.

At times elitism is closely related to social class and stratification. V. Pareto thought that a social system is in constant circulation as the elites are transformed-the old ones decline, the new ones emerge, so the elite circulation takes place. Thus, the society should be considered "the cemetery of elites". V. Pareto asserted that the bourgeoisie which emerged as new aristocracy, or elite as a result of the French revolution, threatens to collapse. For him, revolutions were also circulation of elites as a dominant social class is opposed not by the population but by a new elite which is supported by the population and which comes further and further from it as far as it gets more access to power. The question sounded in E. Durkheim's theory "How is order possible?" in V. Pareto's theory would sound as "How is the society governed?"

It was inevitable in the circumstances that to certain theorists the society should present a picture not of harmony and unity, but of conflict and struggle. *Ludwig Gumplowicz*

(1838-1909), a Polish-Austrian sociologist, was among them. He is well-known for his theory presented in his work, *Race conflict* (1883). In the history of mankind L. Gumplowicz sees a never-ending conflict of hordes, tribes, races, classes and other groups. These struggles may change their forms, but they never change their essential character – the exploitation of the weak by the strong. In other words, a conflict between groups results in subordination of one group by another of which supremacy relations arise, and it serves as the basis for establishing the state. The scientist held that social development rose out of conflict, first among races, then among states, then among other social groups. This is the essence of the sociological theory of the state by L. Gumplowicz which asserts that the state is based on power, and this contradicts the theory of contractual agreements.

In the long run, his views were oriented to give proofs to the theses on inevitability of a social conflict determined by social and biological inequality of races. However, a proposition stating that social groups are basic factors of social life makes sociology of L. Gumplowicz tied up with the present. If to differentiate two theoretic aspects in sociology – the theory of integration and the theory of conflict, the Polish-Austrian researcher can be considered the founding father of the latter.

Maximilian Weber (1864-1920), an outstanding classic of German sociology, is acknowledged as one of the founders of a modern study of sociology and public administration. His three main themes were the effect of religious ideas on economic activities, the relation between social stratification and religious ideas, and the distinguished characteristics of Western civilization.

Weberian sociology is based on the concept of social action understood as behaviour to which human beings attach a specific meaning or set of meanings. It is also behaviour that is guided by or takes account of behaviour of other people (either as individuals or as a group). Meaningful social behaviour, or social action thus contrasts with nonsocial or reactive behaviour, undertaken automatically in response to some stimulus.

Just as people act on the basis of meaning, it's important to understand the source of these meanings and thus motivation behind human social behaviour. To reveal the basis of social action M. Weber used a method of analysis called *Verstehen* (to understand), whereby the motivations of human social behaviour may be fruitfully revealed to the observer. That's why his sociology is often called *Understanding* or *Interpretative Sociology*. It states that any research can never be fully inductive or descriptive without a conceptual apparatus. This apparatus was identified by the sociologist as the *ideal type*. The idea can be summarized as follows: an ideal type is formed of characteristics and elements of the given phenomena but it is not meant to correspond to all of the characteristics of a particular case. For instance, a choleric is a hot, fussy, easy-going person, but a particular individual, John by name, may be a difficult man to get on with. Although being an abstraction, it is essential to understand any particular social phenomena because, unlike physical phenomena, they involve human behaviour which must be interpreted by ideal types.

To M. Weber, social actions fall into four basic types:

(1) action oriented by expectations of behaviour of other people in the surrounding milieu. It means that an individual is rational as he clearly sees the aim, means for its achievement and foresees other people's reaction to it; the criterion of rationality is success;

(2) action oriented to some absolute value as embodied in some ethical, aesthetic, or religious code. In other words, action which is morally guided, and not undertaken simply for one's own gain;

(3) action guided by emotive response to or feelings about the surrounding milieu;

(4) action performed as part of long-standing societal tradition.

Of these four types, the last two are non-social behaviour whereas the first two types are inherently more social forms of human action, because they involve subjective assessment and result from the process of rationalization. Anyway, M. Weber never asserted that any of these types could operate independently of one another in the human individual. Typically, social action is guided by some combination of motivations, including both rational (the first and second types) and non-rational elements (the third and fourth types). M. Weber examined the concept of social action within a number of sociological fields, from class behaviour to politics and religion. Its best-known example is contained in his famous work, *The Protestant Ethic and the Spirit of Capitalism* (1904), in which the sociologist examines the motivation behind social action in the economic sphere. Specifically, he suggests that the spirit that drives modern capitalistic enterprise is motivated by the ethical doctrine of Protestantism.

M. Weber notes a relationship between the zeal for business profit and membership in specific Protestant denominations in Europe in the XVII century. This attitude toward moneymaking is embraced not only by the so-called captains of industry but by ordinary workers and peasants. For M. Weber, this suggests the existence of a new attitude toward work, the one in which the pursuit of gain (living to labour) has gained supremacy over the more traditional view that sees work simply as necessary for survival (labouring to live). This new way of thinking which M. Weber dubs the "spirit of capitalism" appears concurrently with basic changes in religious thinking brought about by the Reformation. Such changes are connected with two prominent developments introduced by Martin Luther and John Calvin. What both M. Luther's and J. Calvin's teachings contributed was the emergence of a new type of Christian – Protestant who valued work as a moral duty, lived an ascetic lifestyle, and as a result achieved considerable success in material terms. This in turn came to be viewed as a sign of God's favour – if one works hard, he will be saved. The notion of predestination became generally accepted that salvation was attainable, but only through a life of "good work".

Ultimately the legacy of early Protestantism, in terms how it motivated capitalistic economic behaviour, became widespread in the Western world. At the same time, individuals largely came to reject the religious roots of the spirit of capitalism and instead became increasingly consumed by the secular passion for profit and acquisition of material goods. That's why M. Weber defines "the spirit of capitalism" as the ideas and habits that favour the rational pursuit of economic gain. And among the tendencies identified by the researcher is a greed for profit with minimum effort, an idea that work is a burden to be avoided, especially when it exceeds what is enough for modest life. In the studies of politics and government, M. Weber unveils the definition of the state that has become so pivotal to Western social thought – the state is that entity which possesses a monopoly on the legitimate use of physical force. Politics is understood as any activity in which the state might engage itself in order to influence the relative distribution of force. Politics thus comes to be understood as deriving from power. M. Weber is also well-known for his study of bureaucratization of the society so many aspects of modern public administration go back to him. In his work, *Economy and Society* (1922), he outlines a description of rationalization (of which bureaucratization is a part) as a shift from a value-oriented organization and action (traditional authority and charismatic authority) to a goal-oriented organization and action (legal-rational authority). The result is that increasing rationalization of human life traps individuals in an "iron cage" of rule-based, rational control.

Georg Simmel (1858-1918) is a German-Jewish sociologist and economist, who analyzed the impact of money relations and division of labour on human culture and alienation of labour in his main work, *The Philosophy of Money* (1890). Through the prism of money G. Simmel considered hidden mechanisms of social life and manifestation of various forms of labour. For him, money is both a pure form of economic relations and economic value. According to G. Simmel, values are fundamental, underlying relations in the society. Another German sociologist *Ferdinand Toennies* (1855-1936) is best known for his distinction between two types of social groups – *communityGemeinschaft or and Gesellschaft* or society. This distinction is based on the assumption that there are only two basic forms of an actor's will. Following his essential will, an actor sees himself as a means to serve the goals of the social group; very often it is an underlying, subconscious force. A group formed around an essential will is called *Gemeinschaft*. Of another type is an arbitrary will: an actor sees a social group as a means to further his individual goals; so it is purposive and future-oriented. A group formed around the arbitrary will is called *Gesellschaft*. Whereas the membership in *Gemeinschaft* is self-fulfilling, *Gesellschaft* is instrumental for its members. In pure sociology (theoretically) these two normal types of will are to be strictly separated; in applied sociology (empirically) they are always mixed.

Thorstein Veblen (1857-1929), an American sociologist, is considered the founding father of the institutional approach due to his study of social institutions. In his central work, *The Theory of the Leisure Class* (1899), he defined a social institution as social patterns of human behaviour and habits of thinking. According to him, mankind and human civilization develop as far as social institutions (those of private property, money competition, demonstrative consumption etc.) change. The engine of the society's development is economy, in particular the development of production that results in change of social institutions and norms of social life; managers and technical intelligentsia play the major role in this development.

He also described capitalism as class struggle but not as happening between the bourgeoisie and the proletariat (according to K. Marx and F. Engels), but between businessmen (bankers, lawyers, brokers, managers) and industry (engineers, designers, technicians, and labour); in short, between those who make money and those who produce goods. His *Theory of Business Enterprise* (1904) further widened his renown. Sociological knowledge grew not only in Western Europe and the USA. On the threshold of the XIX-XX centuries Russian sociological thought was gaining the world level, developing from social philosophy through social theory to sociological theory. In this period fame came to such thinkers as N.K. Michailovski, E.V. de Roberti, M.A. Bakunin, P.A. Sorokin etc.

One of the most influential movements in Russia was anarchism. Its founding fathers were M.A. Bakunin (1814-1876) and P.A. Kropotkin (1842-1921). *Anarchism* is the political belief that the society should have no government, laws, police, or other authority, but should be a free association of all its members.

M.A. Bakunin's ideas are as follows:

- Liberty is the only medium in which intelligence, dignity, and the happiness of man can develop; not official "liberty", licensed, measured and regulated by the state; not individual liberty, selfish, mean and fictitious, which considers the rights of the individual as limited by the rights of the state, and therefore necessarily results in the reduction of the rights of the individual to zero;

- Liberty has a social character as it recognizes no other restrictions than those which are traced for us by the laws of our own nature; such laws are immanent in us, inherent, constituting the very basis of our being, material as well as intellectual and moral; instead, finding them a limit, we must consider them as the real conditions and effective reason for our liberty.

P.A. Kropotkin went further. He borrowed socialist ideas and developed them in the theory of socialism and federalism. Its major postulates are as follows:

- Socialism as the social system must be based on individual and collective liberty and activities of free associations;
- The state must be abolished;
- The relationships between the subjects of society are built on the principles of federalism, i.e. a free union where the subjects have equal rights.

Although the ideas of anarchism (complete individual liberty, rejection of regulation by the state etc.) were naïve, the ideas of equality, justice, individual liberty, federalism in social life are still followed by.

Another famous movement in Russia was *narodnik movement*, or *populism*. Its ideologists were P.L. Lavrov (1823-1900) and N.K. Michailovski (1842-1904). Still of importance are thoughts about power and dictatorship expressed by P.L. Lavrov:

- The possession of great power corrupts the best people, and even the ablest leaders, who meant to benefit the people by decree, failed;
- Every dictatorship must surround itself by compulsory means of defense which must serve as obedient tools in its hands. Every dictatorship is called upon to suppress not only its reactionary opponents but also those who disagree with its methods and actions. Whenever a dictatorship succeeded in establishing itself, it had to spend more time and effort in retaining its power and

defending it against its rivals than upon realization of its programme, with the aid of that power;

- A dictatorship can be wrested from the dictators only by a new revolution.

While solving the problem of interaction between the individual and the society, they asserted that the major engine of historic development were actions undertaken by critically thinking personalities (as a rule, the vanguard of the intelligentsia).

N.K. Michailovski as a founder of the theory of social progress formulated the law of antagonism between the state and personality. Antagonism is given birth because the society develops fast and makes more complex, and man, as a result of social division of labour, turns to the bearer of a particular function of the society. The antagonism could be overcome if a personality were given more liberty with regards to the society (the principle of the personality's supremacy over the society). He asserted that the crowd obeying the impact of leaders loses the ability to critically assess their words and actions.

The psychological movement in Russia of the 1890s is presented by E.V. de Roberti, N.I. Kareev etc. They analyzed such fundamental issues of social development as its primary reasons and motive powers, progress and regress, the role of the mass and personality in history etc. Their analysis proceeded from the assumption that individual and collective psychology is dominant at determining human behaviour. It means that all social phenomena are of psychological character so the society is a system of psychical and practical interactions of people.

Of other Russian researchers who worked in empiric sociology in the first decade after the October revolution of 1917 one can mention P.A. Sorokin who had to flee away abroad, A.V. Chayanov, S.G. Strumilin, A.K. Gastev etc. For instance, an agrarian economist *A.V. Chayanov* (1888-1938) developed a theory of the family labour household in the countryside. He managed to create an integral conception of the organization of peasantry household and make a conclusion about lack of the category of wages in a non-capitalistic peasantry household and its turning to the pure profit of the family members.

Thus, late XIX – early XX centuries were signified by formation of anti-naturalistic doctrines of theoretic sociology with its own perspective of the subject and specificity of sociological knowledge. The classical stage in sociology was finished in the 1920-1940s with active introducing of empiric and applied sociological researches which marked the beginning of the third, contemporary stage.

THE RISE OF FEUDALISM: 850-1000 AD

Before we begin, we should note that the men and women of the middle ages never talked about feudalism. Feudalism is a term invented in the sixteenth century by royal lawyers-primarily in England-to describe the decentralized and complex social, political, and economic society out of which the modern state was emerging. The term "feudalism" came from the German *vieh*, or "cow," the measure of wealth among the early Germans, a term that gave rise to the medieval word *fief*. "Fief" simply meant "something of value." In the agricultural world of the time, "something of value" was usually land. But the sixteenth-century lawyers pictured this land as having been under the control of a powerful king who distributed much of it to his followers, men of distinction whose breeding and upbringing particularly fitted them for governing and giving battle.

It has been argued that historians have interpreted medieval documents and histories in terms of this view, and that, when we examine the documents more closely, there is actually very little evidence that society was really organized in such a fashion. This may very well be true, but a new and different picture of medieval society in the ninth through the fourteenth centuries has yet to be developed. Lacking anything possible better, it is only reasonable that we should turn our attention to the traditional portrayal of feudal society.

The Characteristics of Feudalism

Feudalism is a decentralized organization that arises when central authority cannot perform its functions and when it cannot prevent the rise of local powers.

In the isolation and chaos of the 9th and 10th centuries, European leaders no longer attempted to restore Roman institutions, but adopted whatever would work. The result was that Europe developed a relatively new and effective set of institutions, adapted to a moneyless economy, inadequate transportation and communication facilities, an ineffective central government, and a constant threat of armed attack by raiders such as the Vikings, Magyars, and Saracens. The most well-known of the institutions were manorialism (the organization of the peasants), monasticism (the organization of the churchmen), and feudalism (the institution of the aristocracy).

At the close of the First World War, hundreds of thousands of young men, trained to fight and laden with "war souvenirs" such as Luger pistols, hand grenades, Thompson submachine guns and the like, returned to an America in which there were not enough good jobs for them to fill, and in which the government was busily engaged in cutting expenditures (for such things as policemen) and was bending every effort in a constant (and fruitless) struggle to stop people from drinking alcoholic beverages (Prohibition)

In a feudal society, civil and military powers at the local level are assumed by great landowners or other people of similar wealth and prestige. Much as churchmen assumed governmental authority with the fall of the Roman Empire in the West, local leaders, such as Count Robert of Paris, assumed the role previously exercised by government officials at the local level. Other individuals in other areas gathered retinues of fighting men and took over the role of the government in those territories they could control. Often enough these were imperial officials whom the imperial government could no longer keep in check, but others also emerged as local leaders.

In American cities in the 1920's, neighborhood gangs often arose. Since the neighborhoods were often ethnic, the gangs tended to be dominated by Italians, Irish, Germans, or whatever group was dominant in the district. The leaders of these gangs claimed jurisdiction over their neighborhood-"territory" or "turf"- and collected taxes in the form of "protection money" for the services they performed. These local leaders and their retinues begin to form a warrior class distinct from the people of their territory. The local leaders who emerged during the decay of the Carolingian Empire were generally armed men, particularly armed men mounted on horseback and possessing a fortified residence. As the Frankish empire conquered their neighbors, the Carolingian monarchs had to develop a means of holding and governing these new territories. They accomplished this by entrusting aspects of local government to favoured followers and paying them with grants of land and revenues in the territories they were expected to fortify, garrison, defend and govern.

When the empire ceased to expand, these "class" of fighting men still needed new lands. They had been accustomed to raising large families so that, if one son were to die, there would be another to inherit the father's position. Consequently, their numbers steadily increased, and they found themselves forced to seize the lands of others to provide for their second and third sons. They first took control of the lands on which they were resident and, by doing so, weakened the monarch still further. They then took whatever lands they could from the imperial estates and, finally, began to seize nearby church lands. For the most part, the people of these lands welcomed the change, since they were trading a distant and ineffectual imperial government for a local and effective one.

Municipal governments at first tried to curb the growth of the gangsters, but their police soon found that they were outclassed. The gangsters drew from the trained fighting men of the demobilized army and built and used fast armored cars, submachine guns, hand grenades, and were often highly disciplined. The city governments were no more able to keep them from organizing their territories, than the highway patrols were able to overtake their supercharged cars. Moreover, local residents were not averse to paying protection money to someone in their own neighborhood who would actually provide protection, instead of paying taxes to fuel the graft and bribery of corrupt city governments.

The distinction between private rights and public authority disappears, and local control tends to become a personal and even hereditary matter.

Perhaps the "aristocracy" that emerged as the local leaders in the feudal age were doing no more than the Merovingian and Carolingian monarchs had done by considering their "territory" their private possession. This was not unusual during the middle ages; Various kings named Louis frequently signed their names as *FRANCE*. In any event, the feudal leaders began to treat governmental functions as private property that they could loan, give, away, or pass on to their children. It should be noted that money — silver or gold coins — had gradually vanished from use and that Europe and had adopted a barter system to meet their basic economic needs. Without legal tender, however, it was impossible to hire someone to provide needed services. The fact that the feudal leaders could *lend* someone a territory from which he could derive rents and renders in kind and services was an important factor in the new organization of Western Europe. The feudal structure of society emerged as local leaders gave their followers the income from the dues owed by the residents of a given territory in payment for their services — which could vary considerably.

Perhaps the gangs simply followed the pattern set by city governments of the time, which put their political workers on salary by giving them a position in the city government where they could enjoy a regular income while still devoting their full time to advancing the political fortunes of their bosses. In any event, the gang leaders, or "bosses," who emerged from the mass of neighborhood gang leaders began to divide up their territories, giving their followers, or "boys," the right to a share of the income from a given district.

The feudal leaders often take over responsibility for the economic security of their territories, and dictate how resources are to be used, while at the same time establishing monopolies over some activities. This strengthens their presence at the local level and also makes their possessions even more valuable.

The feudal lords of Western Europe, through the men to whom they had distributed fifes, began to exert economic control over the villages and districts under their control. The woods became the lord's possession, and hardwoods — useful for building and weapons — could not be cut except with the lord's express permission. All fuel had to be used sparingly, and the lord was paid for wood taken from the woodlands, game caught there, pigs put to pasture there, and so on. The lords also build ovens, baths, grain mills and the like as monopolies. Villagers had to patronize the lord's monopolies and pay for the privilege. This gave the lords the opportunity of granting fifes other than land, such as the income from a mill in a certain village, or the revenue from fishing rights in a certain stream.

The gangs were soon aware that people wanted things that the government did not want them to have — primarily alcohol, gambling, and prostitution — and that the government could not prevent the gangs from providing those amenities. They were soon "licensing" or actually establishing illegal activities within their territories — brothels, the numbers game, casinos, and, most of all, saloons ("speakeasies"). The gangs grew wealthy enough so that they could purchase the services of underpaid local officials, increase their own full-time personnel, and still have considerable income left over to invest in "legitimate" businesses

The feudal aristocracies are usually organized on the basis of private agreements, contracts between individuals

By the 900's, some local lords — the duke of Aquitaine, the count of Toulouse, the count of Flanders, and other — had become powerful enough that they began to absorb the lesser lords and territories around them. Sometimes this was a simple matter of conquest, but more often the result of a feudal war was an agreement between the two opponents in which one turned his lands over to the other and received them back as a fief in exchange for service.

In many cities of America, various territorial gangs absorbed their lesser neighbors, and began to take over the turf of their more formidable adversaries. This process, known as "muscling-in," usually took the form of attempting to infringe on one or more of one's neighbor's monopolies, such as the sale of whiskey, but it often led to open warfare. The war in Chicago between the Italian and Polish gangs of the South Side under the leadership of Al Capone against the North Side Irish-German mob of Dion O'Banion and his successor, Buggsy Moran, were particularly bloody and famous, ending with the St. Valentine's Day Massacre of 14 February 1927. Within a few years, each major city was under the control of a single individual — the "Godfather" — who managed the boys in his "family" and conferred with the Godfathers of the families of other cities to keep the peace and work together effectively. It was in this fashion that the "syndicate" emerged.

Homage and Fealty

The private agreements that formed the network of mutual services were called contracts of *homage and fealty,* "homage" because one of the contractants agreed to become the servant (*homme*, or "man" of the other, and *fealty*, because he promised to be "*feal*, faithful" to him. Homage and fealty became formalized, romanticized, and overlaid with symbolism, but it is most easily understood as a simple contract.

The Party of the First Part-the *dominus*, often translated as "lord," but just as easily (and accurately) translated as "boss"-made an arrangement with the Party of the Second Part-the *vassal*, a word derived from the Celtic word for "boy," or *miles*, a word meaning "soldier". The Party of the First Part gave the Party of the Second Part "something of value" (a *fief*, something that would produce an income in services and kind over a long time), and promised him "respect" (meaning that he would not interfere with his enjoyment of the fief except for a very good reason) and justice (meaning that he would protect him against both other lords and, if necessary, other vassals of his.

The Party of the Second Part promised a number of things in return. The three main items were "relief," a payment of some sort that he gave the Party of the First Part for having agreed to take him on; "aid and counsel," which obligated him to attend the court of the Party of the First Part whenever he was called upon to do so, and to support and advise him; and "vassalage," which was usually but not always a period of military service when called. Some men got fifes for service as accountants at the Treasury, or for acting as diplomats, or even for some rather silly things. It is said that one English noble held a nice fief on condition that he appear before the king each year at the royal Christmas court and simultaneously whistle, hop, and break wind. English kings were not noted for the subtlety of their humor.

The Party of the Second Part might additionally pledge to render one or more of a number of traditional services: to give the lord and his retinue three nights hospitality if they were in the neighborhood; to help ransom the Party of the First Part if he were captured and held prisoner; to contribute presents for the wedding of the Party of the First Part's eldest daughter and the knighting of his eldest son, and to contribute money to help defray the cost of the festivities.

There was frequently a ritual of bonding once the contract had been agreed upon by both sides. The Party of the Second Part would kneel before the Party of the First Part, who would take both the vassal's hands between his own as the vassal promised to love and respect the lord. The lord, in turn, would promise to honour and protect the vassal. They would then both rise, kiss, and exchange gifts, the Party of the Second Part giving the Party of the First Part the relief payment, and the Party of the First Part giving the Party of the Second Part a sword or some similarly "honourable" gift. The vassal then became a member of the lord's "familia" (family).

This was a powerful bond. Many of the medieval legends and tales turned upon the relationship between the lord and vassal; Lancelot's tragedy was that his love for Guenevere conflicted with his love for Arthur, while king Alfonso, the Cid's lord, consistently failed to keep his promises to love, respect and protect his outstanding vassal. Indeed, the feudal tie was so powerful that the rituals have persisted in many Western societies. The rituals of homage and fealty, for instance, have persisted in the traditional manner of proposing marriage. Many people think of feudalism as a primitive and inefficient system, but it did not appear to be so. Organized in this fashion, the Western Europeans succeeded in holding off the raiders and restoring a measure of peace that permitted a revival of trade and commerce by about 1000 AD. Besides, the Mafia uses the same organization (and even the same customs and terms) and are not considered either primitive or inefficient. Note also that most franchise enterprises, such as MacDonald's, uses essentially the same system.

TRADITIONAL ECONOMIC STRUCTURE

Modern capitalist mode of production in the womb from the mother out of feudalism, the birth of the initial form is vividly called the seeds of capitalism. Capitalist growth from bud to form a mature economy, not only need a long transition period experienced in Western Europe about 200 years (from the 14th century to 16th century), and related support needs of many conditions, the most important is the institutional environment in which to give the seeds of capitalism to provide much room for development, that is, capitalist production necessary to equal property rights, all kinds of commodity markets and factor markets and the establishment of a variety of institutional trading in the market, the extent to which tools are allowed to produce and develop. Compared to Western Europe, China, the capitalist mode of production through 400 years (from the 15th century to 19th century) competition has not yet left the bud! its roots in the harsh institutional environment, institutionalization of the traditional economic structure of the seeds of capitalism had a strong inhibitory effect.

China's traditional economic structure, economic system of the main body of the landlord, mainly from the production relations, said. In this structure, the feudal landlords of possession of the land, to the use of child slaves, or in the form of self-employed workers to form a host of economic self-. feudal landlords in turn more land sub-family of farmers in farming, collecting rent, the formation of tenant economy. In addition, based on the small land ownership of farmers engaged in independent farming. yeomen economy is not separated from the host system economy separate from the economic system, it is attached to the landlord system, economy, and subject to the constraints and impact. the landlord system, the main economic characteristics of China's traditional economy are: 1. The relative relaxation of feudal relations of personal dependence, and more so more later, 2. Land can be traded freely, 3. Combination of farming organizations. So pre-capitalist era, this economy is the lord than in Western Europe and more efficient economic system a system. Of mainstream economic historians argue that the traditional real estate value by maximizing the economic requirements of some of the rent into reproduction investment, and promote the growth of total economic output of society, its progress and rationality is obvious, some scholars called it "a good economic system in feudal". This is just one aspect of the problem. On the other hand, Strengthening the effectiveness of the traditional economy of its stability, but also enhance its flexibility and tolerance.

on the seeds of capitalism, the traditional economy is a conservative force and inertia, because of its flexible and inclusive to allow capital The emergence of Marxism and even have some bud development, but also because of its stability and powerful, hard to become the seeds of capitalism in general and the Development of relations of production are contained, destroyed.

Flexibility from the traditional economy of its own characteristics: a solid combination of small-scale peasant farming organizations can mitigate the strength of feudal exploitation, while allowing a degree of commodity economy, the development of trade relations between developed land, resulting in real estate, commercial capital and usury capital of mutual transformation, stimulating the further development of commodity economy, but also to consolidate the feudal land relations.

Combination of agriCulture and handicraft production of the basic structure of the traditional economy, including farmers and tenant farmers, including the family is the basic production units. Agro-industrial integration mainly in the rural areas within the family, within the family the balance of production and consumption in order to maintain a food and clothing, this is a one of the small farmers to pursue. To this end they have to be self-sufficient production to direct access to production and livelihood, especially food and clothing and other basic information. However, due to limitations of scale, but it can never be completely self-sufficient, and must be engaged in commodity production, and handicrafts and other farmers switching products. If <<Mencius>> said, they should “more than men millet, women more than fabric,” then you can have transactions with hundreds of hands. In addition to Barter, also need to value exchange, the reproduction process of production and subsistence value of compensation to be achieved through the market. Their reproduction is actually a certain extent, the development of commodity economy. In addition, the possession of the feudal landlords mainly cereal surplus labour rent, very few industrial and agro-processing products, its consumption also depends on the market, after rent money into rent in kind, even more so. If we take into account the cottage Industry production of raw materials and regional geographical conditions, exchange and the existence of the market is even more necessary. so different from Western Europe, China's feudal economy is not the pure form of natural economy, it is a wide range of commercial production as a necessary complement to the highly developed on the basis of the feudal business. feudal Business The existence and development, expanding the feudal landlord class and the exploitation of the scope and number of countries, more play the role of maintaining the feudal economic order.

The development of peasant commodity production and land elements into commodities can be traded freely, the commercial capital of the community increased demand, with the social and economic development, monetary accommodation of usury in the capital's role in social reproduction is increasingly significant. Because the business profits to be higher than the rent, business is profitable, but also because of increasing social demand for money, money lending on interest rates and more generous returns, real estate and rent then the landlord into a large number of commercial capital and usury capital. Meanwhile, with money Merchant wealth envy "does not worry about the fire, do not worry about thieves," the land property, and thus the purchase of land, so from the landlord engaged in commodity production and circulation of commodities, the development of landlords, merchants and usurers of the Trinity. rent, business profits and interest free flow and transform into each other, even if they can put the accumulation of wealth into the most favorable direction, to ensure the maximization of economic benefits, but also to land, commercial capital and usury capital to support each other to ensure their common development, to become the Qing Dynasty The basic structure of the distribution of wealth and social accumulation of the main direction. individual commercial capital of the Ming Dynasty million taels (silver) level, increased taels (silver) level, the market expanded to border areas from the Mainland, the commodity economy is to stimulate further development, At the same time the feudal land relations have been further consolidated. This economic structure is characterized by the export of traditional commodities higher level of economic development and forms the trinity of feudal exploitation, to the feudal rule provides a strong economic base, creating a different from Western Europe centralized state system. It is this centralization of the unified system, using the country's economic functions of the inhibition of the universalization of capitalism embryonic development.

China's economic functions of the centralized feudal state in three aspects: first, engaged in water conservancy, transportation, defense and other public works construction and management, and second, the economic policies through taxes and intervention in social reproduction, the third, direct Jing Ying handicrafts and commerce. The first point directly contributed to social and economic development, has a positive meaning, the second and third points are interrelated, in the early progress of society also play a catalytic role, but the more later, especially in a capitalist bud is produced becomes a hindrance factor. Generally speaking, the commercial development of capitalist relations of production is a necessary condition, Marx also said: "a variety of existing business to use different forms of major production Value of production organization, are more or less plays the role of the disintegration of "So despite the expansion of social division of labour and commodities continue to promote the economic development of the ecoromic prosperity of the landlord, but as a system of economic added landowners commodity production and commercial development in the objective is the negation of the natural economy, and its over-development landlord tenancy system is bound to endanger the economic base and shake the fundamental centralized feudal state, which is intolerable to the landlord class. So the state power of the landlord class through tax intervention in economic policies and social reproduction, trying to suppress the development of commodity economy, in order to consolidate the fundamental rule of the landlord class. dynasties are "Restraining Commerce" as the center of its economic policies, argued reward the farmers farming organizations, while business with a heavy levy taxes, restrict business operations, and other means to belittle the social status of businessmen inhibited the development of commercial capital, commercial capital reduction and weakening of the role of the collapse of small-peasant economy. However, the development of commodity economy, productivity improvement and the specific economic structure of the internal movement requirements and necessity, not a feudal state any economic policy that can suppress the so-called "current law cheap businessman, businessmen have rich men, and respect for the farmer, the farmer is poor and lowly carry" is proof. In the feudal rule of the country and economy need to the struggle between the law of development, the centralized state to intervene directly in the production and business operation, set up a huge government-run industrial and commercial system. Links to free government-run paper handicraft Download Center early Feudal Lord Zhou Dynasty had to correspond with the work of serfdom, slavery exists in the form of the system, the feudal aristocracy was to be the main production of goods and military supplies, is a typical form of natural economy. to the Han Dynasty, the government-run handicraft important changes occurred, the production no longer limited to non-profit activities of daily production of industrial goods and military supplies, but gradually extended to the relationship between the profitability of the importance to the national economy and production, such as salt, metal fabrication and other mining, monetary casting and shipbuilding, the increasing scale of operations, organization of production has become increasingly tight.

Obviously, the centralized feudal state monopoly of production of major industrial products, one aimed at increasing revenue, expanding the economic power of centralized state, and second, inhibition of production of private goods development, consolidation of Tenancy landlord economy. At the same time, feudal country's economic activities also extended to the commercial sector, the state has are lost, stabilization, and other commercial institutions often open, with its strong economic power and ultra-economy established Political forces to the capital as the center of the national commercial network, the implementation of some important goods monopoly system, to a certain extent, maintained control of the circulation and the market, and get a huge profit.

Official business in essence is not a commodity economy, but it has some external features of the commodity economy, it is a perversion of the natural economy. Government-run industrial development, limiting the city folk, especially handicraft handicraft market, blocking the conversion of the commercial capital to industry, while government-run commercial development was further strengthened by the feudal landlord economy on the control of urban and rural handicrafts, inhibit independent development of commercial capital, weaken its role in the collapse of the peasant economy, it had attached to the host economy.

Taking into account the process of development of the feudal economy, to industry in the production patterns, the most positive sense of the urban and rural independent handicraft handicraft. Their development and to the larger, more developed division of labour and cooperation handicraft workshop The transition marks the dawn of capitalism. However, due to government-run industrial and commercial activities on the development of urban and rural handicrafts produced independently extremely limited, so the dawn of capitalism, even if there is also very weak.

First of all. Official control of industrial labour, seriously hampering the development of independent civil craft. Eighth century ago, government-run industry, labour Chuguan slaves and sentences of imprisonment, the large number of services for the lord in the feudal regime, the more visible, builders and Ding Fu, etc., they are basically free labour. this period of government-run industrial use of labour mainly taken the form of labour system. Tang Dynasty to the Ming the middle of the middle of the nature of government-run industrial labour force gradual transition from servitude to the attendant system System, artisans dependency on the feudal regime has been weakened over the previous period, but the national household registration system through the establishment of the handle fixed up the industrial labour force, urban and rural artisans to become an independent government-run handicraft reserve army of labour. This national code of labour households system hinders the independent craftsmen to carry out normal economic activities. craftsmen service locations are generally away from the homeland, and from the need for a long time, when the value of the day, the actual time-consuming two to March, especially in the harsh official interference and exploitation have brought the name To raise the government-run industries employed craftsmen from the same, nearly free labour, and this time, urban and rural artisans neither independence nor the capital to development. of course. Productivity is the most active factor, both government-run handicraft industry engaged in economic activities, and the size greater benefit to some extent the development of social division of labour and Technology level, the spillover effects to stimulate the development of folk handicrafts, the result of this development is to become the antithesis of government-run handicraft. play continuously weakened, the collapse of government-run The role of handicrafts. It was not until the mid Qing Dynasty, government-run industry still controls a number of important industrial sectors.

Second, the government-run handicraft folk handicrafts in the market development is also very obvious limitations. China since the Qin and Han on the establishment of a unified centralized state, but in the natural economy dominated case, as market players or local small and regional markets, as for the development of the handicraft industry to provide more opportunities for important products of the national market, although already there. but basically monopolized by official and exclusive commercial and industrial business, even if the feudal ruling class is required for industrial consumer goods (especially luxury goods) market also due to self-sufficiency of the government-run handicraft production greatly reduced. This of course only urban and rural independent handicraft cottage industries to compete for a small local market. The market expansion is the development of commodity production premise, the existence of government-run handicraft industry has greatly limited the independence of urban and rural handicrafts market. its relatively small scale of operation, production and technological progress and productivity is very slow, while commercial capital into the industry is all the more difficult.

Finally, the government-run business through the monopoly of major commodities business, not only inhibited the development of private commercial capital, weakening its disintegration Zuoyong natural economy, but also prevented the craft of civil society and impact the national market penetration, further strengthening the feudal regime of civil control of the handicraft industry to ensure the dominance of government-run industries. In addition, government-run commercial control and monopoly of international trade, curb market foreign expansion, which for the negative effects of private industrial and commercial development is also not be underestimated.

Capitalism in Europe first appeared in the shipping industry, textile and mining industry, mainly because the production sector in social and economic development has global impact, easy to open up the market, but also the most likely breakthrough productivity sectors. In China, in addition to the three trades. ceramics, shipbuilding is a national significance, higher levels of productivity sectors. but before the middle of the Ming Dynasty, the government-run handicraft production in the dominant industry, the higher the level of productivity in all major sectors not reflected in the urban and rural independent handicrafts, but reflected in the government-run handicrafts. It is very rare in the urban and rural independent handicraft handicraft workshop larger the root causes.

8

The Impact of the Scientific Revolution

The beginning of the seventeenth century is known as the "scientific revolution" for the drastic changes evidenced in the European approach to science during that period. The word "revolution" connotes a period of turmoil and social upheaval where ideas about the world change severely and a completely new era of academic thought is ushered in. This term, therefore, describes quite accurately what took place in the scientific community following the sixteenth century. During the scientific revolution, medieval scientific philosophy was abandoned in favor of the new methods proposed by Bacon, Galileo, Descartes, and Newton; the importance of experimentation to the scientific method was reaffirmed; the importance of God to science was for the most part invalidated, and the pursuit of science itself (rather than philosophy) gained validity on its own terms.

The change to the medieval idea of science occurred for four reasons: (1) seventeenth century scientists and philosophers were able to collabourate with members of the mathematical and astronomical communities to effect advances in all fields; (2) scientists realized the inadequacy of medieval experimental methods for their work and so felt the need to devise new methods (some of which we use today); (3) academics had access to a legacy of European, Greek, and Middle Eastern scientific philosophy they could use as a starting point (either by disproving or building on the theorems); and (4) groups like the British Royal Society helped validate science as a field by providing an outlet for the publication of scientists' work. These changes were not immediate, nor did they directly create the experimental method used today, but they did represent a step toward Enlightenment thinking (with an emphasis on reason) that was revolutionary for the time. Assessment of the state of science before the scientific revolution, examination of the differences in the experimental methods utilized by different "scientists" during the seventeenth century, and exploration into how advances made during the scientific revolution affected the scientific method used in science today will provide an idea of how revolutionary the breakthroughs of the seventeenth century really were and what impact they've had.

SCIENCE AND PHILOSOPHY BEFORE THE REVOLUTION

In immediate contrast to modern times, only a few of Europe's academics at the beginning of the scientific revolution and the end of the sixteenth century considered themselves to be "scientists." The words "natural philosopher" carried much more academic clout and so the majority of the research on scientific theory was conducted not in the scientific realm per se, but in philosophy, where "scientific methods" like empiricism and teleology were promoted widely. In the 17th century, empiricism and teleology existed as remnants of medieval thought that were utilized by philosophers such as William of Ockham, an empiricist (d. 1349), Robert Boyle, a 17th century chemist, teleologist and mechanist, and by the proponents of Plato and Aristotle (1st century teleologists and abstractionists). Both empiricism, as the theory that reality consists solely of what one physically experiences, and teleology, as the idea that phenomena exist only because they have a purpose (i.e. because God wills them to be so), generally negated the necessity of fact-gathering, hypothesis writing, and controlled experimentation that became such an integral part of modern chemistry and biology at the beginning of the 17th century. In other words, the study of science before the scientific revolution was so concentrated on philosophy (such as Aristotle's conception of "ideas" as ultimate truths) as to preclude the development of a scientific method that would necessitate the creation of an informed hypothesis to be tested. Certain medieval philosophers, however, such as Roger Bacon (1214-1294; no relation to Francis), did emphasize the necessity of controlled experimentation in coming to a theoretical conclusion, but they were few and far between, and generally failed to correctly use the experimental method in practice. For example, author Hall wrote that "Bacon [and other advocates were] guilty of misstatements of fact which the most trifling experiment would have corrected" (Hall, p 163).

THE ADVENT OF THE SCIENTIFIC REVOLUTION - 17TH CENTURY

A. R. Hall, in his book The Scientific Revolution 1500-1800, made the observation that a main point dividing scientific thought in the seventeenth century from that of the ancient Greeks and medieval Europeans was the choice of questions each group sought to answer through their methods of research or observation. 2He argued that the first group, that of Copernicus and da Vinci (15th and 16th centuries), focused more on questions of "how can we demonstrate that..." or "how may it be proved that..." that aimed to prove a defined hypothesis true or false, while the second group (that of 17th century chemists and physiologists) emphasized questions phrased as "what is the relationship between..." or "what are the facts bearing upon..." that necessitated fact-finding before a concrete hypothesis could be formulated. The most important point to remember here is that both the questions posed in the 15th century and those of the 17th century form part of the definition of a complete modern "experimental method" – the first type of question cannot stand alone.

A concrete hypothesis (question 1) must be accompanied by sufficient, independently verifiable observations (question 2) in order for the scientist to make a vague inference (a form of hypothesis) that can then be tested with a controlled experiment. The way the scientist/philosopher comes by this "vague inference" that will form a concrete hypothesis differs, and these differences can be described as the scientists' different approaches toward an "experimental method." The following portion of the module will give an idea of the types of experimental methods promoted by 17th century scientists as well as their impact on the standard experimental method utilized and accepted by chemists, biologists, and physicists today.

Scientists and their "Experimental Methods"

Francis Bacon (1561-1626): Bacon represents a first step away from sixteenth century thinking, in that he denied the validity of empiricism (see introduction) and preferred inductive reasoning (the method of deriving a general "truth" from observation of certain similar facts and principles) to the Aristotelian method of deductive reasoning (the method of using general principles to explain a specific instance, where the particular phenomena is explained through its relation to a "universal truth"). Moreover, like Roger Bacon of the 13th century, Francis Bacon argued that the use of empiricism alone is insufficient, and thus emphasized the necessity of fact-gathering as a first step in the scientific method, which could then be followed by carefully recorded and controlled (unbiased) experimentation. Bacon largely differed from his sixteenth century counterparts in his insistence that experimentation should not be conducted to simply "see what happens" but "as a way of answering specific questions." Moreover, he believed, as did many of his contemporaries, that a main purpose of science was the betterment of human society and that experimentation should be applied to hard, real situations rather than to Aristotelian abstract ideas. His experimental method of fact-gathering largely influenced advances in chemistry and biology through the 18th century. 3

Galileo Galilei (1564-1642): Galileo's experimental method contrasted with that of Bacon in that he believed that the purpose of experimentation should not simply be a means of getting information or of eliminating ignorance, but a means of testing a theory and of testing the success of the very "testing method." Galileo argued that phenomena should be interpreted mechanically, meaning that because every phenomenon results from a combination of the most basic phenomena and universal axioms, if one applies the many proven theorems to the larger phenomenon, one can accurately explain why a certain phenomenon occurs the way it does. In other words, he argued that "an explanation of a scientific problem is truly begun when it is reduced to its basic terms of matter and motion," because only the most basic events occur because of one axiom.

For example, one can demonstrate the concept of "acceleration" in the labouratory with a ball and a slanted board, but to fullyexplain the idea using Galileo's reasoning, one would have to utilize the concepts of many different disciplines: the physics-based concepts of time and distance, the idea of gravity, force, and mass, or even the chemical composition of the element that is accelerating, all of which must be individually broken down to their smallest elements in order for a scientist to fully understand the item as a whole. This "mechanic" or "systemic" approach, while necessitating a mixture of elements from different disciplines, also partially removed the burden of fact-gathering emphasized by Bacon. In other words, through Galileo's method, one would not observe the phenomenon as a whole, but rather as a construct or system of many existing principles that must be tested together, and so gathering facts about the performance of the phenomenon in one situation may not truly lead to an informed observation of how the phenomenon would occur in a perfect circumstance, when all laws of matter and motion come into play. Galileo's abstraction of everything concerning the phenomenon except the universal element (e.g. matter or motion) contrasted greatly with Bacon's inductive reasoning, but also influenced the work of Descartes, who would later emphasize the importance of simplification of phenomena in mathematical terms. Galileo's experimental method aided advances in chemistry and biology by allowing biologists to explain the work of a muscle or any body function using existing ideas of motion, matter, energy, and other basic principles.

Rene Descartes (1596-1650):Descartes disagreed with Galileo's and Bacon's experimental methods because he believed that one could only: "(1) Accept nothing as true that is not self-evident. (2) Divide problems into their simplest parts. (3) Solve problems by proceeding from simple to complex. (4) Recheck the reasoning." 4That these "4 laws of reasoning" followed from Descartes' ideas on mathematics (he invented derivative and integral calculus in order to better explain natural law) gives the impression that Descartes, like many 17th century philosophers, were using advances in disciplines outside philosophy and science to enrich scientific theory. Additionally, the laws set forth by Descartes promote the idea that he trusted only the fruits of human logic, not the results of physical experimentation, because he believed that humans ca.. only definitely know that "they think therefore they are." Thus, according to Descartes's logic, we must doubt what we perceive physically (physical experimentation is imperfect) because our bodies are external to the mind (our only source of truth, as given by God). 5Even though Descartes denounced Baconian reasoning and medieval empiricism as shallow and imperfect, Descartes did believe that conclusions could come about through acceptance of a centrifugal system, in which one could work outwards from the certainty of existence of mind and God to find universal truths or laws that could be detected by reason. 6It was to this aim that Descartes penned the above "4 laws of reasoning" – to eliminate unnecessary pollution of almost mathematically exact human reason.

Robert Boyle (1627-1691)

Boyle is an interesting case among the 17th century natural philosophers, in that he continued to use medieval teleology as well as 17th century Galilean mechanism and Baconian induction to explain events. Even though he made progress in the field of chemistry through Baconian experimentation (fact-finding followed by controlled experimentation), he remained drawn to teleological explanations for scientific phenomena. For example, Boyle believed that because "God established rules of motion and the corporeal order – laws of nature," phenomena must exist to serve a certain purpose within that established order. Boyle used this idea as an explanation for how the "geometrical arrangement of the atoms defined the chemical characteristics of the substance." 7Overall, Boyle's attachment to teleology was not so strange in the 17th century because of Descartes' appeal to a higher being as the source of perfection in logic.

Hooke (1635-1703)

Hooke, the Royal Society's first Curator of Experiments from 1662-1677, considered science as way of improving society. This was in contrast to medieval thought, where science and philosophy were done for knowledge's sake alone and ideas were tested just to see if it could be done. An experimentalist who followed the Baconian tradition, Hooke agreed with Bacon's idea that "history of nature and the arts" was the basis of science. 8He was also a leader in publicizing microscopy (not discovering, it had been discovered 30 years prior to his Micrographia).

Sir Isaac Newton (1643-1747)

Newton invented a method that approached science systematically. He composed a set of four rules for scientific reasoning. Stated in the Principia, Newton's four way framework was: "(1) Admit no more causes of natural things such as are both true and sufficient to explain their appearances, (2) The same natural effects must be assigned to the same causes, (3) Qualities of bodies are to be esteemed as universal, and (4) Propositions deduced from observation of phenomena should be viewed as accurate until other phenomena contradict them." His analytical method was a critical improvement upon the more abstract approach of Aristotle, mostly because his laws lent themselves well to experimentation with mathematical physics, whose conclusions "could then be confirmed by direct observation." Newton also refined Galileo's experimental method by creating the contemporary "compositional method of experimentation" that consisted in making experiments and observations, followed by inducted conclusions that could only be overturned by the realization of other, more substantiated truths. Essentially, through his physical and mathematical approach to experimental design, Newton established a clear distinction between "natural philosophy" and "physical science."

All of these natural philosophers built upon the work of their contemporaries, and this collabouration became even simpler with the establishment of professional societies for scientists that published journals and provided forums for scientific discussion. The next section discusses the impact of these societies, especially the British Royal Society.

THE ROLE OF THE ROYAL SOCIETY

Along with the development of science as a discipline independent from philosophy, organizations of scholars began to emerge as centers of thought and intellectual exchange. Arguably the most influential of these was the Royal Society of London for the Improvement of Natural Knowledge, which was established in 1660 with Robert Hooke as the first Curator of Experiments. Commonly known as the Royal Society, the establishment of this organization was closely connected with the development of the history of science from the seventeenth century onwards. The origins of the Royal Society grew out of a group of natural philosophers (later known as "scientists") who began meeting in the mid-1640s in order to debate the new ideas of Francis Bacon. The Society met weekly to witness experiments and discuss what we would now call scientific topics. A common theme was how they could learn about the world through experimental investigation.

The academy became an indispensable part of the development of modern science because in addition to fostering discussing among scientists, the Royal Academy became the de facto academy for scientific study in Europe. Accomplished scientists served as Royal Academy Fellows and exchanged ideas both casually and formally through the publication of articles and findings. These scholars, especially Francis Bacon, served as an important resource for the justification of the new fact-gathering, experiment-based experimental method as well as for the validation of "modern (17th century) science."

Moreover, the work they published through the society helped gain credibility for the society and for science as a discipline. For example, scholars such as Robert Boyle published significant scientific findings in its unofficial journal Philosophical Transactions (Dear, p 140). Other famous scientists that joined the society included Robert Boyle, Isaac Newton and William Petty, all of whom benefited from academic collabouration within the society and from increased publicity generated by their published works.

Dedicated to the free exchange of scientific information, the Royal Society of London-and later, its counterparts throughout Europe such as The Hague and the Academy of Sciences in Paris-proved crucial to the discussion and design of modern science and the experimental method. Although the Royal Society was a governmentally established body, it acted independently as a body dedicated to research and scientific discovery-that is to say, to improving knowledge and integrating all kinds of scientific research into a coherent system. With such a central artery for scientific progress, scientists were able to more quickly and fiercely support and promote their new ideas about the world.

The defining feature of the scientific revolution lies in how much scientific thought changed during a period of only a century, and in how quickly differing thoughts of different natural philosophers condensed to form a cohesive experimental method that chemists, biologists, and physicists can easily utilize today. The modern experimental method incorporates Francis Bacon's focus on use of controlled experiments and inductive reasoning, Descartes' focus on hypothesis, logic, and reason, Galileo's emphasis on incorporation of established laws from all disciplines (math, astronomy, chemistry, biology, physics) in coming to a conclusion through mechanism, and Newton's method of composition, with each successive method strengthening the validity of the next. Essentially, the scientific revolution occurred in one quick bound and the advances made from the 17th century onward appear as little skips in comparison.

However, one must keep in mind that although the Greeks and the philosophers of the 17th century invented and began to perfect the experimental method, their outcomes in their experiments were often flawed because they didn't follow their own advice. Even philosophers like Francis Bacon, the main promoter of fact-gathering and controlled experimentation failed at some point in time to control their experiments or use peer review, or used too much inference/logic and too little mathematic proof/experiment. In short, scientists today must learn from the mistakes of the 17th century philosophers like Galileo who wrote so eloquently about the necessity of a successful scientific method but didn't execute it correctly or failed to recognize the importance of pursuing scientific progress not simply for theoretical excellence, but for how it can improve the human condition.

The lesson to take from the history of the scientific revolution is that the ideas of the 17th century philosophers have the most impact in the context of the progress they made as an academic whole – as singular scientists, they became more prone to faulty logic and uncontrolled experimentation. For instance, non-scientific reasoning such as teleology continued to affect genius philosophers and scientists such as Descartes and Boyle, and today scientists are faced with the problem of intelligent design (teleology) being taught as the equivalent of peer-reviewed, substantiated evolutionary theory. Overall, modern scientists remain just as proneto the same problems as the 17th century philosophers and therefore might consider looking toward the legacy of the successes of the scientific revolution against the backward medieval philosophy for guidance.

SCIENTIFIC REVOLUTION AND ENLIGHTENMENT

The Age of Science of the 1600s and the Enlightenment of the 1700s, also dubbed the Age of Reason, introduced countless new concepts to European society. These ideals still greatly permeate modern society today, and many modern institutions have much of their foundations in the ideals of these times.

An Era of Enlightened Despotism

A new form of government began to replace absolutism across the continent. Whilst monarchs were reluctant to give up their powers, many also recognized that their states could potentially benefit from the spread of Enlightenment ideas. The most prominent of these rulers were Frederick II the Great Hohenzollern of Prussia, Joseph II Hapsburg of Austria, and Catherine II the Great Romanov of Russia. In order to understand the actions of the European monarchs of this period, it is important to understand their key beliefs. Enlightened despots rejected the concept of absolutism and the divine right to rule. They justified their position based on their usefulness to the state. These despots based their decisions upon their reason, and they stressed religious toleration and the importance of education. They enacted codified, uniform laws, repressed local authority, nobles, and the church, and often acted impulsively and instilled change at an incredibly fast rate.

Catherine the Great 1762-1796

Catherine the Great came to power because Peter III failed to bear a male heir to the throne and was killed.

Her enlightened reforms include:

- Restrictions on torture
- Religious toleration
- Education for girls
- 1767 Legislative Commission, which reported to her on the state of the Russian people

- Friends with Diderot, Rousseau, Voltaire
- Trained and educated her grandson Alexander I so that he could progress in society because of his merit rather than his blood line.

However, Catherine also took a number of decidedly unenlightened actions. In 1773 she violently suppressed Pugachev's Rebellion, a massive peasant rebellion against the degradation of the serfs. She conceded more power to the nobles and eliminated state service. Also, serfdom became equivalent to slavery under her.

Foreign Policy

Catherine combated the Ottoman Empire. In 1774 Russia gained a Warm Water Port on the Black Sea.

Frederick II the Great 1740-1786

Frederick II Hohenzollern of Prussia declared himself "The First Servant of the State," believing that it was his duty to serve the state and do well for his nation. He extended education to all classes, and established a professional bureaucracy and civil servants. He created a uniform judicial system and abolished torture. During his tenure, Prussia innovated agriculture by using potatoes and turnips to replenish the soil. Also, Frederick established religious freedom in Prussia.

Joseph II Habsburg 1765-1790

Joseph II Habsburg (also spelled as Hapsburg) of Austria could be considered perhaps the greatest enlightened despot, and he was purely enlightened, working solely for the good of his country. He was anti-feudalism, anti-church, and anti-nobility. He famously stated, "The state should provide the greatest good for the greatest number." He created equal punishment and taxation regardless of class, complete freedom of the press, toleration of all religions, and civil rights for Jews. Under Joseph II a uniform law code was established, and in 1781 he abolished serfdom and in 1789 ordered the General School Ordinance, which required compulsory education for Austrian children. However, Joseph failed because he angered people by making changes far too swiftly, and even the serfs weren't satisfied with their abrupt freedom.

England

As a result of the Glorious Revolution of 1688, England already had a Parliament and thus enlightened despotism did not take a hold in England.

France

After Louis XIV the "Sun King," Louis XV took control from 1715 until 1774. Like his predecessor, he was an absolute monarch who enacted mercantilism. As a result of the influence and control of absolutism in France, France also did not encounter an enlightened despot. In order to consummate an alliance between his nation and Austria, Maria Theresa of Austria married her daughter, Marie Antoinette, to Louis XV's heir, Louis XVI. Louis XV recognized that the fragile institutions of absolutism were crumbling in France, and he famously stated, *"Après moi, le deluge"*, or "After me, the flood."

War of Austrian Succession

The war of Austrian Succession of 1740 to 1748 pitted Austria, England, and the Dutch against Prussia, France, and Spain. Upon Maria Theresa's acquisition of the Austrian throne, Frederick the Great of Prussia attacked Silesia, and war broke out. In 1748 peace came at the Treaty of Aix la Chapelle. The treaty preserved the balance of power and the *status quo ante bellum*. Austria survived but lost Silesia, which began "German Dualism" or the fight between Prussia and Austria over who would dominate and eventually unite Germany.

The Seven Years War

The peace in 1748 was recognized as temporary by all, and in 1756 Austria and France allied in what was known as the Diplomatic Revolution. The reversal of the traditional France versus Austria situation occurred as a result of both nation's fear of a rising, militant Prussia. To consummate the marriage, Louis XVI married Marie Antionette. The Seven Years War engaged Austria, France, Russia, Spain, Sweden, and Saxony against Prussia and England. The purpose of the war was to annihilate Prussia, and took place at a number of fronts: in Europe, in America (where American citizens know it as the French and Indian War) and in India. At the Peace of Paris in 1763, the war concluded, and Prussia retained all of its territory, including Silesia. France ceded Canada to Britain and the North American interior to Spain, and removed its armies from India. It did, however, get to keep its West Indies colonies. At this point, Great Britain became the supreme naval power and it began its domination of India.

The Partitioning of Poland

Poland was first partitioned on February 19, 1772, between Russia, Austria, and Prussia, in an agreement between them to gain more land and power in Europe. Poland was able to be partitioned because it was weak and had no ability to stop the larger and more powerful nations. The balance of power was not taken into consideration by France or England because the partitioning did not upset the great powers of Europe. The second partition involved Russia and Prussia taking addition land from Poland. After the second partition, which occurred on January 21, 1792, the majority of their remaining land was lost to Prussia and Russia. The third partition of Poland took place in October of 1795, giving Russia, Prussia, and Austria the remainder of the Polish land. Russia ended up with 120,000 square kilometres, Austria 47,000 square kilometres, and Prussia 55,000 square kilometres. This took Poland off of the map.

Science and Technology

The Enlightenment was notable for its scientific revolution, which changed the manner in which the people of Europe approached both science and technology. This was the direct result of philosophic enquiry into the ways in which science should be approached.

The most important figures in this change of thinking were Descartes and Bacon. The philosopher Descartes presented the notion of deductive reasoning-that is, to start with a premise and to then discard evidence that doesn't support the premise. However, Sir Francis Bacon introduced a new method of thought. He suggested that instead of using deductive reasoning, people should use inductive reasoning-in other words, they should gather evidence and then reach a conclusion based on the evidence. This line of thought also became known as the Scientific Method.

Changes in Astronomy

The Scientific Revolution began with discoveries in astronomy, most importantly dealing with the concept of a solar system. These discoveries generated controversy, and some were forced by church authorities to recant their theories.

Pre-Revolution: Aristotle and Ptolemy

Ancient Greek philosophers Aristotle and Ptolemy had a geocentric, or Earth-centred, view of the universe. Of the ten spheres of the heavens, Earth and heavy objects (such as sinners) were at the centre, and lighter objects (such as angels) were in the higher spheres. This view was adopted as Church doctrine.

Nicolaus Copernicus (1473-1543)

During the Renaissance, study of astronomy at universities began. Regiomontanus and Nicolas of Cusa developed new advances in mathematics and methods of calculation. Copernicus, although a devout Christian, doubted whether the views held by Aristotle and Ptolemy were completely correct. Using mathematics and visual observations with only the naked eye, he developed the Heliocentric, or Copernican, Theory of the Universe, stating that the Earth revolves around the sun.

Tycho Brahe (1546-1601)

Tycho Brahe created a mass of scientific data on astronomy during his lifetime; although he made no major contributions to science, he laid the groundwork for Kepler's discoveries.

Johannes Kepler (1571-1630)

Kepler was a student of Brahe. He used Brahe's body of data to write Kepler's Three Laws of Planetary Motion, most significantly noting that planets' orbits are elliptical instead of circular.

Galileo Galilei (1564-1642)

Galileo is generally given credit for invention of the telescope; although the device itself is not of Galileo's design, he was the first to use it for astronomy. With this tool, he proved the Copernican Theory of the Universe. Galileo spread news of his work through letters to friends and colleagues.

Although the Church forced him to recant his ideas and spend the rest of his life under house arrest, his works had already been published and could not be disregarded.

Isaac Newton (1642-1727)

Newton is often considered the greatest scientific mind in history. His *Principia Mathematica* (1687) includes Newton's Law of Gravity, an incredibly ground-breaking study. Newton's work destroyed the old notion of an Earth-centred universe. Newton also had a great influence outside of science. For example, he was to become the hero of Thomas Jefferson.

Developments in Medicine

Vesalius studied human cadavers, a practice forbidden by church doctrine. His writing *The Structure of the Human Body* in 1543 renewed and modernized the study of the human body.

Bibliography

Angel, R: *Relativity: The Theory and its Philosophy*, Oxford, Pergamon Press, 1980.

Berlin, Isaiah: *Karl Marx: his Life and Environment,* New York, Oxford University Press, 1963.

Bernard McGinn: *Classics of Western Spirituality,* Paulist Press, New York, 1978.

Bottomore, Tom: *A Dictionary of Marxist Thought,* Cambridge, Harvard University Press, 1983.

Bruun, Hans Henrik: *Science, Values and Politics in Max Weber's Methodology*. Copenhagen: Munksgaard, 1972.

Bryson, Valerie: *Feminist Political Theory*. Macmillan, London, 1992.

Dalton, Dennis : *Gandhi's Power : Nonviolence in Action*, New Delhi, OUP, 2001.

David Held: *Classes, Power, and Conflict: Classical and Contemporary Debates,* Berkeley, University of California Press, 1982.

Derrett, J. : *Religion, Law, and the State in India*, London, Faber, 1968.

Eisenstein, Zillah: *The Radical Future of Liberal Feminism*. Boston: Notheastern University Press, 1986.

Grant, G. P.: *Philosophy in the Mass Age*, Copp Clark, Toronto, 1959.

Gyford J: *The Politics of Local Socialism*, London, George Allen and Unwin, 1985.

Heimanson, Rudolph: *Dictionary of Political Science and Law*, N.Y.: Oceana Publications, 1967.

Hoggett, P.: *The Politics of Decentralisation*, Basingstoke, MacMillan, 1994.

Hughes, H. S.: *Consciousness and Society: Reorientation of European Social Thought*. New York: Vintage Books, 1977.

Jonathan H.: *The Structure of Sociological Theory*, Belmont, Ca., Wadsworth, 1991.

Kewal Krishan: *Materialism in Indian Thought,* Munshiram Manoharlal Publishers, New Delhi, 1974.

Kim, Sung Ho.: *Max Weber's Politics of Civil Society*. Cambridge: Cambridge University Press, 2004.

Leo, S.: *Political Philosophy*, The Bobbs Merrill Co., New York, 1975.

Michael, B.: *The Politics of Succession in India*, Connecticut, Greenwood, 1976.

Mommsen, Wolfgang: *Max Weber and German Politics, 1980-1920*, Chicago: University of Chicago Press, 1984.

Rattansi, Ali: *Marx and the Division of Labour,* London, Macmillan, 1982.

Richard W.: *Sociological Theory: An Introduction to the Classical Tradition*, Peterborough, Broadview Press, 1997.

Ritzer, George: *Sociological Theory*, New York, McGraw-Hill, 1992.

Seidman, Steven: *Liberalism and the Origins of European Social Theory,* Berkeley, University of California Press, 1983.

Stammer. Otto: *Max Weber and Sociology Today*. New York: Harper, 1971.

Sydie, Rosalind: *Natural Women, Cultured Men: A Feminist Perspective on Sociological Theory*. Toronto: Methuen, 1987.

Taylor, Charles: *Sources of the Self: The Making of the Modern Identity*. Cambridge, MA: Harvard University Press, 1989.

Thompson, J.: *Organizations in Action*, New York, McGraw-Hill, 1967.

Tong, Rosemarie: *Feminist Thought: A Comprehensive Introduction*. Boulder: Westview Press, 1989.

Victor G. : *Law as a Political Instrument,* New York, Random House, 1955.

Wright Mills: *From Max Weber: Essays in Sociology*, New York, Oxford University Press, 1958.

Index

❑❑❑